Financial Crime

Other titles available from Law Society Publishing:

Anti-Money Laundering Toolkit, 3rd edition
Alison Matthews

Assessing and Addressing Risk and Compliance in Your Law Firm
Rebecca Atkinson

COFAs Toolkit, 2nd edition
Jeremy Black and Tom Vose

COLPs Toolkit, 3rd edition
Michelle Garlick

Retained EU Law
Eleonor Duhs and Indira Rao

Solicitors and the Accounts Rules, 4th edition
Andrew Allen and Janet Taylor

Titles from Law Society Publishing can be ordered from all good bookshops or direct (telephone 0370 850 1422, or visit our online shop at **www.lawsociety.org.uk/bookshop**).

FINANCIAL CRIME

A Compliance Manual

Rebecca Atkinson

All rights reserved. No part of this publication may be reproduced in any material form, whether by photocopying, scanning, downloading onto computer or otherwise without the written permission of the Law Society except in accordance with the provisions of the Copyright, Designs and Patents Act 1988. Applications should be addressed in the first instance, in writing, to Law Society Publishing. Any unauthorised or restricted act in relation to this publication may result in civil proceedings and/or criminal prosecution.

The author has asserted the right under the Copyright, Designs and Patents Act 1988 to be identified as author of this work.

Whilst all reasonable care has been taken in the preparation of this publication, neither the publisher nor the author can accept any responsibility for any loss occasioned to any person acting or refraining from action as a result of relying upon its contents.

The views expressed in this publication should be taken as those of the author only unless it is specifically indicated that the Law Society has given its endorsement.

© The Law Society 2021

Crown copyright material is reproduced with the permission of the Controller of Her Majesty's Stationery Office

ISBN-13: 978-1-78446-178-2

Published in 2021 by the Law Society
113 Chancery Lane, London WC2A 1PL

Typeset by Columns Design XML Ltd, Reading
Printed by Hobbs the Printers Ltd, Totton, Hants

The paper used for the text pages of this book is FSC® certified. FSC (the Forest Stewardship Council®) is an international network to promote responsible management of the world's forests.

Contents

Preface	ix
Acknowledgements	x
About the author	xi
Table of cases	xii
Table of statutes	xiii
Table of statutory instruments	xv
Table of European legislation	xviii
Abbreviations	xix

PART I: ANTI-BRIBERY AND CORRUPTION

1 Anti-bribery and corruption — 3

   1.1 Bribery Act 2010 — 3
   1.2 Practical examples — 7
   1.3 How to implement compliance — 9
   1.4 What to do if bribery is suspected — 12

PART II: ANTI-MONEY LAUNDERING

2 Legislation and regulation — 17

   2.1 Anti-money laundering legislation — 17
   2.2 Financial Action Task Force – what is it and what is its role? — 17
   2.3 Outline of the legislation as it applies to law firms — 19
   2.4 Proceeds of Crime Act 2002 offences, defences and tipping off — 22
   2.5 Terrorism Act 2000 — 30
   2.6 Other terrorist property offences legislation — 35

3 Risk assessment and internal controls — 36

   3.1 UK national risk assessment and SRA's AML risk assessment — 36

CONTENTS

	3.2	Who is who – supervisors and guidance providers	40
	3.3	Firm-wide AML risk assessment	42
	3.4	Role of MLRO and MLCO and crossover with COLP and COFA	44
	3.5	Suspicious activity reports and privilege	47
	3.6	Policies, controls, procedures – regulations 19 and 20	53
	3.7	Internal controls – regulations 21 and 24	56

4 Client due diligence — **62**

	4.1	Client due diligence	62
	4.2	Politically exposed persons (regulation 35), sanctions and adverse media checks	94
	4.3	Reliance and record-keeping – regulations 39 and 40	98
	4.4	Trustee obligations – regulations 44 and 45	101
	4.5	Note on pooled client accounts	103
	4.6	Beneficial owners, officers and managers approval	104
	4.7	Client due diligence centralisation and different standards for non-regulated and regulated work	106

5 Guidance, reviews, visits, regulations and compliance — **109**

	5.1	Legal Sector Affinity Group guidance and Solicitors Regulation Authority guidance	109
	5.2	Law Society of England and Wales guidance	110
	5.3	SRA warning notices	112
	5.4	OPBAS and its review of the SRA	119
	5.5	SRA thematic reviews, outcomes and what is next	121
	5.6	What are the SRA's plans for 2021 and beyond?	132
	5.7	SRA visits – what to expect and how to handle them	134
	5.8	6AMLD and Brexit regulations	138
	5.9	Firms and solicitors – disciplinary action	139
	5.10	AML compliance – where do I start?	142

PART III: CRIMINAL FINANCES AND INVESTIGATIONS

6 Criminal Finances Act 2017 and tax evasion — **149**

	6.1	Background to the Criminal Finances Act 2017	149
	6.2	Outline of the Criminal Finances Act 2017	150
	6.3	Associated persons	151
	6.4	Investigations and penalties	152
	6.5	Prosecutions to date and HMRC research	152
	6.6	Unexplained wealth orders	154
	6.7	Account freezing orders	157

	6.8	Implementing compliance	158
	6.9	Practical examples of tax evasion	162
	6.10	Other tax avoidance rules	163
	6.11	Professional conduct, SRA warning notices and the SDT	164
	6.12	SRA visits	169
7	**Responding to a criminal investigation**		**170**
	7.1	Introduction	170
	7.2	Production orders	170
	7.3	Notice to disclose	171
	7.4	Other orders	172
	7.5	Practical considerations	172

PART IV: SANCTIONS, WHISTLEBLOWING AND REPORTING CONCERNS

8	**Sanctions**		**179**
	8.1	Relevant legislation	179
	8.2	UK sanctions regime key players	180
	8.3	What sanctions are and why sanctions are imposed	180
	8.4	Who needs to comply?	181
	8.5	International sanctions – the reach of the Office of Foreign Assets Control	182
	8.6	Where to find sanctions lists	182
	8.7	Checking clients for sanctions	183
	8.8	Obligation to report to the Office of Financial Sanctions Implementation	185
	8.9	Privilege	187
	8.10	Exceptions and licences (specific and general)	187
	8.11	Compliance and breaching the terms of a licence	193
	8.12	Other reporting obligations – suspicious activity reports	193
9	**Whistleblowing and reporting concerns**		**194**
	9.1	Introduction	194
	9.2	Whistleblowing legislation	194
	9.3	Reporting concerns under the SRA Codes of Conduct	200
	9.4	How to implement compliance in your firm	205
	9.5	What if you have offices in different countries?	207

CONTENTS

APPENDICES

A	**Anti-bribery and corruption**	**209**
	A1 Template anti-bribery and corruption risk assessment	211
	A2 Template anti-bribery and corruption policy	214
B	**Anti-money laundering**	**217**
	B1 Template firm-wide anti-money laundering risk assessment	219
	B2 Template suspicious activity report	224
	B3 Privilege decision template from Legal Sector Affinity Group anti-money laundering guidance	225
	B4 Flowchart from Legal Sector Affinity Group anti-money laundering guidance	228
	B5 Template anti-money laundering policy	229
	B6 Template client and matter risk assessment	240
	B7 Template high-risk register	245
	B8 Template ongoing anti-money laundering risk monitoring form	247
	B9 Template anti-money laundering audit table	248
C	**Criminal finances and investigations**	**255**
	C1 Template Criminal Finances Act 2017 risk assessment	257
	C2 Template anti-tax evasion policy	260
D	**Sanctions, whistleblowing and reporting concerns**	**265**
	D1 Template whistleblowing policy	267
	D2 Guidance note: Solicitors Regulation Authority reporting obligations – what are they and when do they kick in?	270

Index   273

Preface

So vast is the financial crime legislative framework that designing a plan for compliance can be daunting and, if not done correctly, ineffective and costly.

In this book the reader will find a comprehensive review of the financial crime legislation and regulations that affect the vast majority of legal practitioners.

The aim of the book is to break down what the law or regulation requires and how firms and legal practitioners might then go about ensuring compliance in their practice. To that end, the book provides sample policies, procedures, guidance and risk registers.

The book is as up to date as it can be at the time of writing and takes into account the Legal Sector Affinity Group (LSAG) guidance which was released on 20 January 2021.

It is important for anyone tasked with compliance and risk management in their firm to understand that bringing a firm up to where it should be in terms of compliance is a marathon and not a race. There is a lot to do, and so take time to do it and do it carefully.

The law is stated as at April 2021.

Rebecca Atkinson

Acknowledgements

A big thank you to Melissa Oxby, client on-boarding manager at Howard Kennedy LLP, for her structure charts with explanations found at **4.1.1.15**. She clearly had some honey and tea that day.

About the author

Rebecca Atkinson is director of risk and compliance for London law firm Howard Kennedy LLP. Rebecca heads up the risk function at her firm and is the money laundering compliance officer (MLCO), money laundering reporting officer (MLRO), data protection officer (DPO), whistleblowing officer (WBO) and anti-bribery and corruption officer (ABCO). Rebecca was called to the Bar in 2006 and recently qualified as a New York attorney. Rebecca is a regular writer of articles on the subject of risk and compliance and you may hear her deliver podcasts and webinars.

Table of cases

Alexander Dobrovinsky and Partners LLP July 2020, SRA 5.9.4
Bowman *v.* Fels [2005] EWCA Civ 226 .... 2.4.1.4, App.B5
Child & Child 2019, SDT 5.9.3
Clyde & Co and partners 2017, SDT 5.9.5
Fuglers LLP *v.* SRA [2014] EWHC 179 (Admin) 5.3.3
Hajiyeva *v.* National Crime Agency [2020] EWCA Civ 108 .... 6.6.2.1
Mounteney, Jonathan Peter, SDT 6.11
NCA *v.* Baker [2020] EWHC 822 (Admin) 6.6.2.3
Patel, Premji Naram Patel *v.* SRA [2012] EWHC 3373 (Admin) 5.3.3
R *v.* Anwoir [2008] EWCA Crim 1354 .... App.B3
R *v.* Da Silva [2006] EWCA Crim 1654; [2007] 1 WLR 303 .... 2.4, 3.5.1, App.B3
Seatons Law Ltd (Seatons) 20 November 2020, SRA 5.9.2
SFO *v.* Eurasian Natural Resources Corp Ltd [2018] EWCA Civ 2006 .... 7.5.2
Simpson Millar, SRA 6.11
SRA *v.* Chan, Ali and Abode Solicitors [2015] EWHC 2659 (Admin) 6.11
SRA *v.* Podger (12065-2020) 5.5.3.8
Taylor Vinters LLP (TV) 28 August 2020, SRA 5.9.1
Three Rivers DC *v.* Governor and Company of the Bank of England [2004] UKHL 48 .... 7.5.2
Zambia (Attorney General of Zambia) *v.* Meer Care & Desai [2008] EWCA Civ 1007 .... 5.3.3

Table of statutes

Administration of Justice Act 1985 .. 3.4.1
Affordable Care Act (USA) 9.2.4.3
Anti-terrorism, Crime and Security Act
    2001 .... 2.5.3, 8.1, 8.8, 8.10.4
Basic Standard of Enterprise Internal
    Control (PRC) 9.2.4.4
Bribery Act 2010 ..... 1.1, 1.1.1.1, 1.1.1.2,
    1.2, 1.3, 1.3.2, 1.3.5, 1.3.8,
    App.A2
    s.1 .... 1.1.1, 1.2.1
    s.2 .... 1.1.1
    s.6 .... 1.1.1
        (5)–(7) 1.1.1.3
    ss.7, 8 .... 1.1.2
    s.11 .... 1.1.3
British Nationality Act 1981 .... 1.1.1.1
Companies Act 2006
    s.1162 .... 4.1.1.3, 4.6.1
    Sched.1A, Part 1 ...... 4.1.1.3, 4.6.1
    Sched.7 .... 4.1.1.3, 4.6.1
Companies Act 2008 (South
    Africa) 9.2.4.2
Corporate and Criminal Fraud
    Accountability Act 2002
    (Sarbanes-Oxley) (USA) 9.2.4.3,
    9.2.5
Counter-Terrorism Act 2008 ... 8.1, 8.10.4
Criminal Finances Act 2017 ...... 6.1, 6.4,
    6.5, 6.8, 6.8.1, 6.8.2, 6.8.4,
    6.8.5, 6.10, 6.10.2, App.C1,
    App.C2
    Part 1
        s.1 .... 6.6.1
        s.16 .... 6.7
    Part 3 .... 6.2, App.C2
        s.44(2) 6.2
            (4) 6.3
        s.45(5) 6.2
        s.46 .... 6.2
Criminal Justice Act 1987
    s.2 .... 7.3

Criminal Justice Act 1991 .... 2.3.1
Data Protection Act 2018 .... 7.5.2
Data Protection Act (France) 9.2.4.1
Dismissal Protection Act
    (Germany) 9.2.4.1
Drug Trafficking Act 1994 .... 2.3.1
Employment Ordinance (Hong
    Kong) 9.2.4.4
Employment Rights Act 1996 .... 9.2.3
Finance Act 2013
    Part 5 .... 6.10.1
    s.208 .... 6.10.1
Financial Services and Markets Act
    2000
    Part 4A 8.4
Financial Services (Banking Reform) Act
    2013 .... 8.10.3
Labor Relations Act (South
    Africa) 9.2.4.2
Labour Code (France) 9.2.4.1
Legal Services Act 2007 .... 3.4.1
Limited Liability Partnerships Act
    2000 .... 4.6.1
Occupational Safety and Health Act 1970
    (USA) 9.2.4.3
Organised and Serious Crimes Ordinance
    (Hong Kong) 9.2.4.4
Police and Criminal Evidence Act 1984
    Sched.1 .... 7.2
Prevention of Corruption Act 1916 ..... 1.1
Proceeds of Crime Act 2002 .... 2.3.1,
    2.4.1.1, 2.4.1.2, 2.4.3.2, 2.5,
    2.5.1.4, 3.5.3.1, 3.5.3.6,
    3.5.4.3, 4.7.2, 5.3.4, 5.5.3.5,
    6.6.2.1, 7.3, 8.12, App.B5
    Part 1
        s.3 .... 3.7.3
    Part 5
        s.303Z 6.7

TABLE OF STATUTES

Proceeds of Crime Act 2002 – *continued*
Part 7 .... 3.4.1, 3.6
  ss.327–329 ... 2.4, 2.4.2, 2.4.2.1,
                           3.5.3.4, App.B2
  s.327(3) 2.4.1.3
  s.328 .... 2.4.1.4
  s.329 .... 2.4.1.5
  ss.330–332 .... 2.4.1.6, 2.4.3
  s.330 ... 2.4.2.2, 3.5.3.4, App.B2
    (6) App.B3
  s.333 .... 2.4
  s.333A 2.4, 2.4.4.2
    (1), (3), (4) 2.4.4.1
  s.333B(4) 2.4.4.2
  s.333C(2) 2.4.4.2
  s.333D(1), (2) 2.4.4.2
  s.336A 2.4.4.2
  s.336ZH 7.4.2
  s.338 .... 2.4.2.1
  s.339ZB 2.4.4.2
Part 8
  s.342(1) 2.4.4.1
    (3), (4), (6) 2.4.4.2
    (7) 2.4.4.1
  s.345 .... 7.2
  ss.362A–362T 6.6.1
Protected Disclosures Act 2000 (South Africa) 9.2.4.2
Public Bodies Corrupt Practices Act 1889 .... 1.1
Public Interest Disclosure Act 1998 .... 9.2.3

Regulation on Labor Security Supervision and Criminal Procedure Law of the PRC 9.2.4.4
Rules of the People's Procuratorate on Whistleblowing Work (PRC) 9.2.4.4
Sanctions and Anti-Money Laundering Act 2018 .... 2.6, 8.1, 8.4
Serious Organised Crime and Police Act 2005
  s.62 .... 7.3
Solicitors Act 1974 .... 3.4.1
  s.43 .... 3.7.1
Taxes Management Act 1970
  s.20BA 7.2
Terrorism Act 2000 ..... 2.3.1, 2.5.4, 3.1.1,
              3.4.1, 3.5.3.1, 4.1.7, 4.7.2
  Part 3 .... 3.6
  s.14(1) 2.5
  ss.15–18 .... 2.5.2, 5.3.4
  s.15 .... 2.5.1.1
  s.16 .... 2.5.1.2
  s.17 .... 2.5.1.3
  s.18 .... 2.5.1.4
  s.19 .... 2.5.3
  ss.21, 21ZA, 21ZB,
    21ZC 2.5.2
  s.21A 2.5.3
  s.21D(1), (3) 2.5.5.1
  s.21E(4) 2.5.5.2
  s.21F(2)(a) 2.5.5.2
  s.21G 2.5.5.2
United Nations (Anti-Terrorism) Ordinance (Hong Kong) 9.2.4.4

Table of statutory instruments

Counter-Terrorism (International Sanctions) (EU Exit) Regulations 2019,
  SI 2019/573 .... 2.6
Counter-Terrorism (Sanctions) (EU Exit) Regulations 2019, SI 2019/577 .... 2.6
Extraterritorial US Legislation (Sanctions against Cuba, Iran and Libya) (Protection of
  Trading Interests) (Amendment) Order 2018, SI 2018/1357 .... 8.5
ISIL (Da'esh) and Al-Qaida (United Nations Sanctions) (EU Exit) Regulations 2019,
  SI 2019/466 .... 2.6
Money Laundering and Terrorist Financing (Amendment) (EU Exit) Regulations 2019,
  SI 2019/253 .... 5.8
Money Laundering and Terrorist Financing (Amendment) (EU Exit) Regulations 2020,
  SI 2020/991 .... 4.4
Money Laundering and Terrorist Financing (Amendment) Regulations 2019,
  SI 2019/1511 .... 3.7.5, 4.1.1.4, 4.1.1.5, 4.1.7, 4.3.1, 5.7.5
    reg.4(8) 3.1
    reg.5(4) 4.1.7
Money Laundering Regulations 1993, SI 1993/1933 .... 2.3.1
Money Laundering Regulations 2003, SI 2003/3075 .... 2.3.1
Money Laundering Regulations 2007, SI 2007/2157 .... 2.3.1, 4.5, 5.2
    reg.14(5) 4.2.1
Money Laundering, Terrorist Financing and Transfer of Funds (Information on the
  Payer) Regulations 2017, SI 2017/692 .... 2.1, 2.3.1, 2.3.2, 2.4, 3.2.5, 3.7, 4.1,
                      4.1.1.2, 4.1.1.11, 4.1.4.3, 4.2.3, 4.7.1, 5.1, 5.3.1, 5.3.3,
                      5.3.4, 5.5, 5.5.1, 5.5.3.10, 5.6.3, 5.7.2, 5.9.1, 5.9.4, 5.9.5,
                                                              6.12, 8.7.2, App.B5
    reg.3 .... 4.6.2, 4.6.3, 5.9.2
      (1) 4.2.1
    reg.5 .... 4.6.1
      (1) 4.1.1.3
    reg.6(1) 4.1.1.7
    reg.11(d) 2.3.2, 4.7.2
    reg.12(1), (2) 2.3.2
    reg.16(2), (3) 3.1
    reg.17(9) 3.1, 4.1.6
    reg.18 .... 3.1, 3.1.2, 5.3.2, 5.5.2, 5.10.2
      (1) 3.3, 3.6, 3.7.4, 4.1.2, App.B9
      (2)(a), (b) App.B9
      (3), (4) App.B9
    reg.19(1) 3.6
      (a), (b) App.B9
      (2) 3.6
      (a), (b) App.B9

TABLE OF STATUTORY INSTRUMENTS

Money Laundering, Terrorist Financing and Transfer of Funds (Information on the Payer) Regulations 2017, SI 2017/692 – *continued*
- reg.19(3) 3.6, App.B9
  - (4) App.B9
    - (a)–(e) 3.6
    - (5)(b) 3.6
    - (6) 3.6, App.B9
- regs.20–24 .... 3.6
- reg.21 .... 5.5.3.1, 5.5.3.5
  - (1)(a)–(c) 3.7.1, App.B9
  - (2) 3.7.1, 5.5.3.8, App.B9
  - (3) 3.4.1, 3.7.2
  - (4), (5) 3.7.2
  - (8), (9) 3.7.3
  - (10) 3.7.4
- reg.24(1) 3.7.5
  - (a) App.B9
  - (2), (3) 3.7.5
- reg.26 .... 4.6, 5.10.1
- regs.27–38 .... 3.6
- reg.27 .... 4.1.7
  - (1) App.B9
    - (b) 4.1.7
  - (2) 4.1.1.1, 4.1.7
  - (8) 4.1.1.1
  - (9) 4.1.1.1, App.B9
- reg.28 .... App.B9
  - (2) 4.3.1
    - (a), (b) 4.1.1.1
  - (3)–(5) 4.1.1.3, 4.3.1
  - (6) 4.1.1.4, 4.3.1
  - (7) 4.1.1.4
  - (9) 4.1.1.3
  - (10) 4.1.1.13, 4.3.1
  - (11) 4.1.5, App.B9
  - (12)(a)(i) 4.1.2
    - (ii) App.B9
  - (13) 4.1.2, 4.1.3, App.B9
  - (19) 4.1.7
- reg.30 .... App.B9
  - (3) 4.1.1.14
  - (7) 4.1.1.7
- reg.30A 4.1.1.5, 4.3.1
- reg.31 .... 4.1.1.14
- reg.33 .... 4.1.3, 4.1.5
  - (1)(b), (f) 4.1.7
  - (2) 4.1.7
  - (3A) 4.1.7, App.B9
  - (4)–(6) 4.1.7
- reg.34 .... 4.1.7
- reg.35 .... 4.1.5
  - (1), (5) App.B9
  - (9)–(11) 4.2.1

TABLE OF STATUTORY INSTRUMENTS

reg.35(12)(a) 4.2.1
    (14) 4.2.1
reg.37 .... App.B9
    (3)(b) 4.1.6
        (iii) 4.1.1.10
    (5), (6) 4.5
reg.39 .... 3.6, 4.3.1, 5.5.3.2, App.B5, App.B9
    (2), (3) 4.3.1
reg.40 .... 3.6, 4.1.2, 4.1.5
    (1) App.B9
    (2) App.B9
        (b) 4.3.2
    (3) App.B9
        (b)(i) 4.3.2
    (4) 4.3.2
    (5) 4.3.2, App.B9
reg.43(9) 4.1.7
regs.44, 45 .... 4.4
reg.47 .... 3.1, 4.1.6
reg.58 .... 3.6
Sched.3 .... 4.6.4
Sched.3A 4.4
Scottish Partnerships (Register of People with Significant Control Regulations 2017
    Sched.1, Part 1 .... 4.6.1
Terrorism Act 2000 and Proceeds of Crime Act 2002 (Amendment) Regulations 2007,
    SI 2007/3398 .... 2.3.2

Table of European legislation

Directive 91/308/EEC First Money Laundering Directive 2.3.1
Directive 2001/97/EC Second Money Laundering Directive 2.3.1
Directive 2002/87/EC 4.4
Directive 2005/60/EC Third Money Laundering Directive 2.3.1
Directive 2006/48/EC 4.4
Directive 2006/49/EC 4.4
Directive 2006/70/EC 2.3.1
Directive 2009/138/EC 2.3.1
Directive 2013/36/EU 2.3.1, 4.4
Directive (EU) 2015/849 Fourth Money Laundering Directive 2.3.1, 4.1.6
Directive (EU) 2018/843 Fifth Directive on Money Laundering 2.3.1, 2.3.2, 3.1, 3.7.5, 4.1.1.4, 4.1.7, 4.4, 4.7.2, 5.5.3, 5.7.5, App.B5
Directive (EU) 2018/1673 Sixth Directive on Money Laundering 5.8
Regulation (EU) 648/2012 .... 2.3.1
Regulation (EU) 2015/847 .... 4.1.1.1

Abbreviations

5AMLD/AMLD V	fifth anti-money laundering directive (EU) 2018/843
ABCO	anti-bribery and corruption officer
ABO	anti-bribery officer
AFO	account freezing order
AML	anti-money laundering
AML Regulations	Money Laundering, Terrorist Financing and Transfer of Funds (Information on the Payer) Regulations 2017, SI 2017/692
ATCSA 2001	Anti-terrorism, Crime and Security Act 2001
BA 2010	Bribery Act 2010
BOOM	beneficial owner, officer or manager
BSB	Bar Standards Board
BVI	British Virgin Islands
CDD	client/customer due diligence
CEO	chief executive officer
CFT	countering/combating the financing of terrorism
CGT	capital gains tax
CJA 1987	Criminal Justice Act 1987
COFA	compliance officer for finance and administration
COLP	compliance officer for legal practice
CPS	Crown Prosecution Service
CQS	Conveyancing Quality Scheme
CTA 2008	Counter-Terrorism Act 2008
DAML	defence against money laundering
DASVOIT	disclosure of tax avoidance schemes for VAT and other indirect taxes
DBS	Disclosure and Barring Service
DOTAS	disclosure of tax avoidance schemes
DPO	data protection officer
DPP	Director of Public Prosecutions
ECJU	Export Control Joint Unit
EDD	enhanced due diligence
EEA	European Economic Area
EU	European Union

ABBREVIATIONS

FATF	Financial Action Task Force
FCA	Financial Conduct Authority
FCDO	Foreign, Commonwealth and Development Office
FSMA 2000	Financial Services and Markets Act 2000
FSRB	FATF-Style Regional Body
GAAR	general anti-abuse rule
HMRC	Her Majesty's Revenue and Customs
ID&V	identification and verification
IHT	inheritance tax
JMLSG	Joint Money Laundering Steering Group
KYC	know your client
LLP	limited liability partnership
LPP	legal professional privilege
LSAG	Legal Sector Affinity Group
ML	money laundering
MLCO	money laundering compliance officer
MLR 2019	Money Laundering and Terrorist Financing (Amendment) Regulations 2019, SI 2019/1511
MLRO	money laundering reporting officer
NCA	National Crime Agency
OFAC	Office of Foreign Assets Control
OFSI	Office of Financial Sanctions Implementation
OPBAS	Office for Professional Body Anti-Money Laundering Supervision
PCPs	policies, controls and procedures
PEP	politically exposed person
POCA 2002	Proceeds of Crime Act 2002
PSC	people with significant control
REL	registered European lawyer
RFL	registered foreign lawyer
SAMLA 2018	Sanctions and Anti-Money Laundering Act 2018
SAR	suspicious activity report
SDLT	stamp duty land tax
SDT	Solicitors Disciplinary Tribunal
SEC	Securities and Exchange Commission (US)
SFO	Serious Fraud Office
SOCPA 2005	Serious Organised Crime and Police Act 2005
SRA	Solicitors Regulation Authority
STAR	serial tax avoidance regime
TA 2000	Terrorism Act 2000
TF	terrorist financing
UHNW	ultra high net worth
UWO	unexplained wealth order

ABBREVIATIONS

VADR	VAT avoidance disclosure regime
VAT	value added tax
WBO	whistleblowing officer

PART I

Anti-bribery and corruption

CHAPTER 1

Anti-bribery and corruption

1.1 BRIBERY ACT 2010

Prior to the Bribery Act (BA) 2010, which came into force on 1 July 2011, legislation that criminalised bribery was based on the Public Bodies Corrupt Practices Act 1889, the Prevention of Corruption Act 1906 and the Prevention of Corruption Act 1916. Further, a body of common law grew to define this area of law.

The further development of anti-bribery and corruption law was debated over a number of years, culminating in a draft Bribery Bill in 2002. Thereafter, a consultation was conducted and a white paper was produced before the Bill was given royal assent on 8 April 2010, creating BA 2010. Further consultations took place putting back the date by which the Act came into force, and after the publication of government guidance the Act came into force on 1 July 2011.

1.1.1 Individual offences

BA 2010 creates three main offences as follows:

(a) bribing a person to induce them to perform or reward them for performing a relevant function (s.1);
(b) improperly requesting, accepting or receiving a bribe as a reward for performing a relevant function (s.2); and
(c) improperly using a bribe to influence a foreign public official to gain a business advantage (s.6).

1.1.1.1 *Bribing a person to induce them to perform or reward them for performing a relevant function*

The Act sets out that an offence will be committed if a person offers, promises or gives a financial or other advantage to another person and the person making the offer/promise/advantage intended the advantage to induce a person to perform improperly a relevant function or activity or to reward a person for the improper performance of such a function.

The Act goes on to state that it is also an offence where a person offers, promises or gives a financial or other advantage to another and that person knows or believes that the acceptance of the advantage would itself constitute the improper performance of a relevant function or activity.

In relation to this offence, the Act goes on to state that it does not matter whether the person to whom the advantage is offered, promised or given is the same person as the person who is to perform, or has performed, the function or activity concerned. Further it does not matter whether the advantage is offered, promised or given by the person directly or through a third party.

It is unlikely that hospitality undertaken for the purposes of courting a client or prospective client would be considered the act of bribing a person. However, firms should have a policy around what is and is not an acceptable level of hospitality, and a process for signing such activity off (see **1.3.4** on gifts and hospitality).

The offence itself does not have to take place in the UK, but the person committing the offence must have a close connection with the UK. 'Close connection' with the UK means being:

- a British citizen;
- a British overseas territories citizen;
- a British national (overseas);
- a British overseas citizen;
- a person who under the British Nationality Act 1981 was a British subject;
- a British protected person within the meaning of that Act;
- an individual ordinarily resident in the UK;
- a body incorporated under the law of any part of the UK;
- a Scottish partnership.

Offers of bribes can also be implied, such as holding a meeting over an open briefcase full of money.

'Relevant function' is defined as any of the following:

- a function of a public nature;
- an activity connected with a business, trade or profession;
- an activity carried out in the course of employment;
- an activity carried out on behalf of a body of persons (corporate or unincorporated);

and which is performed with one or more of the following relevant expectations:

- in good faith;
- with impartiality;
- that by virtue of performing the activity, the person doing so is in a position of trust.

The function does not have to have been performed in the UK and can have been performed elsewhere. This is particularly relevant to fee earners who may conduct business abroad.

Whether the relevant expectations apply to the act in question will depend on whether a reasonable person in the UK would expect it to apply. If the act is undertaken abroad, then local law is considered but custom and practice are not (which ensures that local custom to offer and accept bribes does not legitimise the act itself).

1.1.1.2 Improperly requesting, accepting or receiving a bribe as a reward for performing a relevant function

BA 2010 sets out that a person is guilty of an offence where they request, agree to receive or accept a financial or other advantage intending that, in consequence, a relevant function or activity should be performed improperly whether by the person or another.

The Act further sets out that a person is guilty of an offence where they request, agree to receive or accept a financial or other advantage and the request, agreement or acceptance itself constitutes the improper performance by the person of a relevant function or activity.

A further offence is where a person requests, agrees to receive or accepts a financial or other advantage as a reward for the improper performance (either by themselves or by another person) of a relevant function or activity.

Finally, the Act creates an offence where in anticipation of or in consequence of the person requesting, agreeing to receive or accepting a financial or other advantage, a relevant function or activity is performed improperly by the person or another at the person's request, assent or acquiescence.

For these offences it does not matter whether the person requests, agrees or accepts the advantage directly or through a third party, nor whether the advantage is for the benefit of the person or another.

Further, it does not matter whether the person knows or believes that the performance of the function or activity is improper. If another person is performing the act, then it does not matter whether that person knows or believes that the performance of the function or act is improper. To that end, therefore, the threshold for knowledge is lower than what one might expect.

1.1.1.3 Improperly using a bribe to influence a foreign public official to gain a business advantage

A person commits an offence if they bribe a foreign public official with the intention of influencing the official in their capacity as a foreign official. In doing so, the person bribing must intend to obtain or retain business or an advantage.

The act of bribery here occurs only if the person directly or through a third party offers, promises or gives any financial or other advantage to the foreign official or another person at the official's request or with their assent or acquiescence. Further, an offence is only committed if the official is not permitted nor required by written law applicable to be influenced in their capacity as a foreign official by the offer, promise or gift.

The Act goes on to define what is meant by 'written law applicable' in this context (s.6(7)):

(a) where the performance of the functions of [the official] which [the person] intends to influence would be subject to the law of any part of the United Kingdom, the law of that part of the United Kingdom,

(b) where paragraph (a) does not apply and [the person being bribed] is an official or agent of a public international organisation, the applicable written rules of that organisation,

(c) where paragraphs (a) and (b) do not apply, the law of the country or territory in relation to which [the official] is a foreign public official so far as that law is contained in–

  (i) any written constitution, or provision made by or under legislation, applicable to the country or territory concerned, or
  (ii) any judicial decision which is so applicable and is evidenced in published written sources.

A 'foreign public official' is a person who (s.6(5)):

(a) holds a legislative, administrative or judicial position of any kind, whether appointed or elected, of a country or territory outside the United Kingdom (or any subdivision of such a country or territory),

(b) exercises a public function–

  (i) for or on behalf of a country or territory outside the United Kingdom (or any subdivision of such a country or territory), or
  (ii) for any public agency or public enterprise of that country or territory (or subdivision), or

(c) is an official or agent of a public international organisation [an example could be the World Health Organization].

'Public international organisation' is further defined (s.6(6)) as an organisation whose members are any of the following:

(a) countries or territories,
(b) governments of countries or territories,
(c) other public international organisations,
(d) a mixture of any of the above.

It may seem that the chances of a law firm coming into contact with a foreign public official are slim, and that may well be the case depending on the type of work that the firm undertakes. If a firm undertakes work for foreign governments where a tender process is involved, contact between the firm or those within it and a foreign public official may occur.

It is important to remember that bribery is not limited to the handing over of cash. Gifts, hospitality and entertainment can be bribes if they are intended to influence a decision.

ANTI-BRIBERY AND CORRUPTION

1.1.2 Corporate offence

Under BA 2010, s.7, if one of the above offences is committed by a person associated with a firm with the intention of gaining or retaining a business advantage for the firm, then that firm will also be guilty of a corporate offence if it failed to prevent bribery in its firm.

An 'associated person' is defined under the Act (s.8) as a person who performs services for or on behalf of the firm whether that be an employee, an agent or a subsidiary. Whether the person performed services on behalf of the firm will be determined on the facts (this is a rebuttable presumption) and not purely by reference to the relationship between the person and the firm.

'Associated person' may also include contractors, and therefore it is important to vet contractors to a firm carefully (see **1.3.8**).

Where a firm has committed an offence and a senior officer has consented to or conspired in the commission of the offence, then the senior officer can also be held liable for the offence. In the context of a law firm, this could be the compliance officer for legal practice (COLP), compliance officer for finance and administration (COFA), money laundering reporting officer (MLRO) or perhaps the chief executive or managing partner who gave their blessing to the act. It could also be a person within a firm's business development team who sanctioned the act.

A law firm will have a defence to a corporate offence if it took all reasonable steps to prevent an act of bribery in the organisation.

1.1.3 Penalties

Under BA 2010, bribery by individuals is punishable by up to 10 years' imprisonment and/or an unlimited fine (s.11). If a law firm is found to have taken part in bribery or to lack adequate procedures to prevent bribery, it too could face an unlimited fine.

A conviction for a bribery- or corruption-related offence would of course have severe reputational and financial consequences for a firm.

1.2 PRACTICAL EXAMPLES

To assist in illustrating how bribery might crop up in law firms, below are some examples. The first three examples are taken from the Law Society's practice note, 'Bribery Act 2010' (25 November 2019) (**www.lawsociety.org.uk/en/topics/regulation/bribery-act-2010**).

1.2.1 A firm currently gives Christmas gifts each year to local estate agents

The firm should consider:

- What is the purpose of the gifts – are they to cement good business relations, or are they intended as some form of inducement?
- Does the firm have a policy on gifts which is clear and transparent, and do these gifts comply with the policy?
- Is the recipient given the impression that they are under some obligation to confer business on the firm as a result of accepting the gift?
- Is the gift lavish?
- Is a record made of the gift and the cost entered into the accounts?

It's unlikely that a small token of appreciation sent to local estate agents at Christmas will engage BA 2010, s.1. However, firms should consider carefully the intent behind gifts. They should also ensure that they have a clear policy on gifts, and record both the giving and the receiving of gifts.

1.2.2 A firm is considering setting up an overseas operation in a country that has a high level of corruption

There are particular risks that occur during the setting up of the firm, for instance:

- gaining the appropriate government licences for the firm;
- acquiring planning permission for building new offices or changing existing ones;
- applying for visas for staff who will be working in the new offices.

These are all transactions where there is a risk of being asked to pay a bribe. Many of these issues may be dealt with by a local agent. Using a third party also creates a risk, as the firm will have less control over the third party.

1.2.3 A firm has instructed a professional firm based overseas on behalf of a client regarding a dispute in another country

There is a high level of corruption within this country. The firm is concerned that a bribe may have been paid by the professional firm in order to resolve the dispute. The firm is not clear on whose behalf the bribe has been paid.

In most cases, the bribe is likely to have been paid on behalf of the client, as the professional firm is providing services on their behalf. However, this may vary depending on the retainer that has been put in place.

If the retainer makes it clear that the professional firm has been retained on behalf of the firm, then the firm may be liable for any bribe paid. Firms should consider carrying out appropriate due diligence on firms they refer work to. The due diligence required will depend on the risk, including:

- the country in which the firm operates;
- current knowledge such as the firm's reputation, previous experience of dealing with the firm;

- the nature of the transaction – for example, is the work a simple research exercise, or does it involve contract negotiations or dealing with government officials where the risk is likely to be higher?

1.2.4 A client has informed the solicitor acting in the sale of the client's business that contracts with those the business makes supplies to came about after a 'grease payment' was made

The business and contracts are in the UK. See also **1.3.5**.

The solicitor should report the matter to the firm's COLP and MLRO. The solicitor and COLP need to consider whether the solicitor will be drafting any warranties in the company sale documentation that warrant that bribery has not taken place, as to do so would be misleading, potentially dishonest and show a lack of integrity. If the solicitor has already done this, thought needs to be given about whether the position should be corrected. If the solicitor has not drafted such warranties, thought needs to be given as to whether the solicitor can, and what should be said to the client.

The MLRO needs to consider whether there is a suspicion of money laundering and whether criminal property is in existence. If so, the MLRO needs to consider whether a defence should be sought.

Generally the firm and solicitor need to consider whether they want to continue acting – and if not, whether it is appropriate to stop acting (it may prejudice the client's position, or tip the client off (see **2.4** for an explanation of tipping off)).

1.3 HOW TO IMPLEMENT COMPLIANCE

Where a corporate offence is alleged, a law firm will have a defence if it had adequate procedures in place to prevent bribery. To that end, law firms need to have procedures in place that provide for adequate steps to be taken to prevent bribery and which will stand up to scrutiny when pleaded in defence.

The Law Society practice note on BA 2010 sets out that: 'For some firms there will be no need to put bribery prevention procedures in place as there is no risk of bribery on their behalf.' The author is not aware of a law firm that would have no bribery risk. In litigation there are judges who might have attempts of bribery aimed at them; in property there may be local counsellors who may have attempts of bribery aimed at them; and generally speaking, although much less of a main theme of law firms currently, hospitality and gifts from law firms to clients or prospective clients still occur. It is recommended that some measures are put in place in all law firms. What those measures look like will need to be proportionate to the risk faced by the firm. Below are some suggested steps that firms may want to take and aspects to consider.

1.3.1 Risk assessment

As a starting point firms should conduct a bribery risk assessment to assess the extent and nature of the risk that the firm's activities might involve the risk of bribery. This assessment should record the type of risk and the means by which the firm prevents or mitigates exposure to such risk. The assessment should be reviewed each year, and firms may wish to make it part of their firm-wide risk assessment. There is no magic to such risk assessments, and a simple layout will do. See **Appendix A1** for a suggested template.

1.3.2 Policy implementation

Firms should implement a policy setting out what the bribery offences are under BA 2010; what the firm's stance on bribery and corruption is; what steps people should take to prevent bribery; and whom to report it to. The policy should also set out who the anti-bribery officer (ABO) in the firm is. See **Appendix A2** for a suggested template policy.

1.3.3 Anti-bribery officer

Where it is deemed proportionate to do so, firms should have a designated ABO who is responsible for overseeing the firm's policy on anti-bribery and corruption and ensuring it is upheld in both word and spirit.

The ABO's responsibilities should include:

- an annual review of the policy;
- an annual review of the risk assessment of issues relating to the policy;
- overseeing training and communications relating to the topic.

Although the ABO should have responsibility to oversee bribery compliance overall, the firm may want to make it clear that ultimately all partners of the practice remain accountable for the policy's implementation and ensuring compliance.

1.3.4 Gifts and hospitality

Firms need to have a policy on gifts and hospitality that is proportionate to the work undertaken and types of clients the firm deals with.

Gifts and hospitality are commonly used in business to build relationships and market services or products. Hospitality often takes the form of entertainment, meals and gifts. If the provider of the hospitality does not attend, then it should be regarded as a gift rather than as entertainment/meals.

While this is all normal practice, it should be recognised by law firms, and reflected in their policies, that gifts and hospitality can be used to influence and corrupt third parties, and on occasion to manoeuvre employees into a position of obligation.

When considering whether to accept or provide a gift or hospitality, what matters is the intention behind it. If it is offered as a bribe, it should be refused or not given; but if it is offered as a genuine gift – as, say, a thank you for a job well done or a thank you to a client for an instruction after the work has been completed – it may be accepted provided that all aspects of the firm's policy are complied with.

Ultimately, firms should prevent the giving or receiving of gifts, hospitality or paying of expenses if it might influence, or be perceived to influence, a business decision.

Firms therefore should decide what value of gifts, entertainment and hospitality either given or received must be reported to the ABO and whether this is before or after the event and recorded by either the ABO or other appropriate business services team (such as business development/marketing). The value to be reported and recorded will depend on the type of client and/or work – so, for example, a threshold of £500 might be appropriate for a London City law firm that has completed a piece of work that generated large fees, but might not be appropriate for a 'high street' firm acting for private individuals.

Reporting and recording gifts, entertainment and hospitality will allow the ABO to monitor both the level and the number of instances to assess whether the nature of the relationship is appropriate.

1.3.5 'Grease payments'

Formally known as 'facilitation payments', grease payments are small payments demanded by officials to provide a service they are obligated to perform. There is no exemption for these payments under BA 2010, though other countries such as the US carve such payments out from the offence of bribery.

The Law Society practice note, however, states that the government does recognise that there is an issue faced by organisations which operate in some parts of the world where grease payments are considered the norm and expected.

It goes on further to state that guidance for prosecutors sets out that factors that would make it more likely that a prosecution would occur include where making such payments is seen as a standard part of conducting business, and where payments are repeated or large. Further, an individual's failure to follow the firm's procedures on making facilitation payments might also be a factor.

Where the payments are seen as a one-off, or where there has been self-reporting and remedial actions taken, prosecution is less likely.

1.3.6 Donations to connected charities

Many firms donate monies to charity. When that charity is connected to a client or an organisation which might be providing work in the future, caution needs to be exercised. If the charity is not connected to the firm and its workflow, then there is far less likely to be an issue.

1.3.7 Communication and training

It is important that members of the firm are aware of the firm's policy and stance on bribery. To that end, the policy content needs to be clearly communicated. Further, appropriate training should be provided. Where the bribery risk is deemed to be low, training might be done by way of a 'mandatory read' of the policy and attendance by the ABO or other relevant person at team meetings. Where the bribery risk is deemed to be higher, then more formal training may be needed, either face to face (physical or virtual) or by way of online module.

In addition, firms may also want to diarise sending a bribery story or small piece of guidance around the firm once or twice a year.

1.3.8 Third party due diligence

The scope of BA 2010 requires firms to identify third party business relationships that may provide opportunities for a third party to use bribery while acting on the firm's behalf. To that end, appropriate due diligence should be undertaken before a third party is engaged. Ordinarily this would be done during the procurement phase of suppliers being selected, and to that end firms may wish to devise a questionnaire that asks about the supplier's own anti-bribery and corruption practices (alongside other aspects of compliance and risk management, such as modern slavery compliance, money laundering prevention measures and so on) and also conduct searches via open channels (such as Google) for any adverse news which might suggest that bribery might be part of the supplier's practices.

Where the risk of bribery is potentially higher (perhaps because of the location of the supplier in a high-risk jurisdiction), then the firm may wish to ask the supplier to agree to follow the terms of the firm's own policy and also ensure that those who supply to the supplier also have appropriate measures in place to tackle bribery. If the supplier is wholly UK-based and not in an industry linked to bribery, then the due diligence conducted can be lighter in touch.

In contracts with suppliers the firm should also have the ability to terminate the agreement if bribery is detected or if the firm's policy is not followed (if it is a term that the supplier agrees to follow it). Contracts should also have clear terms about what is being supplied.

1.4 WHAT TO DO IF BRIBERY IS SUSPECTED

Bribery may be suspected as occurring either internally or externally. Internally, a report may be made under the whistleblowing policy (see **Chapter 9** for more information on whistleblowing) of an employee who has attempted to bribe or accepted a bribe or of a supplier who has attempted to bribe or accepted a bribe. Externally, a client may inform their solicitor that they have been bribed or have been bribing others.

ANTI-BRIBERY AND CORRUPTION

If a firm is faced with an internal report of bribery, this needs to be investigated straight away (usually by the ABO) and a view taken as to whether the report is accurate or not. Further, the firm needs to consider whether it should report a possible offence to the police and the Solicitors Regulation Authority (SRA) under its reporting obligations (see **9.3** for more information about reporting obligations). The COLP should be informed about the allegation so that they may consider whether they need to make a report to the SRA; and further the MLRO should be informed to consider whether they need to make a suspicious activity report (SAR) to the National Crime Agency (NCA) (see **3.5** for more information on SARs).

If the firm has been informed by one of its clients that the client has accepted bribes or has itself been bribing others, then the firm needs to think about the following:

- privilege;
- MLROs and SARs;
- SRA Principles and Codes;
- reputation.

1.4.1 Privilege

It is very likely that what has been divulged is privileged, and therefore the solicitor needs to consider whether they are able to take any further steps in relation to the information and whether the crime/fraud exception applies (see **3.5.4** for guidance on privilege).

1.4.2 MLROs and SARs

The MLRO needs to consider whether the act of bribery has caused criminal property to come into play and therefore a SAR needs to be made requesting a defence from the NCA. This will depend on the facts before the firm and whether there is a transaction that is yet to occur – for example, if the firm is acting on the sale of a business that has income derived as a result of bribery.

1.4.3 SRA Principles and Codes

The solicitor and COLP need to consider whether the solicitor/firm can continue to act in the circumstances of what is now known and in accordance with the SRA Principles and Codes (**www.sra.org.uk/solicitors/standards-regulations/**). The following could be relevant:

- Principle 1 – acting in a way that upholds the constitutional principle of the rule of law, and the proper administration of justice;
- Principle 2 – acting in a way that upholds public trust and confidence in the solicitors' profession;
- Principle 4 – acting with honesty;

ANTI-BRIBERY AND CORRUPTION

- Principle 5 – acting with integrity; and
- Codes of Conduct (Code of Conduct for Firms, para.1.4 on misleading others could be relevant).

The COLP also needs to consider whether a report needs to be made if the solicitor or firm has not met the standards required. The client may also be asking the solicitor to put forward a position that is contrary to what the client has informed them – for example, to put forward declarations that no bribery has occurred to a buyer of a business when the client has in fact confirmed that it has taken place.

1.4.4 Reputation

The solicitor and firm need to consider whether they want to continue acting from a reputational standpoint. If it is known or suspected that bribery has occurred and the information is press-worthy, does the firm want to be linked to it?

PART II

Anti-money laundering

CHAPTER 2

Legislation and regulation

2.1 ANTI-MONEY LAUNDERING LEGISLATION

By way of introduction to Part II of this book, acknowledgement is given to its length. Preventing money laundering under the Money Laundering, Terrorist Financing and Transfer of Funds (Information on the Payer) Regulations 2017, SI 2017/692 ('AML Regulations') is by far the most complicated and costly area of compliance in financial crime prevention, and possibly in all aspects of law firm compliance. There is a lot to it, and there really is no way of getting around that. If the reader finds this section a little overwhelming, there is a relatively short 'to do' list at the end of Part II which might help focus efforts.

There is a lot to be said for reading the AML Regulations in full to really understand them, and for any money laundering reporting officer (MLRO) this is highly encouraged. In lieu of doing this, Part II will greatly assist in understanding and implementing the AML Regulations in law firms.

2.2 FINANCIAL ACTION TASK FORCE – WHAT IS IT AND WHAT IS ITS ROLE?

Established by the G7 Summit in Paris in 1989, the Financial Action Task Force (FATF) is an intergovernmental organisation set up to develop policies and standards to combat money laundering. From 2001 FATF also took on the role of developing policies in the area of terrorist financing. FATF currently has 39 members, comprising 37 countries and two regional organisations (the European Commission and the Gulf Co-operation Council). It also has nine associated regional members that have similar objectives of setting up systems to fight money laundering and terrorist financing (FATF-Style Regional Bodies (FSRBs)); and approximately 30 observer members, including the International Monetary Fund (IMF), the United Nations (UN) and the World Bank.

As set out on the FATF website (**www.fatf-gafi.org**), the objectives of FATF are to set standards and promote effective implementation of legal, regulatory and operational measures for combating money laundering, terrorist financing and other related threats to the integrity of the international financial system. Starting with its own members, FATF monitors countries' progress in implementing the

FATF Recommendations; reviews money laundering and terrorist financing techniques and counter-measures; and promotes the adoption and implementation of the FATF Recommendations globally.

Shortly after its creation, FATF provided its 'Forty Recommendations' (or 'Standards') in relation to anti-money laundering (AML) and its 'Nine Special Recommendations on Terrorist Financing' (**www.fatf-gafi.org/publications/fatfrecommendations**). These recommendations are seen globally as the benchmark for anti-money laundering. These recommendations were revised in 1996 and again in 2003. The 2003 recommendations require member states to:

- implement relevant international conventions;
- criminalise money laundering and enable authorities to confiscate the proceeds of money laundering;
- implement customer due diligence, record-keeping and suspicious transaction reporting requirements for financial institutions and designated non-financial businesses and professions;
- establish a financial intelligence unit to receive and disseminate suspicious transaction reports; and
- co-operate internationally in investigating and prosecuting money laundering.

These recommendations were updated once again in subsequent years with the latest update given in October 2020 (**www.fatf-gafi.org/publications/fatfrecommendations/documents/fatf-recommendations.html**).

In 2004 FATF published a document, 'Methodology for assessing technical compliance with the FATF Recommendations and the effectiveness of AML/CFT systems', setting out the methodology for assessing compliance with the recommendations, and it is this methodology that FATF uses to assess a country's performance (**www.fatf-gafi.org/publications/mutualevaluations/documents/fatf-methodology.html** as revised in 2013 and with latest update November 2020). This methodology includes whether the member state has a legal and institutional framework and adequate powers and procedures are held by the authorities in this regard. Further, the methodology looks at whether the framework held by the member states is working and producing the desired results.

In addition to its recommendations, FATF also issued a list of countries that it now terms 'High-Risk Jurisdictions subject to a Call for Action' (**www.fatf-gafi.org/publications/high-risk-and-other-monitored-jurisdictions/documents/call-for-action-february-2021.html**), sometimes referred to as the 'FATF blacklist'. This list was first published in 2000 and comprised 15 jurisdictions that FATF considered were unco-operative with others in international efforts against money laundering and terrorist financing (by way of unwillingness or inability to provide information relating to bank account records, customer due diligence and beneficial owner information relating to such accounts and the use of shell companies or other financial vehicles commonly used in money laundering). As of 21 February 2021, two countries are on the FATF blacklist: Iran and North Korea.

In addition to the blacklist, FATF also issues a 'grey list' – properly titled 'Jurisdictions Under Increased Monitoring'. The countries on this list represent a higher risk of money laundering and terrorist financing and have committed to working with FATF to develop their plans to tackle their deficiencies and therefore help prevent money laundering from occurring. Countries on the grey list can find themselves the subject of sanctions. As of February 2021, the following countries are on the FATF grey list: Albania, Barbados, Botswana, Cambodia, Ghana, Jamaica, Mauritius, Myanmar, Nicaragua, Pakistan, Panama, Syria, Uganda, Yemen and Zimbabwe.

Countries on either the blacklist or the grey list should feature as part of a firm's firm-wide risk assessment and also client and matter risk assessment. See **3.3** and **4.1.2** for more information on those assessments.

Whilst neither list carries sanctions, placing a country on such a list brings a certain level of international pressure and is a powerful tool used to encourage change.

The impact of FATF in the UK should not be underestimated. FATF brings about change to its members, who in turn implement regulations and laws to adhere to the FATF standards.

2.3 OUTLINE OF THE LEGISLATION AS IT APPLIES TO LAW FIRMS

2.3.1 Prior AML legislation

Following FATF's recommendations, 1991 saw the First EU Money Laundering Directive (Council Directive 91/308/EEC of 10 June 1991 on prevention of the use of the financial system for the purpose of money laundering). This directive applied to financial institutions and was enshrined into UK law by the Criminal Justice Act 1991, the Drug Trafficking Act 1994 and the Money Laundering Regulations 1993, SI 1993/1933.

In 2001, the Second Money Laundering Directive was issued (Directive 2001/97/EC of the European Parliament and of the Council of 4 December 2001 amending Council Directive 91/308/EEC on prevention of the use of the financial system for the purpose of money laundering). This directive extended AML obligations to a set of activities provided by service professionals including legal professionals, accountants, auditors, tax advisers and real estate agents. This directive was incorporated into UK law via the Proceeds of Crime Act (POCA) 2002 and the Money Laundering Regulations 2003, SI 2003/3075. It is here that law firms and solicitors were first subject to AML regulations.

The Third Money Laundering Directive was issued in 2005 (Directive 2005/60/EC of the European Parliament and of the Council of 26 October 2005 on the prevention of the use of the financial system for the purpose of money laundering and terrorist financing). This directive extended due diligence measures to beneficial owners, recognised the concept of a risk-based approach to such due diligence and required enhanced due diligence to be undertaken when the circumstances warranted it. This directive was incorporated into UK law by the Money Laundering Regulations 2007, SI 2007/2157 and the Terrorism Act 2000 and Proceeds of Crime Act 2002 (Amendment) Regulations 2007, SI 2007/3398.

In 2015 the Fourth European Union (EU) Directive on Money Laundering was issued (Directive (EU) 2015/849 of the European Parliament and of the Council of 20 May 2015 on the prevention of the use of the financial system for the purposes of money laundering or terrorist financing, amending Regulation (EU) No 648/2012 of the European Parliament and of the Council, and repealing Directive 2005/60/EC of the European Parliament and of the Council and Commission Directive 2006/70/EC). The fourth directive implemented the requirements issued by FATF in 2012. This directive effected a number of changes and was implemented in the UK via the AML Regulations. It is these regulations that are the focus of this chapter, together with the Fifth EU Directive on Money Laundering outlined below. These regulations came into force on 26 June 2017.

The Fifth EU Directive on Money Laundering ('5AMLD' or 'AMLD V') took effect on 10 January 2020 (Directive (EU) 2018/843 of the European Parliament and of the Council of 30 May 2018 amending Directive (EU) 2015/849 on the prevention of the use of the financial system for the purposes of money laundering or terrorist financing, and amending Directives 2009/138/EC and 2013/36/EU). The fifth directive required amendments to the UK's 2017 AML Regulations. Where those amendments affected the application of the AML Regulations for solicitors, they are covered in this book.

2.3.2 Summary of AML legislation today

Before getting into the nitty gritty of the AML Regulations later in this chapter, we will first cover some basics.

Money laundering is the process by which proceeds of crime are cleaned. The stages of money laundering in general terms are: placement of monies into non-cash items; layering transactions to complicate tracing; and integration of the funds.

Proceeds of crime will not always take the form of cash and can be an asset. See **3.5.2** for an explanation of unexpected proceeds of crime.

The AML Regulations term those that need to adhere to them as 'relevant persons'. Depending on the regulation being considered, 'relevant persons' can be read to be the firm or the conducting fee earner. The term 'relevant persons' has been used in this chapter where necessary.

Not all work types that are conducted by solicitors are in scope of the regulations. Generally speaking, litigation work types and wills are out of scope/non-regulated and therefore the AML Regulations do not need to be followed for this work. However (and it is a big however), 5AMLD brought with it a new definition of 'tax adviser' (see AML Regulations, reg.11(d)) which means that those areas that are non-regulated can become regulated if an element of the matter requires tax advice

LEGISLATION AND REGULATION

meaning the relevant person is providing material aid, or assistance or advice on tax affairs including when provided through a third party. For more information on that, see **4.7.2**.

In summary, the AML Regulations in place today apply to persons acting in the course of business carried out in the UK in credit institutions or financial institutions; auditors; insolvency practitioners; accountants; tax advisers; trust or company service providers; estate agents; high value dealers; casinos; and, importantly for this chapter, independent legal professionals.

Regulation 12(1) of the AML Regulations sets out that 'independent legal professional' means a firm or sole practitioner who by way of business provides legal or notarial services to other persons, when participating in financial or real property transactions concerning:

(a) the buying and selling of real property or business entities;
(b) the managing of client money, securities or other assets;
(c) the opening or management of bank, savings or securities accounts;
(d) the organisation of contributions necessary for the creation, operation or management of companies; or
(e) the creation, operation or management of trusts, companies, foundations or similar structures,

and, for this purpose, a person participates in a transaction by assisting in the planning or execution of the transaction or otherwise acting for or on behalf of a client in the transaction.

Regulation 12(2) goes on to state that 'trust or company service provider' means a firm or sole practitioner who provides services for the purpose of forming companies or other legal persons; acting or arranging for another person to act as a director or secretary of that company, as a partner of a partnership or in a similar capacity in relation to legal persons; providing registered offices services; or acting as or arranging for another to act as trustee of an express trust or similar legal arrangement or nominee shareholder for a person other than a company whose securities are listed on a regulated market.

The AML Regulations do not apply to work undertaken by a notary as a public certifying officer where they have no substantive role in the underlying transaction. Therefore, the AML Regulations do not apply to many aspects of a notary's practice including, for example, the taking of affidavits and declarations, protests, translating, certifying the execution of documents and authentication work in general. Note, however, that notaries have their own obligations under their own practice rules.

Generally speaking, the following will not be viewed as participation in a financial transaction such that the AML Regulations apply:

- payment on account of costs to a legal professional or payment of a legal professional's bill;
- provision of legal advice;
- participation in litigation or a form of alternative dispute resolution;

- will-writing, although you should consider whether any accompanying taxation advice is covered;
- work funded by the Legal Services Commission.

In deciding whether a firm is operating within the regulated sector for the purposes of the AML Regulations, the definitions of those caught by the regulations need to be consulted. Some firms may wish to take a broad approach and treat all activities as regulated.

Those who are caught by the AML Regulations need to have appropriate policies, controls and procedures (PCPs) as well as a firm-wide AML risk assessment. These are explored in depth in **Chapter 3**.

2.4 PROCEEDS OF CRIME ACT 2002 OFFENCES, DEFENCES AND TIPPING OFF

POCA 2002 establishes a number of money laundering offences, together with a regime of disclosure of suspicions about money laundering and seeking a defence to what might be a money laundering offence under that disclosure regime. In order to understand the steps required under the AML Regulations, these offences too need to be understood.

POCA 2002 not only creates principal money laundering offences (ss.327–329), but also creates the offences of failing to report suspicious activity (ss.330–332) and tipping off (ss.333–33A).

Save for failing to report and tipping off, POCA 2002 applies to everyone and not just regulated persons.

For a person to be convicted of an offence under POCA 2002, the prosecution must prove knowledge, suspicion or reasonable grounds for suspicion. Further, the prosecution must prove that the property involved was criminal property, i.e. that it was obtained through criminal conduct and that at the time of the alleged offence the individual knew or suspected it was criminal property.

What constitutes suspicion has been the subject of case law, and current guidance can be found in the case of *R* v. *Da Silva* [2007] 1 WLR 303 where the judge commented that suspicion is where a defendant must think that there is a possibility which is more than fanciful that the relevant facts exist, i.e. facts leading to a possibility of money laundering, and that 'a vague feeling of unease would not suffice' (para.16).

The Legal Sector Affinity Group's (LSAG's) 'Anti-money laundering guidance for the legal sector' (20 January 2021, **www.lawsociety.org.uk/en/topics/anti-money-laundering/anti-money-laundering-guidance**) comments that (para.16.7.2): 'There is no requirement for the suspicion to be clear or firmly grounded on specific facts, but there must be a degree of satisfaction, not necessarily amounting to belief, but at least extending beyond speculation.'

A person does not need to be clear that money laundering or some crime is occurring – but if they suspect something might be, they should discuss this with the firm's MLRO. Suspicion does not extend only to a firm's clients, and may arise due to suspicion about another party involved in a transaction. If this is the case, then the relevant person should discuss this with the MLRO. For further guidance on suspicion and making suspicious activity reports (SARs) to the National Crime Agency (NCA), see **3.5**.

2.4.1 Offences

2.4.1.1 A note about legal advice

This book is not a substitute for legal advice. If a relevant person (individual or firm) is concerned that they are in danger of committing an offence under POCA 2002, or needs advice on whether they have a suspicion to report, this book should help. However, the LSAG guidance should be consulted and if the relevant person remains unsure, legal advice should be sought.

2.4.1.2 Criminal property

Naturally POCA 2002 is concerned with criminal property. This is defined as a person's benefit from criminal conduct and where the alleged offender knows or suspects that it constitutes or represents such benefit.

Where there is no criminal property, no money laundering offence can follow.

2.4.1.3 POCA 2002, s.327 – concealing

A person commits an offence if he or she conceals, disguises, converts, transfers criminal property or removes criminal property from England and Wales, Scotland or Northern Ireland.

POCA 2002, s.327(3) goes on to state that concealing or disguising criminal property includes concealing or disguising its nature, source, location, disposition, movement or ownership or any rights with respect to it.

2.4.1.4 POCA 2002, s.328 – arrangements

A person commits an offence if they enter into or become concerned in an arrangement which they know or suspect facilitates (by whatever means) the acquisition, retention, use or control of criminal property by or on behalf of another person.

'Arrangement' is not defined under POCA 2002 and should arguably therefore be given its ordinary meaning.

The LSAG guidance helpfully sets out the position of what an arrangement is *not*. The view contained in the LSAG guidance is that the handling of criminal property in accordance with a court judgment is not becoming involved in an arrangement. Further settlements, negotiations, out-of-court settlements, alternative dispute resolution and tribunal representations are not arrangements. LSAG advises, however, that the criminal property in question will still be criminal property and relevant persons may need to advise their clients to take independent legal advice on any consequences of holding such property. For further reading on the meaning of an arrangement, *Bowman* v. *Fels* [2005] EWCA Civ 226 and the LSAG guidance should be consulted.

2.4.1.5 POCA 2002, s.329 – *acquisition, use or possession*

A person commits an offence if they acquire, use or have possession of criminal property.

2.4.1.6 POCA 2002, ss.330, 331 and 332 – *failure to disclose offences*

For a POCA 2002, s.330 offence ('Failure to disclose: regulated sector') to be committed, the following conditions need to be met. A person commits an offence if:

- they know or suspect, or have reasonable grounds for knowing or suspecting, that another person is engaged in money laundering; and
- the information on which their suspicion is based comes in the course of business in the regulated sector; and
- they fail to disclose that knowledge or suspicion, or reasonable grounds for suspicion, as soon as practicable to a nominated officer or the NCA.

A s.331 offence ('Failure to disclose: nominated officers in the regulated sector') will be committed if the nominated officer (MLRO), having received a disclosure under section 330 and forming the required knowledge or suspicion or reasonable grounds to know or suspect money laundering, fails to disclose this as soon as practicable to the NCA.

A s.332 offence ('Failure to disclose: other nominated officers') will be committed where a nominated officer appointed in a firm that conducts non-regulated activities fails to make a disclosure when they know or suspect that another person is engaged in money laundering. This test is a subjective one, not an objective one. Practically it means that where an MLRO receives information in relation to a piece of non-regulated work, for example litigation, the MLRO needs to consider whether they have an obligation to make a disclosure and not simply to decide not to do so on the basis that the work itself is unregulated.

2.4.2 Defences to offences under POCA 2002, ss.327, 328 and 329

POCA 2002, ss.327, 328 and 329 all state that a person does not commit an offence under those sections if they make an authorised disclosure under s.338 and are given the appropriate consent, intended to make a disclosure but had a reasonable excuse for not doing so, acquired or used or had possession of the property for adequate consideration (in the case of s.329) or the act undertaken is done in carrying out a function the person has relating to the enforcement of any provision of POCA 2002 or of any other enactment relating to criminal conduct or benefit from criminal conduct.

2.4.2.1 POCA 2002, s.338 – authorised disclosure

In order to avoid committing an offence under POCA 2002, ss.327, 328 and 329, s.338 allows an authorised disclosure of the actual or suspected money laundering in defence of a principal money laundering offence. The section sets out that the disclosure must be made before money laundering has occurred, whilst it is occurring but as soon as there is suspicion or after it has occurred if there was good reason not to disclose earlier and the disclosure is made as soon as practicable. Where a disclosure is an authorised one, regulatory requirements such as confidentiality will not be breached.

Where a firm has an MLRO, this disclosure should be made to that person and that person should consider making a disclosure to the NCA. Where a firm does not have an MLRO, the relevant person (normally the conducting fee earner) needs to make a disclosure directly to the NCA.

Where necessary, the MLRO (or relevant person in the absence of an MLRO) will seek a defence from the NCA via a SAR. This is often referred to as the seeking of 'consent', but this term is in fact incorrect and it is not 'consent' that the NCA can provide; instead it will be able to provide a defence to a money laundering offence committed by the relevant persons should one occur.

For more guidance on the submission of SARs, see **3.5.3**.

2.4.2.2 Reasonable excuse not to make a disclosure

Here a defence to a principal money laundering offence is available if a person intended to make an authorised disclosure but had a reasonable excuse not to do so. 'Reasonable excuse' has not been defined by the courts and LSAG advises that in its view information giving rise to knowledge or suspicion of money laundering which is privileged (and the crime/fraud exception does not apply) will afford the relevant person a reasonable excuse defence on not making a disclosure. For more guidance on legal professional privilege, see **3.5.4**.

The LSAG guidance also sets out the following possible reasonable excuses (para.16.4.3):

- If it is clear that a regulator or enforcement authority (in the UK or elsewhere) is already aware of the suspected criminal conduct or money laundering and the reporter does not have any additional information which might assist the regulator or enforcement authority.
- If the only information that a reporter would be providing for the purposes of an authorised disclosure or a report under s.330 is information entirely within the public domain.
- If all the suspected predicate offending occurs outside the UK and all the suspected money laundering occurs outside the UK and there is otherwise no UK nexus to the suspected criminality.
- If the criminal activity derives from an administrative offence; for example, one of 'strict liability' where no mens rea, or criminal intent, is required.

The LSAG guidance notes that this is not an exhaustive list and that ultimately it will be for a court to decide whether the defence of reasonable excuse is available. Subject to privilege not coming into play, those who should report may do well to simply report anyway even if they are aware a report has already been made or the information is in the public domain. That way no criticism can be levied. If a decision not to report is made, this should be well documented for future reference and ultimately possible scrutiny.

2.4.2.3 Adequate consideration defence

This defence applies if there was adequate consideration for acquiring, using and possessing the criminal property, unless the person knows or suspects that those goods or services may help another carry out criminal conduct.

The LSAG guidance notes that guidance given to the Crown Prosecution Service (CPS) prosecutors is that this defence applies where professional advisers, such as legal professionals or accountants, receive money for or on account of costs or disbursements, whether from the client or from another person on the client's behalf. However, the fees charged must be reasonable, and the defence is not available if the value of the work is significantly less than the money received.

Note, however, that returning funds to a client may be a money laundering offence if the relevant person knows or suspects that the money is criminal property. If that is the case, then a defence should be sought via a SAR to the NCA.

The LSAG guidance (para.16.4.2) sets out that other instances where this defence might apply are where:

- a third party seeks to enforce a debt and is given criminal property in payment for that debt;
- a person provides goods or services as part of a legitimate arm's length transaction but is paid from a bank account which contains the proceeds of crime.

2.4.3 Defences to offences under POCA 2002, ss.330, 331 and 332

There are three defences to offences under POCA 2002, ss.330, 331 and 332 as set out within those sections: reasonable excuse; privileged circumstances; or that the relevant person did not receive the appropriate training from their employer. The first defence applies to all three offences. The second and third only apply to those who are not nominated officers.

2.4.3.1 Reasonable excuse

There is no judicial guidance on what might constitute a reasonable excuse. Again, the LSAG guidance sets out that LSAG's view is that information received is privileged and the crime/fraud exception does not apply; this will be a reasonable excuse for not making a disclosure. LSAG repeats the possible reasonable excuses outlined above.

2.4.3.2 Privileged circumstances

The concept of information being provided in privileged circumstances is not the same as legal professional privilege and is a design of POCA 2002 to accord with the exemptions from reporting set out in the EU directives.

Information provided in privileged circumstances means information communicated:

- by a client, or a representative of a client, in connection with the giving of legal advice to the client;
- by a client, or by a representative of a client, seeking legal advice from you; or
- by a person in connection with legal proceedings or contemplated legal proceedings.

If the goal of the giving of the information is to further a criminal purpose, then the exemption will not apply.

2.4.3.3 Lack of training

This defence is available for those employees within the regulated sector. Should this defence be successfully run, a law firm's money laundering compliance officer (MLCO) will no doubt be open to prosecution for failing to fulfil their role. See **3.7.1** for further guidance on the role of an MLCO.

2.4.4 Tipping off offences and defences under POCA 2002

2.4.4.1 Offences

DISCLOSING A SAR

Under POCA 2002, s.333A(1) a person commits an offence if they disclose that they have made a SAR to a constable, HM Revenue and Customs (HMRC), the MLRO of their firm or the NCA and that disclosure is likely to prejudice any investigation that might be conducted following the SAR. For this offence to occur, the information needs to come to the person in the course of business in the regulated sector.

This offence can only be committed after a disclosure to the NCA and if the person knows or suspects that by disclosing the information they are likely to prejudice any investigation related to that SAR.

For this reason, all relevant persons need to understand through training that when they have a suspicion they need to report it to their MLRO and take advice from the MLRO as to what they can and cannot say to their client or anyone else. See **3.5** for further guidance on SARs.

DISCLOSING AN INVESTIGATION

Under POCA 2002, s.333A(3) a person commits an offence if they disclose that an investigation into allegations that an offence has been committed is being contemplated or is being carried out and the disclosure is likely to prejudice the investigation. Again, for this offence to occur the information on which the SAR is based needs to come to the person in the course of business in the regulated sector.

PREJUDICING AN INVESTIGATION OFFENCE UNDER S.342(1)

POCA 2002, s.342(1) contains another offence of prejudicing an investigation. A person commits this offence if the person knows or suspects that an appropriate officer is acting in connection with a confiscation investigation, civil recovery investigation or money laundering investigation which is being or is about to be conducted and makes a disclosure about it which is likely to prejudice an investigation or that person falsifies, conceals, destroys or otherwise disposes of, or causes or permits the falsification, concealment, destruction or disposal of, documents which are relevant to the investigation.

PENALTIES FOR TIPPING OFF OFFENCES

For an offence under POCA 2002, s.333A a person found guilty is liable (s.333A(4)):

(a) on summary conviction to imprisonment for a term not exceeding three months, or to a fine not exceeding level 5 on the standard scale, or to both;
(b) on conviction on indictment to imprisonment for a term not exceeding two years, or to a fine, or to both.

For a s.342 offence, a person found guilty is liable (s.342(7)):

(a) on summary conviction, to imprisonment for a term not exceeding six months or to a fine not exceeding the statutory maximum or to both, or
(b) on conviction on indictment, to imprisonment for a term not exceeding five years or to a fine or to both.

A s.342 offence therefore carries a heavier possible penalty.

2.4.4.2 Defences to tipping off offences

POCA 2002, S.333B – DISCLOSURES WITHIN AN UNDERTAKING OR GROUP, ETC.

POCA 2002, s.333B provides a defence if an employee, officer or partner of a firm discloses that a SAR has been made to another employee, officer or partner of the same undertaking. Same undertaking here means same firm.

Section 333B(4) provides that a professional legal adviser or relevant professional adviser does not commit an offence of tipping off under s.333A if:

(a) the disclosure is to professional legal adviser or a relevant professional adviser,
(b) both the person making the disclosure and the person to whom it is made carry on business in the United Kingdom or an EEA state or in a country or territory imposing equivalent money laundering requirements, and
(c) those persons perform their professional activities within different undertakings that share common ownership, management or control.

POCA 2002, S.333C – OTHER PERMITTED DISCLOSURES BETWEEN INSTITUTIONS, ETC.

Under POCA 2002, s.333C(2) a person does not commit an offence under s.333A if:

(a) the disclosure relates to–
   (i) a client or former client of the institution or adviser making the disclosure and the institution or adviser to whom it is made,
   (ii) a transaction involving them both, or
   (iii) the provision of a service involving them both;
(b) the disclosure is for the purpose only of preventing an offence under this Part of this Act;
(c) the institution or adviser to whom the disclosure is made is situated in the United Kingdom or an EEA state or in a country or territory imposing equivalent money laundering requirements; and
(d) the institution or adviser making the disclosure and the institution or adviser to

whom it is made are subject to equivalent duties of professional confidentiality and the protection of personal data.

POCA 2002, S.333D – OTHER PERMITTED DISCLOSURES, ETC.

POCA 2002, s.333D(1) sets out that an offence is not committed under s.333A if the disclosure is to a supervisory authority (such as the Solicitors Regulation Authority (SRA)); for the purpose of proceedings under s.336A (power of court to extend the moratorium period); made in good faith by virtue of s.339ZB (disclosures within the regulated sector); or for the purposes of detection, investigation or prosecution of a criminal offence, investigation under the Act or enforcement of any court order under the Act.

POCA 2002, s.333D(2) goes on to state that:

> A professional legal adviser or a relevant professional adviser does not commit an offence under section 333A if the disclosure–
> (a) is to the adviser's client, and
> (b) is made for the purpose of dissuading the client from engaging in conduct amounting to an offence.

POCA 2002, S.342 DEFENCE

POCA 2002, s.342(3) and (6) set out the circumstances when a s.342 offence will not be made out. These are when a person did not know or suspect that a disclosure was likely to prejudice an investigation or that person did not intend to conceal any facts disclosed by the documents from any appropriate officer or proper person carrying out the investigation.

Further, under s.342(4) no s.342 offence is committed if the disclosure is made by a legal representative to a client or another representative of a client in connection with giving legal advice to the client or to any person in connection with legal proceedings or contemplated legal proceedings.

2.5 TERRORISM ACT 2000

The UK government's 'National risk assessment of money laundering and terrorist financing 2020' (December 2020, **www.gov.uk/government/publications/national-risk-assessment-of-money-laundering-and-terrorist-financing-2020**) sets out that terrorist financing in the legal sector is considered to be a low risk (the risk of money laundering is high – see **3.1.1**). However, law firms need to be aware of the principal offences and defences under the Terrorism Act (TA) 2000. That said, because there are parallels with the offences and defences under POCA 2002, these are explored here briefly and readers are advised to consult the legislation directly and the LSAG guidance, and if necessary seek legal advice.

All persons are required to abide by TA 2000. TA 2000 created four principal offences (fundraising; use and possession; funding arrangements; and money laundering) and two tipping off offences for those who are in the regulated sector.

'Terrorist property' is defined (s.14(1)) as:

(a) money or other property which is likely to be used for the purposes of terrorism (including any resources of a proscribed organisation),
(b) proceeds of the commission of acts of terrorism, and
(c) proceeds of acts carried out for the purposes of terrorism.

2.5.1 Principal offences under the Terrorism Act 2000

2.5.1.1 TA 2000, s.15 – fundraising

TA 2000, s.15 sets out that a person commits an offence if:

(a) the person invites another to provide money or other property and intends that it should be used, or has reasonable cause to suspect that it may be used, for the purposes of terrorism;
(b) the person receives money or other property and intends that it should be used, or has reasonable cause to suspect that it may be used, for the purposes of terrorism;
(c) the person provides money or other property and knows or has reasonable cause to suspect that it will or may be used for the purposes of terrorism.

It is not a defence that the monies or other property are for payment of goods and services.

2.5.1.2 TA 2000, s.16 – use and possession

Here a person commits an offence if they use money or other property for the purposes of terrorism. The offence is committed if the person possesses money or other property and intends that it should be used or has reasonable cause to suspect that it may be used for the purposes of terrorism.

2.5.1.3 TA 2000, s.17 – funding arrangements

Here a person commits an offence if they enter into or become concerned in an arrangement as a result of which money or other property is made available or is to be made available to another and that person knows or has reasonable cause to suspect that it will or may be used for the purposes of terrorism.

2.5.1.4 TA 2000, s.18 – money laundering

TA 2000, s.18 provides that:

ANTI-MONEY LAUNDERING

(1) A person commits an offence if he enters into or becomes concerned in an arrangement which facilitates the retention or control by or on behalf of another person of terrorist property–
   (a) by concealment,
   (b) by removal from the jurisdiction,
   (c) by transfer to nominees, or
   (d) in any other way.

(2) It is a defence for a person charged with an offence under subsection (1) to prove that he did not know and had no reasonable cause to suspect that the arrangement related to terrorist property.

For the purposes of this offence, the meaning of 'arrangement' is the same as under POCA 2002. See **2.4.1** for guidance.

2.5.2 Defences to principal offences under TA 2000

In addition to an existing defence of the co-operation of the police, the Terrorism Act 2000 and Proceeds of Crime Act 2002 (Amendment) Regulations 2007, SI 2007/3398 created three new defences to the principal offences under TA 2000 (set out at points 2–4 below). The defences can be found at TA 2000, ss.21, 21ZA, 21ZB and 21ZC, and are as follows:

1. **Police co-operation (s.21)** – A person does not commit an offence under TA 2000, ss.15–18 if they act with the express consent of a constable and a disclosure is made as to the person's suspicion or belief that the money or other property is terrorist property and provides the information on which that suspicion or belief is based. The defence does not apply if the constable forbids the person to continue involvement in the transaction or arrangement and the person continues that involvement. The section sets out that this defence is also available to employees who report their suspicions internally using the procedure specified by their employer.
2. **Prior consent (s.21ZA)** – A person does not commit an offence under TA 2000, ss.15–18 if they made a disclosure of their suspicion and consent is given to becoming involved in the transaction or arrangement. The disclosure has to have been made prior to involvement. This disclosure would be made by way of a SAR (see **3.5**).
3. **Consent (s.21ZB)** – A person does not commit an offence under TA 2000, ss.15–18 if after becoming involved the person makes a disclosure and there is a reasonable excuse for the person's failure to make the disclosure before becoming involved. Again, this disclosure would be made by way of a SAR (see **3.5**). The defence does not apply if an authorised person forbids the person to continue involvement in the transaction or arrangement and the person continues that involvement.
4. **Reasonable excuse for failure to disclose (s.21ZC)** – It is a defence for a person charged with an offence under TA 2000, ss.15–18 if they intended to

LEGISLATION AND REGULATION

make a disclosure but had a reasonable excuse for not doing so. For meaning of reasonable excuse, see guidance at **2.4.2**.

2.5.3 Failure to disclose offences under TA 2000

There are two offences of failure to disclose a terrorism offence. One relates to the non-regulated sector and one to the regulated sector.

TA 2000, s.19 sets out that anyone commits an offence if they do not disclose as soon as reasonably practicable a belief or suspicion that another person is committing a terrorist financing offence and the information on which that belief or suspicion is based.

TA 2000, s.21A (inserted by the Anti-terrorism, Crime and Security Act 2001) creates an offence for those in the regulated sector who fail to make a disclosure to a constable or the firm's nominated officer where they know or suspect or have reasonable grounds to suspect that another person is committing or attempting to commit an offence under the Act.

2.5.4 Defences to the failure to disclose offences under TA 2000

There are two defences available to those who stand accused of failure to disclose offences under TA 2000:

(a) reasonable excuse for not making a disclosure (see **2.4.2** for guidance); or
(b) the information on which the belief or suspicion is based was given in privileged circumstances without an intention to further a criminal purpose. This defence applies to those who are employed by or are in partnership with a professional legal adviser and the information is given in privileged circumstances. See **3.5.4** for further guidance on privilege.

2.5.5 Tipping off offences and defences under TA 2000

2.5.5.1 Offences

DISCLOSING A SAR

Under TA 2000, s.21D(1) a person commits an offence if they disclose that a SAR was made and that disclosure is likely to prejudice any investigation that might be conducted following the SAR. The information which is disclosed should have come to the person in the course of business in the regulated sector.

DISCLOSING AN INVESTIGATION

Under TA 2000, s.21D(3) it is an offence to disclose that an investigation into allegations that an offence under the Act has been committed is being contemplated or is being carried out and that disclosure is likely to prejudice that investigation and the information on which the disclosure is based came to the person in the course of a business in the regulated sector. The person does not need to be aware that a SAR has been submitted.

2.5.5.2 Defences

TA 2000, S.21E – DISCLOSURES WITHIN AN UNDERTAKING OR GROUP

TA 2000, s.21E sets out that it is not an offence for an employee, officer or partner of a practice to disclose a SAR if the disclosure is to an employee, officer or partner of the same undertaking. Further, under s.21E(4) a legal professional adviser will not commit an offence under section if:

(a) the disclosure is to a professional legal adviser or a relevant professional adviser,
(b) both the person making the disclosure and the person to whom it is made carry on business in the United Kingdom or an EEA state or in a country or territory imposing equivalent money laundering requirements, and
(c) those persons perform their professional activities within different undertakings that share common ownership, management or control.

TA 2000, S.21F – OTHER PERMITTED DISCLOSURES BETWEEN INSTITUTIONS

Under TA 2000, s.21F(2)(a) a legal professional will not commit the offence of tipping off if the disclosure relates to:

(i) a client or former client of the institution or adviser making the disclosure and the institution or adviser to whom it is made,
(ii) a transaction involving them both, or
(iii) the provision of a service involving them both ...

The disclosure must be made for the purpose of preventing an offence under the Act and the person to whom the disclosure is made must be situated in an EEA state or country/territory imposing equivalent money laundering requirements. Further, both parties must have equivalent duties of confidentiality and protection of personal data.

TA 2000, S.21G – OTHER PERMITTED DISCLOSURES

Under TA 2000, s.21G a person will not commit an offence of tipping off if the disclosure is to a client for the purposes of dissuading the client from engaging in conduct that amounts to an offence. This only applies to the regulated sector.

2.6 OTHER TERRORIST PROPERTY OFFENCES LEGISLATION

There are other pieces of legislation that firms ought to be aware of at a high level; these are contained in the LSAG guidance and are summarised below.

The Sanctions and Anti-Money Laundering Act 2018 empowers the Secretary of State to make regulations that enables the freezing of terrorist assets.

Asset freezing offences can be found in the following regulations:

- Counter-Terrorism (Sanctions) (EU Exit) Regulations 2019, SI 2019/577;
- Counter-Terrorism (International Sanctions) (EU Exit) Regulations 2019, SI 2019/573; and
- ISIL (Da'esh) and Al-Qaida (United Nations Sanctions) (EU Exit) Regulations 2019, SI 2019/466.

As stated in the LSAG guidance, these regulations contain prohibitions against:

- dealing with the funds or economic resources owned, held or controlled by designated persons;
- making funds or financial services or economic resources available, directly or indirectly to designated persons;
- making funds or financial services or economic resources available to any person for the significant benefit of a designated person; and
- knowingly and intentionally participating in activities that would directly or indirectly circumvent the financial restrictions, enable, or facilitate the commission of any of the above offences.

As set out in the LSAG guidance, it is a defence if persons did not know nor had any reasonable cause to suspect that they were undertaking a prohibited act with respect to a designated person.

In relation to funds, 'deal with' is defined by the legislation as:

- using, altering, moving, allowing access to or transferring;
- dealing with in any other way that would result in any change in volume, amount, location, ownership, possession, character or destination; or
- making any other change that would enable use of the funds (including portfolio management).

In relation to economic resources, 'deals with' is defined as:

- exchanging or using the resources for funds, goods, or services (including by pledging them as security).

CHAPTER 3

Risk assessment and internal controls

3.1 UK NATIONAL RISK ASSESSMENT AND SRA'S AML RISK ASSESSMENT

As outlined at **3.3** below, 'relevant persons' must conduct a firm-wide anti-money laundering (AML) risk assessment in accordance with Money Laundering, Terrorist Financing and Transfer of Funds (Information on the Payer) Regulations 2017, SI 2017/692 ('AML Regulations'), reg.18. In doing so, the relevant person must take into account information made available by the supervisory body under regs.17(9) and 47. The supervisor's risk assessment must take into account the risk assessment undertaken by the Treasury and Home Office under reg.16. This risk assessment is termed the 'UK national risk assessment'.

The purpose of the risk assessment by the Treasury and Home Office is set out at reg.16(2) as follows:

(a) identify any areas where relevant persons should apply enhanced customer due diligence measures, and where appropriate, specify the measures to be taken;
(b) identify, where appropriate, the sectors or areas of lower and greater risk of money laundering and terrorist financing;
(c) consider whether any rules on money laundering and terrorist financing made by a supervisory authority applying in relation to the sector it supervises are appropriate in the light of the risks of money laundering and terrorist financing applying to that sector;
(d) provide the information and analysis necessary to enable it to be used for the purposes set out in paragraph (3).

Regulation 16(3) goes on to state that the Treasury and Home Office must consider the appropriate allocation and prioritisation of resources to counter money laundering and terrorist financing and whether the exclusions provided for in reg.15 are being abused. Following the Fifth EU Directive on Money Laundering (EU) 2018/843 (5AMLD), implemented by the Money Laundering and Terrorist Financing (Amendment) Regulations 2019, SI 2019/1511 (MLR 2019), reg.16 was amended to provide that the risk assessment by the Treasury and Home Office must also set out (see reg.4(8) of MLR 2019):

(a) the institutional structure and broad procedures of the United Kingdom's anti-money laundering and counter-terrorist financing regime, including the role of the financial intelligence unit, tax agencies and prosecutors;

(b) the nature of measures taken and resources allocated to counter money laundering and terrorist financing.

As indicated above, reg.17 sets out the requirements for a risk assessment to be conducted by supervisory bodies. In the case of most law firms this will be the Solicitors Regulation Authority (SRA). Regulation 17 also provides the requirements for supervisory bodies to keep risk profiles on relevant persons.

Although the firm-wide risk assessment that must be carried out by relevant persons needs to take into account the supervisory body's risk assessment and the regulations do not require the relevant person to consider the risk assessment of the Treasury and Home Office, it would be remiss, in the author's opinion, to focus solely on the risk assessment of the supervisor.

There is no substitute for reading the relevant risk assessments and indeed they should be read. However, below there is a summary of each assessment (correct as at early 2021).

3.1.1 UK National risk assessment of money laundering and terrorist financing 2020

The UK published its 'National risk assessment of money laundering and terrorist financing 2020' on 17 December 2020 (**www.gov.uk/government/publications/ national-risk-assessment-of-money-laundering-and-terrorist-financing-2020**). The assessment is over 150 pages long, and readers are encouraged to read the 'Executive summary' and chapter 10 which relates to legal services. In summary, the latter section sets out the following:

1. The risk of money laundering in legal services remains high. Legal service providers offer a range of services and 'the services most at risk of exploitation by criminals and corrupt elites for money laundering purposes continue to be conveyancing, trust and company services and client accounts'.
2. The risk of money laundering in firms increases when legal professionals fail to carry out their obligations under the regulations or 'take a tick box approach to compliance'. Further, 'there also remains a risk that some legal professionals are complicit and willingly enable money laundering'.
3. The risk assessment acknowledges that there have been improvements in the supervision of legal professionals in part, it says, due to the Office for Professional Body Anti-Money Laundering Supervision (OPBAS). See **5.4** in relation to OPBAS; and **5.7** for a rundown of the SRA's AML visits.
4. The risk of legal services being used to fund terrorism is low. See **2.5** for guidance on the Terrorism Act 2000.
5. In relation to conveyancing, there is no evidence that the risks have changed and both residential and commercial property transactions remain high risk for money laundering. The risk assessment sets out that although further evidence is needed to ascertain geographical risks, criminals are likely to favour high value residential properties in London and university towns due to

high demands and rental returns. The risk assessment goes on to set out some conveyancing red flags as follows (para.10.4):

- clients seeking anonymity buying property through complex corporate structures, such as companies based in secrecy jurisdictions which can mask the ultimate beneficial owner.
- clients buying the property without a mortgage from a financial institution with no verifiable source of income justifying their wealth.
- conveyancing transactions that involve multiple LSPs [legal service providers].
- customers that are PEPs [politically exposed persons] from high corruption-risk jurisdictions and those charged with or alleged to have committed corruption offences.

6. There is a risk that legal professionals negligently or unwittingly facilitate money laundering through providing trust and company services (paras.10.6–10.9). If trust and company services provision is coupled with other risk factors such as complex structures intended to conceal beneficial ownership or parties outside the UK, the risk may increase. The risk assessment refers to the SRA's review of law firms who provide trust and company services. See **5.5.1** for more information.

7. There is risk of client accounts being exploited for money laundering (paras.10.10–10.11). The assessment notes that solicitors have strict rules on what a client account can be used for (see **5.3.3** for details of the SRA's warning notice).

8. Other risks such as sham litigation and notary services are also noted in the assessment (paras.10.12–10.15).

9. Key non-compliance trends observed by those who supervise legal service providers are (para.10.20):

    (a) many legal service providers treating AML compliance as a low priority or a tick-box exercise which comes second to their day job;
    (b) insufficient or weak risk-based controls in place;
    (c) a lack of legal sector specific AML training available for legal service professionals.

10. There has been an increase in the number of suspicious activity reports (SARs) made by legal service professionals in 2019–2020 by 13 per cent from 2017–2018 (para.10.28). (See **3.5** for guidance on SARs.)

3.1.2 SRA's AML risk assessment

The SRA's latest risk assessment is 'Sectoral risk assessment – anti-money laundering and terrorist financing' (28 January 2021, **www.sra.org.uk/sra/how-we-work/reports/aml-risk-assessment/**) and as stated above this must be considered by those conducting the firm's AML risk assessment under reg.18. However, below is a brief summary of some of the key aspects of the risk assessment. This risk

RISK ASSESSMENT AND INTERNAL CONTROLS

assessment is liable to frequent change and so care must be taken to regularly check for updated versions.

1. Under 'Emerging risks', the risk assessment notes the impact of COVID-19. The SRA's view is that COVID-19 may have left some firms in a vulnerable financial position which results in them taking on clients that they would otherwise have avoided. The SRA notes that COVID-19 has 'accelerated the trend for firms not meeting clients face to face, which can make it inherently more difficult to identify and verify the identity of these clients'. In the author's opinion, the converse is true in practice as law firms embrace video technology to meet clients with some being clients they would not have met anyway.
2. Following on from the COVID-19 theme, the risk assessment sets out the risk in decreasing sufficient resourcing of AML work in law firms due to economic pressure.
3. Getting special mention is work where funds have come from legal cannabis growing abroad, and the issues around proceeds of crime.
4. Under 'Observations from our proactive supervision work', the SRA sets out that during supervision visits it has observed AML weaknesses such as inadequate source of funds checks, independent audits, screening of staff and completion of matter risk assessments. Further, the SRA sets out its concerns about centralised compliance teams which might lead to fee earners not having access to an underlying risk assessment and due diligence information and being prevented from conducting effective ongoing monitoring of risk.
5. The SRA sets out that it has found that some firms have an overly simplistic view of PEPs. This was based on its thematic reviews. See **5.5**.
6. Under 'Products and services', the risk assessment sets out that conveyancing, trust and company formation are considered to be at high risk of being used to launder money. Further mentioned is tax advice where that advice is used to evade tax, and also acting as a 'family office' for ultra-high net worth individuals offering a range of services where the firm might be open to influence.
7. Client accounts are also at risk of being used to launder money, with the assessment setting out that:

    Criminals target client accounts as a way of moving money from one individual to another through a trusted third party under the guise of a legal transaction without attracting the attention of law enforcement.

    You must never allow your client account to be used as a banking facility, or to pass funds through it without a legitimate underlying transaction. Firms should be aware of any attempt to pay funds into a client account without a genuine reason, or to get a refund of funds from a client account (particularly to a different account from which the original funds were paid).

    See **5.3.3** for details of the SRA's warning notice on the use of a client account as a banking facility.

8. Under 'Client risk', the assessment sets out that clients who are PEPs, come from cash intensive or higher risk sectors and clients who seek anonymity or who cannot prove their identity are considered to be higher risk. The SRA's assessment notes that in some cases it might be natural that a person cannot produce identification documentation, such as the elderly.
9. Under 'Transaction risk', transactions such as large or high value transactions, payments in cash, transactions that don't fit in with the client's normal pattern of behaviour or are not of the type of transaction that the firm would normally do and transactions that are complex to obscure source of funds or ownership are all highlighted as risks of money laundering.
10. Under 'Delivery channel risk', delivery channels of offering services such as not meeting clients (though note comments above); combining services which may not be high risk in themselves but when combined might be; and receiving payments from third parties are all considered to increase the risk of money laundering.
11. Under 'Geographic risk', geographical aspects of services such as dealing with countries that do not have equivalent AML standards or countries that have significant levels of corruption or are subject to sanctions, are considered to be high risk.

All of these risk factors need to be considered and addressed in the firm's AML risk assessment and also factored into the client and matter risk assessment (see **3.3** and **4.1.2**).

3.1.3 NCA National strategic assessment of serious and organised crime 2020

A further risk assessment that relevant persons may want to consider (but are not obliged to do so) is the NCA's 'National strategic assessment of serious and organised crime 2020' (**www.nationalcrimeagency.gov.uk/news/nsa2020**). This assessment does not focus solely on money laundering and covers modern slavery, immigration crime, cybercrime and fraud, amongst others.

3.2 WHO IS WHO – SUPERVISORS AND GUIDANCE PROVIDERS

It is important for firms to understand who the regulators and supervisors are that operate to prevent law firms being involved with money laundering. In this section we provide a brief rundown.

RISK ASSESSMENT AND INTERNAL CONTROLS

3.2.1 Financial Action Task Force

The Financial Action Task Force (FATF) is an intergovernmental organisation set up to develop policies and standards to combat money laundering. Its recommendations are often enshrined into legislation. See **2.2** for further information.

3.2.2 Office for Professional Body Anti-Money Laundering Supervision

Housed within the Financial Conduct Authority (FCA) office, OPBAS was set up in 2018 with the aim of improving the supervision of the implementation of AML measures by regulators of those they regulate. OPBAS does not therefore oversee what those who are regulated do, but rather is there to supervise the regulators. The watchers have now become the watched.

OPBAS oversees not only the SRA, but also many other legal and accountancy regulators.

Ultimately it is pressure from OPBAS which has led to tighter supervision of law firms by the SRA. See **5.4** for further information about OPBAS and its review of the SRA.

3.2.3 Solicitors Regulation Authority

The SRA supervises those it regulates for AML compliance and is able to take disciplinary action and make referrals to the Solicitors Disciplinary Tribunal for non-compliance with penalties ranging from rebukes to fines and striking off. See **5.9** for examples. It is the SRA's views and guidance that law firms must take heed of, and the reader will find that throughout this chapter the SRA's guidance and views are explored to enable the reader to consider the same.

3.2.4 National Crime Agency

The National Crime Agency (NCA) is the national law enforcement agency in the UK. It replaced the Serious Organised Crime Agency in 2013. It is this organisation that SARs are made to and by which a money laundering defence may be given.

3.2.5 The Law Society of England and Wales

The Law Society of England and Wales provides guidance to solicitors on the implementation of the AML Regulations. The Law Society has no supervisory role but instead is a representative body for solicitors. See **5.2** for Law Society guidance.

3.2.6 Legal Sector Affinity Group

The Legal Sector Affinity Group (LSAG) is made up of AML supervisors for the legal sector and produces the 'Anti-money laundering guidance for the legal sector'

(January 2021, **www.lawsociety.org.uk/en/topics/anti-money-laundering/anti-money-laundering-guidance**). This guidance should be consulted by all relevant persons in law firms when needed, and the reason for any deviation from it should be recorded in case the SRA asks for an explanation for that deviation. See **5.1** for more information about this guidance.

3.2.7 Joint Money Laundering Steering Group

The Joint Money Laundering Steering Group (JMLSG) produces guidance to assist those in financial industry sectors represented on the JMLSG by their trade member bodies, to comply with their obligations in terms of the AML Regulations and counter-terrorist financing legislation. This guidance is unlikely to be relevant to law firms unless they have an FCA regulated arm.

3.3 FIRM-WIDE AML RISK ASSESSMENT

Under reg.18(1) of the AML Regulations, a law firm is obliged to undertake a firm-wide AML risk assessment to identify and assess the money laundering risk, and consider and put in place policies, controls and procedures (PCPs) to tackle those risks. This requirement has been in place since June 2017.

On 20 January 2021, the LSAG provided new, detailed and well-written guidance in this area, and this should be consulted.

Further, the SRA, after having conducted a thematic review (see **5.5** for more on this) has produced guidance on the requirement for a firm-wide AML risk assessment which should also be read: 'Guidance – Firm risk assessments' (25 November 2019, **www.sra.org.uk/solicitors/guidance/firm-risk-assessments/**). Additionally, the SRA has issued a warning notice on this subject: 'Warning notice – Compliance with the money laundering regulations – firm risk assessment' (25 November 2019, **www.sra.org.uk/solicitors/guidance/compliance-money-laundering-regulations-firm-risk-assessment/**; see **5.3**).

In summary, the SRA guidance sets out that the SRA expects a firm's risk assessment to:

- take into account information that the SRA publishes – this could be guidance and warning notices;
- address risk factors set out in the AML Regulations, namely:
    - the firm's clients;
    - the countries or geographic areas in which the firm operates;
    - the products or services which the firm provides;
    - the firm's transactions;
    - how the firm's products and services are delivered;
- take into account, and be appropriate to, the size and nature of the firm.

RISK ASSESSMENT AND INTERNAL CONTROLS

Each firm needs to read the SRA guidance and LSAG guidance for itself – but below are a few aspects for firms to consider.

- **Checklist** – The SRA has produced a checklist, 'Anti-money laundering (AML) firm risk assessment checklist', to help firms prepare for a risk assessment (**www.sra.org.uk/globalassets/documents/solicitors/anti-money-laundering-aml-firm-risk-assessment-checklist.docx?version=4a4d74**). This is worth using if a firm is conducting a risk assessment for the first time or is revisiting its current assessment (which it should do on a regular basis, particularly when it has changed its AML policy or client due diligence (CDD) requirements, for example, or the SRA has released a new risk assessment of its own).
- **Templates** – The SRA has produced a template risk assessment that firms may wish to use (**www.sra.org.uk/globalassets/documents/solicitors/firm-wide-risk-assessment-template.docx?version=4a4d74**). The SRA does not mandate use of this template and there are many ways of writing the assessment. A firm may decide to do it by way of a spreadsheet and/or a table or in written form. Each firm should tailor its risk assessment to suit its firm. At **Appendix B1** you will see a suggested template, and you are encouraged to review the SRA's template found on its website. However, note that when the SRA conducted a review of 400 law firms' risk assessments, it found that the use of templates had an impact on the quality of a firm's risk assessment, i.e. the quality was lower and the assessment did not match the firm's risk profile. See **5.5** for more information on SRA reviews. It is recommended, therefore, to view a few templates and if possible, firms should create their own. That said, a firm shouldn't waste time reinventing the wheel if it felt that a template fitted it well.
- **Review** – Firms should make space in the assessment document to note when it was reviewed last, so the firm can show that it is regularly reviewing it. There are no set review times, but it would be advisable to review it at least once a year, and two or three times a year is definitely preferable especially if the firm conducts work in a high-risk category. Whilst a firm is reviewing the assessment it can also review the firm's AML policy and record that also.
- **Points to cover in an assessment** – As outlined above, the firm's assessment needs to take into account the following:
    - *The firm's clients* – What kind of clients instruct the firm; where they are based; are they based in high-risk jurisdictions; where their assets come from; do fee earners know what is usual behaviour for the firm's clients; are fee earners good at collating and understanding source of funds and wealth information; whether the clients operate in high-risk sectors, are PEPs, are sanctioned or there is adverse media about the client, large cash businesses and so on.
    - *Countries and geographical areas in which the firm operates* – Does the firm operate in jurisdictions with equivalent AML regulations as the UK;

is the firm referred work from persons/entities based in jurisdictions that are high risk; is geographic risk captured; etc.
- *The services the firm provides and the transactions the firm is involved with* – For example, company formation, trust formation, sham litigation, tax havens and how risky those activities are.
- *How the firm delivers its services, i.e. face to face or remotely* – What safeguards does the firm deploy to mitigate any risk; does the firm accept payments from non-clients and if so what steps are taken.
- *Transactions* – Does the firm ever receive unsolicited payments and if so what is the process to resolve those; does the firm deal with complex transactions or transactions that facilitate anonymity.
- *SARs and disclosure* – The nature of the firm's SARs and the disclosures that are made to the money laundering reporting officer (MLRO).

- **Policies, controls and procedures** – The firm should set out in its assessment how the risks it has identified are mitigated by way of PCPs and what work there is to do. That work should be diarised with deadlines, and the work then carried out.

3.4 ROLE OF MLRO AND MLCO AND CROSSOVER WITH COLP AND COFA

It is important for all firms to understand the different regulatory roles and how they overlap and link to one another.

3.4.1 Regulatory roles

Regulation 21(3) of the AML Regulations requires all practices within the regulated sector to have a nominated officer who is tasked with receiving disclosures under Part 7 of the Proceeds of Crime Act (POCA) 2002 and the Terrorism Act (TA) 2000, and subsequently making disclosures to the NCA. This officer is also known as the *money laundering reporting officer* (MLRO).

If a firm does not provide services within the regulated sector, it does not have to appoint a nominated officer – but it should consider doing so as good practice.

In terms of who is the appropriate person to be the MLRO, it needs to be someone who has sufficient seniority and access to client files and business information to enable them to make decisions on reporting and actually report.

The MLRO is responsible for ensuring that information which gives knowledge of or suspicion of money laundering is reported to the relevant authority, the NCA, via a SAR, and if necessary a defence sought (see **3.5**). It is acceptable for the MLRO to nominate a deputy MLRO to assist, and this is likely to be more prevalent in larger firms that conduct a significant amount of regulated work.

RISK ASSESSMENT AND INTERNAL CONTROLS

Naturally the MLRO will also liaise with the NCA and/or police and respond to any queries that they may have, taking into consideration privilege (see **3.5** on privilege).

The role of the *money laundering compliance officer* (MLCO) is, put simply, to be responsible for the firm's compliance with the regulations. This means they are responsible for making sure that all PCPs are in place and working. This includes (but is not limited to):

- ensuring that the firm has conducted a firm-wide risk assessment and that any actions are completed and the risk assessment is regularly reviewed;
- ensuring that the firm has adequate policies in place and that these are adhered to;
- ensuring that the firm has adequate procedures in place, such as due diligence measures, and that these are adhered to;
- ensuring that adequate training is provided for relevant staff, and that this is done;
- ensuring that employees are screened appropriately;
- keeping and maintaining records of high-risk clients and ensuring that they are regularly checked.

The role of the *compliance officer for legal practice* (COLP) is to:

- take all reasonable steps to ensure compliance with the terms and conditions of the firm's authorisation, including compliance with the SRA Standards and Regulations (**www.sra.org.uk/solicitors/standards-regulations/**);
- take all reasonable steps to ensure compliance with any statutory obligations for example, the duties imposed by the Legal Services Act 2007, the Solicitors Act 1974 and the Administration of Justice Act 1985;
- take all reasonable steps to record breaches, in order to be able to recognise material breaches that must be reported to the SRA; and
- report material breaches of the regulatory arrangements to the SRA as soon as reasonably practicable.

The role of the *compliance officer for finance and administration* (COFA) is to:

- take all reasonable steps to ensure compliance with the SRA Accounts Rules (**www.sra.org.uk/solicitors/standards-regulations/accounts-rules/**);
- take all reasonable steps to record breaches, in order to be able to recognise serious breaches of the SRA Accounts Rules that must be reported to the SRA; and
- report serious breaches to the SRA promptly.

ANTI-MONEY LAUNDERING

3.4.2 How do these roles overlap?

It is often the case that one individual will take on some or all of these roles, depending on the size of the firm. These roles certainly overlap, and if undertaken by more than one person can provide an environment of support amongst role holders.

It is the MLRO's sole decision as to whether there exists suspicion or knowledge such that a report to the NCA needs to be made by the MLRO. How that information came to the attention of the MLRO is of interest to the MLCO, as they are tasked with making sure that relevant members of staff are aware of their regulatory obligations. Likewise, this will be of interest to the COLP who has an interest in ensuring that the relevant SRA Principles and aspects of the SRA Codes of Practice are complied with. In terms of the Principles that may be relevant to a suspicion of money laundering, these could be to act in a way that upholds the constitutional principle of the rule of law, and the proper administration of justice (principle 1); to act in a way that upholds public trust and confidence in the solicitors' profession and in legal services provided by an authorised person (principle 2); to act with honesty (principle 4); and to act with integrity (principle 5).

Of relevance also are the reporting requirements of solicitors who are obliged to report to the SRA any facts or matters which they reasonably believe are capable of amounting to a serious breach of the regulatory requirements (SRA Code of Conduct for Solicitors, RELs and RFLs, para.7.7). A solicitor will have discharged this obligation by reporting the same to the COLP on the understanding that the COLP will make a report to the SRA (SRA Code of Conduct for Solicitors, RELs and RFLs, para.7.12).

The COLP will therefore have an interest in ensuring that relevant staff understand their reporting obligations.

The COFA, mainly concerned with compliance with the SRA Accounts Rules, will need to ensure adherence to rule 3.3 of the SRA Accounts Rules in particular and it must be remembered that the genesis of that rule was in fact money laundering. This rule sets out that no monies must come through the firm's client account that do not relate to the delivery of regulated services. In essence this means that monies cannot be sent by the client or other party for the purchase of goods or payments that do not relate to the work at hand. If money laundering is occurring through the firm, it is possible that this rule is also being breached. Thus, the COFA has a role to play in the fight against money laundering within the firm also.

Understanding how these roles overlap highlights that ensuring that money laundering does not occur never sits in one place within the firm and instead is a collective responsibility in practice.

3.5 SUSPICIOUS ACTIVITY REPORTS AND PRIVILEGE

3.5.1 What is suspicion?

When a relevant person holds a suspicion of money laundering, a SAR must be made. In practice, members of staff within a law firm will report their suspicions to the MLRO, and the MLRO will consider whether a SAR needs to be made to the NCA and a defence sought (officially known as a 'defence against money laundering' (DAML)).

The challenging aspect of the regime is to understand when suspicion arises. There are situations which are relatively black and white and it is clear a SAR should be made (e.g. a client has informed a relevant person they have committed a crime which has produced the funds they are using for a property purchase). At other times it will not be so clear whether suspicion has been formed.

So, what is suspicion really?

As outlined in **2.4**, suspicion is not defined by statute, and what constitutes suspicion has been the subject of case law. Current guidance can be found in the case of *R* v. *Da Silva* [2007] 1 WLR 303 where the judge commented that suspicion is where a defendant must think that there is a possibility which is more than fanciful that the relevant facts exist, i.e. facts leading to a possibility of money laundering, and that 'a vague feeling of unease would not suffice' (para.16).

The LSAG guidance comments that: 'There is no requirement for the suspicion to be clear or firmly grounded on specific facts, but there must be a degree of satisfaction, not necessarily amounting to belief, but at least extending beyond speculation' (para.16.7.2 'Suspicion').

A person does not need to be clear that money laundering or some crime is occurring, but if they suspect something might be amiss they should discuss this with the firm's MLRO. Suspicion does not extend only to a firm's clients, and may arise due to suspicion about another party involved in a transaction. If this is the case, then the relevant person should discuss this with the MLRO.

3.5.2 Unexpected proceeds of crime

There are less obvious ways in which proceeds of crime can be produced and therefore for suspicion to arise.

Where there are legal requirements upon a client which if not met constitute a criminal offence and criminal property is created, suspicions of money laundering should arise and a SAR (internal to the MLRO and/or external to the NCA) made. Examples could be the legal requirement to produce an energy certificate on a property being sold, or any legal requirements to obtain licences before running certain businesses. It will not always be the case that criminal property is gained from the criminal activity, but it must be remembered that there is no de minimis or scale of importance when it comes to suspicions and SARs. The regime and the

NCA expect to be told about the activity regardless of value. Training on unexpected proceeds of crime should be part of a firm's training for its people.

Another consideration should be activity which is a criminal offence abroad but not in the UK. This might be, for example, breaching money transfer regulations in China where nationals are limited to the amount of monies they can transfer and reasons for the transfer. Whilst a criminal offence may be committed abroad, it is unlikely that proceeds of crime will result and therefore there may be no money laundering (although thought needs to be given as to whether the person transferring has committed fraud when providing reasons for the transfer). The converse situation is cannabis growing, which is illegal in the UK but not in some other countries. Where a client wishes to use their gains from this cannabis growing abroad, consideration needs to be given as to whether the firm will be handling proceeds of crime.

If in doubt about whether a suspicion has arisen and a SAR needs to be made, firms should take independent legal advice.

3.5.3 Suspicious activity reports

3.5.3.1 Overview

Relevant persons have an obligation under POCA 2002 and TA 2000 to make SARs. In practice, a SAR to the NCA will be made by a firm's MLRO. SARs should be made as soon as possible after suspicion has been formed.

3.5.3.2 Making a SAR

Whilst it is possible to make a SAR by post or fax, the majority of SARs will be filed online using the NCA's SAR form (**www.ukciu.gov.uk**). Those who report need to register with the NCA website and log on to enable a SAR to be filed. The online SAR system is outdated and clunky. A good portion of the form does not feel applicable to law firms, and there may be some information that the reporter does not have (if that is the case, the SAR should say this to ensure that the NCA does not ask the law firm for the missing information). The NCA has been promising a review of the form and online system for a significant amount of time.

3.5.3.3 Purpose of a SAR

The purpose of a SAR is to request a defence from the NCA to a specific act which, if undertaken by the relevant person, may constitute a money laundering offence. These are called 'defence against money laundering' (DAML) SARs. It is also possible to submit what might be termed an 'FYI' SAR or 'information only' SAR. This is not a SAR where a defence is sought, but rather a report of suspicious activity. This might be where the firm has decided not to act where a client has been evasive about their source of funds or wealth.

Colloquially people still call a DAML 'consent'. This is not technically correct, and the NCA has taken steps to distance itself from this term. When a defence is given by the NCA, it is not giving 'consent' to proceed.

3.5.3.4 Content of a SAR

Producing a clear SAR is vital to obtaining a defence. Solicitors have been heavily criticised for their SARs, with the NCA frequently calling them deficient. The NCA is eager to show solicitors what a 'bad' SAR looks like, but is unable or unwilling to produce a 'good' SAR or a template. It has, however, produced guidance about submitting a SAR:

- 'Submitting a suspicious activity report (SAR) within the regulated sector' (March 2021, **www.nationalcrimeagency.gov.uk/who-we-are/publications/ 233-submitting-a-suspicious-activity-report-sar-within-the-regulated-sector/file**);
- 'Guidance on submitting better quality suspicious activity reports (SARs)' (May 2020, **www.nationalcrimeagency.gov.uk/who-we-are/publications/ 446-guidance-on-submitting-better-quality-sars-1/file**);
- 'SARs regime good practice – frequently asked questions – suspicious activity reports' (July 2020, **www.nationalcrimeagency.gov.uk/who-we-are/ publications/462-sars-faq-july-2020/file**).

These are all highly recommended reading.

In terms of how to structure a SAR, it needs to be logical and contain certain elements. At **Appendix B2** you will find a template SAR.

SARs are not in fact a challenge to write, but when written from the perspective of someone who understands the retainer and the client, they can be deficient in the information needed by the NCA to consider whether to provide a defence or not. SARs should be written from the point of view of telling a story and on the basis that the person reading it is coming to the story cold. It needs to be a standalone document where anyone can pick it up and understand what is happening and what is being asked of the NCA. The more SARs a reporter does, the better they will get. To that end, below is a suggested structure:

1. Outline of the reporter – i.e. name of the firm, where located and what it does.
2. Confirmation that the report is made under POCA 2002, s.330.
3. The proposed activity for which a defence is sought – i.e. set out the act to which the firm is seeking a defence in a succinct way.
4. Set out that there is suspicion that there may be proceeds of crime and what offences under POCA 2002 (s.327 and/or s.328 and/or s.329) may be committed.
5. Outline of the matter, including who the firm acts for; details of the retainer;

what monies have been received and from where; what the proposed activity is; when it will take place (the NCA wants to have a timescale); and what the suspicion is (firms are encouraged to use the NCA's 'Suspicious activity report (SAR) glossary codes and reporting routes' (May 2021, **www.nationalcrimeagency.gov.uk/who-we-are/publications/517-glossary-codes-and-reporting-routes-may-2021/file**) to speed up the SAR).
6. Summarise again what the defence is sought for.

Here are some things *not* to do when making a SAR:

- A reporter should not ask for 'consent' to proceed. The NCA will not give this, and it may lead to the SAR being rejected or a defence being refused.
- A reporter should not omit a timescale for the act. Even if the firm is not sure precisely when monies will pass or an act will happen, give an estimated timescale such as six months. The NCA is likely to reject a SAR without a timescale.
- A reporter should not ask for a defence to act. The NCA will not provide a blanket defence to acting in a matter. It needs to have a specific act put to it, such as an exchange and completion of a property purchase.
- A reporter should not ask a hypothetical question, e.g. if the firm were to do XYZ would the NCA provide a defence? The NCA will reject this.
- A report should not be vague, illogical in structure or not set out what the suspicion is.

If the firm does not have certain information – for example, the bank account to which monies will be sent – at the time of the making of a SAR, the SAR needs to set this out and confirm when information will become available.

In complicated matters SARs can be tricky, and legal advice should be considered.

3.5.3.5 *What happens after a SAR is submitted?*

The NCA has seven working days (starting the day after the submission) to consider a firm's SAR and either provide a defence or refuse a defence. It is possible that the NCA will not return to the reporter at all. If this is the case, then the relevant person has deemed consent/defence.

Where a defence is refused, a moratorium period of 31 calendar days begins from the date of refusal. During this moratorium period (and the seven working day period), the firm must not undertake the prohibited act. The purpose of the moratorium period is to allow the enforcement agencies to investigate further and potentially injunct the firm from taking steps. If no NCA/enforcement action comes, the firm is able to proceed – however, careful thought needs to be given as to whether the firm should. Note the moratorium period can be increased by court order.

RISK ASSESSMENT AND INTERNAL CONTROLS

There is a possibility that the NCA provides a reply which is neither a defence nor a refusal to provide one. These are rare, and again legal advice should be sought should this occur.

3.5.3.6 What can a relevant person inform a client once a SAR has been made?

Once a SAR has been made (internal or external), there is a real risk of tipping off, which is an offence under POCA 2002. See **2.4.4** for guidance on the offence of tipping off.

Relevant persons should be informed through training, firm policy and the MLRO that they must not inform a client about a SAR. So, what can relevant persons say to a client to explain why action is not being taken or a transaction concluded? There is no silver bullet here. It is very difficult, and what the individual must try and do is stall the client whilst trying to act ethically and honestly. For example, blaming others would not be correct conduct.

The relevant person must not say something that might alert the client to there having been a SAR made, for example by mentioning the MLRO or a risk team.

What might be appropriate to say will depend on the facts, and again legal advice can be taken.

If the moratorium period is extended by way of court application, then the relevant person can inform the client of that application but must only provide such information as is necessary – and if they go further, may risk tipping off. The extension of moratorium periods is rare and so hopefully this will not arise for most firms.

3.5.4 The role of privilege

Privilege is a fundamental right enabling clients to be frank with their legal advisers without concern that the information will be disclosed later. This is an absolute right that only statute or waiver can override.

When deciding whether to make a SAR, relevant persons need to consider whether privilege applies or whether the information was obtained in privileged circumstances and whether any exceptions bite.

3.5.4.1 Legal advice privilege

Communications between a legal professional acting in their capacity as a legal professional and a client are privileged if that communication is confidential and for the purpose of seeking legal advice or providing it. Communications are not privileged purely by being made between a legal professional and a client, nor because they are labelled 'privileged'. A solicitors' bill of costs, or information imparted by prospective clients for the purpose of indicating the advice needed

ANTI-MONEY LAUNDERING

might be considered to be privileged as opposed to notes of open correspondence, meetings between opposing legal professionals and conveyancing documents which may not.

Communications between a client and a legal professional will attract privilege even if the document itself contains no advice, as long as the documents relate to the underlying transaction.

Privilege can be a difficult area to navigate, and a law firm faced with a challenging privilege question may wish to take its own legal advice.

The 2021 version of the LSAG guidance has been comprehensively rewritten in this area and this should be consulted. It contains a useful decision template, which is reproduced at **Appendix B3**. Further, the Law Society's practice note, 'Legal professional privilege' (13 November 2019, **www.lawsociety.org.uk/en/topics/client-care/legal-professional-privilege**) is useful.

3.5.4.2 Litigation privilege

Litigation privileged information comprises confidential communications made after litigation has started or is reasonably in prospect between a legal professional and a client, an agent or a third party; and that communication is for seeking or giving advice, obtaining evidence to be used in relation to the advice or obtaining information leading to obtaining such evidence. Litigation privilege is wider than legal advice privilege.

3.5.4.3 Privileged circumstances

The concept of information being provided in privileged circumstances is not the same as legal professional privilege, and is a design of POCA 2002 to accord with the exemptions from reporting set out in the EU directives.

Information provided in privileged circumstances means information communicated:

- by a client, or a representative of a client, in connection with the giving of legal advice to the client;
- by a client, or by a representative of a client, seeking legal advice from the professional adviser; or
- by a person in connection with legal proceedings or contemplated legal proceedings.

If the goal of the giving of the information is to further a criminal purpose, then the exemption will not apply.

If a legal professional forms a genuine but mistaken belief that the privileged information exemption applies, then the legal professional will be able to rely on the reasonable excuse defence.

If this exemption is used as a reason not to report a suspicion, that analysis and decision should be recorded.

3.5.4.4 Crime/fraud or iniquity exception

Information that is subject to legal professional privilege cannot be disclosed. There is an exception to this, and that is the crime/fraud – or otherwise called the iniquity – exception.

Information gathered with the intention of furthering a criminal purpose is not privileged. However, advice given to a client to avoid them committing a crime or warning them about their proposed actions is subject to privilege.

If the relevant person knows that the transaction they are instructed to advise on is a principal criminal offence, then the relevant person may be committing an offence themselves and such communications in the retainer are not privileged.

If a relevant person has a suspicion that money laundering is occurring then privilege will not attach if that conclusion is correct – but if it is incorrect, privilege remains.

Privilege is a challenging area to navigate, and law firms should seek advice where necessary. At **Appendix B4** readers will find a flowchart provided within LSAG's guidance which may help decide whether information can be disclosed or not.

3.6 POLICIES, CONTROLS, PROCEDURES – REGULATIONS 19 AND 20

It is advisable that whoever in the firm has overall responsibility for the application of the AML Regulations reads and understands the wording of the regulations themselves rather than relying solely on guides. For that reason, this section will repeat some of the legislation in a step-by-step process so that it can be understood, and with understanding implemented better.

Regulation 19 sets out what a firm must do to ensure it has PCPs to manage the risk of money laundering occurring. Under reg.19(1), a relevant person must:

(a) establish and maintain policies, controls and procedures to mitigate and manage effectively the risks of money laundering and terrorist financing identified in any risk assessment undertaken by the relevant person under regulation 18(1);
(b) regularly review and update the policies, controls and procedures established under sub-paragraph (a);
(c) maintain a record in writing of–
   (i) the policies, controls and procedures established under sub-paragraph (a);
   (ii) any changes to those policies, controls and procedures made as a result of the review and update required by sub-paragraph (b); and
   (iii) the steps taken to communicate those policies, controls and procedures, or any changes to them, within the relevant person's business.

A firm therefore needs to have a robust set of policies which sets out what money laundering is; how solicitors and those in the law firm can encounter it; and what to do when money laundering is suspected. The policies must be written to take into account the firm's AML risk assessment (see **3.3** for guidance) and should not therefore be a template not adapted to the firm's work type, client type and so on.

The policies need to also set out the firm's procedures around the undertaking of CDD to include identification, PEP/sanction/adverse media checking, risk assessments, understanding purpose and nature of the transaction and so on.

There needs also to be a recording mechanism for the review of the firm's policies – this could be a table at the end of each policy setting out when it was last reviewed and by whom, and if that gets too visually busy then perhaps a separate document setting out when reviews occurred. Naturally if there is a change in the firm's AML risk assessment it may necessitate at that time a change in the firm's PCPs and if this is the case, this needs to be documented. However, on top of that ongoing regular review it is recommended to review all the firm's risk and compliance policies once a year (in the summer months is a good time, if the firm is quieter during that time).

Regulation 19(2) goes on to set out:

(2) The policies, controls and procedures adopted by a relevant person under paragraph (1) must be–

(a) proportionate with regard to the size and nature of the relevant person's business, and
(b) approved by its senior management.

Regulation 19(3) sets out:

(3) The policies, controls and procedures referred to in paragraph (1) must include–

(a) risk management practices;
(b) internal controls (see regulations 21 to 24);
(c) customer due diligence (see regulations 27 to 38);
(d) reliance and record keeping (see regulations 39 to 40);
(e) the monitoring and management of compliance with, and the internal communication of, such policies, controls and procedures.

Regulation 19(4) goes on to state:

(4) The policies, controls and procedures referred to in paragraph (1) must include policies, controls and procedures–

(a) which provide for the identification and scrutiny of–
  (i) any case where–
    (aa) a transaction is complex or unusually large, or there is an unusual pattern of transactions, or
    (bb) the transaction or transactions have no apparent economic or legal purpose, and
  (ii) any other activity or situation which the relevant person regards as particularly likely by its nature to be related to money laundering or terrorist financing;
(b) which specify the taking of additional measures, where appropriate, to prevent the use for money laundering or terrorist financing of products and transactions which might favour anonymity;
(c) which ensure that when new products, new business practices (including

RISK ASSESSMENT AND INTERNAL CONTROLS

new delivery mechanisms) or new technology are adopted by the relevant person, appropriate measures are taken in preparation for, and during, the adoption of such products, practices or technology to assess and if necessary mitigate any money laundering or terrorist financing risks this new product, practice or technology may cause;

(d) under which anyone in the relevant person's organisation who knows or suspects (or has reasonable grounds for knowing or suspecting) that a person is engaged in money laundering or terrorist financing as a result of information received in the course of the business or otherwise through carrying on that business is required to comply with–

    (i) Part 3 of the Terrorism Act 2000; or
    (ii) Part 7 of the Proceeds of Crime Act 2002;

(e) which, in the case of a money service business that uses agents for the purpose of its business, ensure that appropriate measures are taken by the business to assess–

    (i) whether an agent used by the business would satisfy the fit and proper test provided for in regulation 58; and
    (ii) the extent of the risk that the agent may be used for money laundering or terrorist financing.

Regulation 19(4)(a), (b) and (d) can and should be covered in the firm's AML policy (see **Appendix B5** for template policy) and the client and matter risk assessments (see **Appendix B6** for template client and matter risk assessments). Naturally what might be an unusual pattern of transactions for one firm might not be for another and all assessments must be taken in the context of what is normal for that firm. That being said, the firm should be alive to the fact that what happened in the past may have been money laundering and so whilst the context of the firm's work is highly relevant, the firm shouldn't take the view that 'my client has always done this and so there is nothing to be concerned about'. Each transaction should be scrutinised afresh.

Regulation 19(4)(c) requires the firm to assess the AML risk when using new technology. The 2021 version of the LSAG guidance now has a chapter on the use of technology for electronically verifying a client's identification, which should be consulted by those who use such methods or are planning to.

Regulation 19(4)(e) covers money service businesses which are business that provide currency exchange and conversion services. This is not relevant to law firms and so not explored here.

Regulation 19(5) sets out:

(5) In determining what is appropriate or proportionate with regard to the size and nature of its business, a relevant person may take into account any guidance which has been–

    (a) issued by the FCA; or
    (b) issued by any other supervisory authority or appropriate body and approved by the Treasury.

ANTI-MONEY LAUNDERING

The LSAG guidance is explored at **5.1** and it is this guidance which is referred to in reg.19(5)(b). If the firm has an FCA arm then it will need to take into account the JMLSG guidance.

Finally, reg.19(6) sets out:

> (6) A relevant person must, where relevant, communicate the policies, controls and procedures which it establishes and maintains in accordance with this regulation to its branches and subsidiary undertakings which are located outside the United Kingdom.

This is of course relevant if the firm has overseas offices, and in that instance the firm's PCPs must be communicated to those branches.

Regulation 20 sets out the PCPs required at group level, and in summary these are:

(a) to ensure that all the PCPs set out in reg.19 are applied to all overseas offices which are carrying out an activity in respect of which a relevant person is subject to the AML Regulations;
(b) to establish and maintain group PCPs for data protection and the sharing of information across branches to assist in the prevention of money laundering and terrorist financing;
(c) to maintain records of the PCPs, to amend them where necessary after regular review and communicate those PCPs;
(d) where a branch is in a European Economic Area (EEA) state, the branch must follow the law of the EEA state that implements the AML Regulations;
(e) where the branch operates in a third country where there are AML measures that are not as strict as those in the UK, the firm must ensure that the branch offices apply measures equivalent to the AML Regulations as far as permitted by the third country's laws;
(f) if the third country does not allow the implementation of equivalent AML measures, then the firm must inform the SRA and take measures to handle the risk of money laundering and terrorist financing.

International firms therefore have to consider what AML procedures they should adopt in each jurisdiction in which they operate.

3.7 INTERNAL CONTROLS – REGULATIONS 21 AND 24

In this section we explore the internal controls as required under the AML Regulations.

3.7.1 MLCO appointment, screening and independent audit

Regulation 21(1) sets out the following:

RISK ASSESSMENT AND INTERNAL CONTROLS

21 Internal controls

(1) Where appropriate with regard to the size and nature of its business, a relevant person must–

    (a) appoint one individual who is a member of the board of directors (or if there is no board, of its equivalent management body) or of its senior management as the officer responsible for the relevant person's compliance with these Regulations;

    (b) carry out screening of relevant employees appointed by the relevant person, both before the appointment is made and during the course of the appointment;

    (c) establish an independent audit function with the responsibility–

        (i) to examine and evaluate the adequacy and effectiveness of the policies, controls and procedures adopted by the relevant person to comply with the requirements of these Regulations;

        (ii) to make recommendations in relation to those policies, controls and procedures; and

        (iii) to monitor the relevant person's compliance with those recommendations.

Regulation 21(1)(a) sets out the requirement to appoint the MLCO (see **3.4** for further guidance on this role). Notice, however, how this requirement is in accordance with the size and nature of the firm – and therefore arguably if the firm is small or conducts solely unregulated work (for example, litigation), it may be considered that the firm does not need to appoint such an officer. Although note at **5.5.3** the SRA's thematic review report where it sets out that it expects each firm to have an MLCO.

Regulation 21(1)(c) outlines the requirement for an independent audit of the firm's PCPs to evaluate whether they are adequate and effective.

This audit does not have to be carried out by someone outside the firm. It should, however, be carried out by someone not involved in the day-to-day due diligence gathering, and so should not be the firm's central risk team if they gather and sign off identification documentation, for example. If there does not seem to be anyone within the firm that seems suitable, it is open, it seems, for firms to audit each other and for very small firms this may be a good way to seek an independent view without too much (or at no) cost. There are legal and accounting businesses that will audit firms for a fee, and of course the larger the firm, the more there is to audit and the higher the cost.

To consider screening requirements under reg.21(1)(b) we need to also consider reg.21(2) as set out below:

(2) For the purposes of paragraph (1)(b)–

    (a) 'screening' means an assessment of–

        (i) the skills, knowledge and expertise of the individual to carry out their functions effectively;

        (ii) the conduct and integrity of the individual;

    (b) a relevant employee is an employee whose work is–

(i)   relevant to the relevant person's compliance with any requirement in these Regulations, or
(ii)   otherwise capable of contributing to the–
    (aa) identification or mitigation of the risks of money laundering and terrorist financing to which the relevant person's business is subject, or
    (bb) prevention or detection of money laundering and terrorist financing in relation to the relevant person's business.

Screening therefore should be undertaken on all persons within a law firm who have a role to play in the prevention or detection of money laundering. Although the regulation speaks in terms of 'employee' it should be read to include partners and consultants of a firm.

A firm may decide to undertake criminal records checks on incoming and ongoing employees or people. To undertake such a check requires the consent of that person, and this must be freely given. Consent for an incoming employee is not so much of an issue as consent can, on the face of it, be freely given. However, for an existing employee there is an imbalance of power and arguably an employee could not give consent freely on the basis that if they do not give consent they may be concerned about suspicion arising and the consequences of that.

The SRA does not mandate that criminal records checks are conducted and instead takes the view that it is for each firm to consider what is best for that firm. That being the case therefore, whatever a firm decides, this should be documented somewhere.

For screening on existing staff, the firm may want to conduct adverse media checks by simply Googling the individual's name (the firm needs to consider whether this needs to be included in any documentation about what data the firm processes and retains on its people) and having an annual declaration to confirm that there is nothing to make the firm aware of that would affect the firm or the SRA's assessment of integrity of the individual. Be aware, however, that any person who lacks integrity could well lie on such a declaration and therefore there is only so much weight that can be given to such a declaration.

Another check would be to run the person's name through the SRA's 'Check a solicitor's record' search function found on its website (**www.sra.org.uk/consumers/solicitor-check/**) to see whether there are any adverse findings against the solicitor or non-solicitor employee.

It is possible for the SRA to issue an order under the Solicitors Act 1974, s.43 against non-solicitors to control how and where the individual works in SRA-regulated entities. To employ a person subject to such an order requires approval from the SRA, and failing to obtain that can in itself lead to disciplinary action against the firm.

The 2021 version of the LSAG guidance sets out a useful table of screening options (para.9.4). Note that firms do not have to undertake all screening options in that table.

RISK ASSESSMENT AND INTERNAL CONTROLS

3.7.2 MLRO appointment and role

Regulation 21(3) sets out that an individual in the firm must be appointed as a nominated officer (see **3.4** for further guidance on the role of MLRO).

Regulation 21(4) sets out that the firm must, within 14 days of the appointment of the nominated officer and the MLCO, inform the SRA of their identity, and if the individuals change the identities of their successors.

Regulation 21(5) sets out:

> (5) Where a disclosure is made to the nominated officer, that officer must consider it in the light of any relevant information which is available to the relevant person and determine whether it gives rise to knowledge or suspicion or reasonable grounds for knowledge or suspicion that a person is engaged in money laundering or terrorist financing.

This is of course referring to the MLRO's responsibility to consider whether there are grounds for suspicion and as such a SAR needs to be made to the NCA. For guidance on what suspicion actually means and the making of SARs, see **3.5**.

3.7.3 Establish and maintain system enabling relevant person to respond to requests for information

Regulation 21(8) and (9) sets out:

> (8) A relevant person must establish and maintain systems which enable it to respond fully and rapidly to enquiries from any person specified in paragraph (9) as to–
>
> (a) whether it maintains, or has maintained during the previous five years, a business relationship with any person; and
> (b) the nature of that relationship.
>
> (9) The persons specified in this paragraph are–
>
> (a) financial investigators accredited under section 3 of the Proceeds of Crime Act 2002 (accreditation and training);
> (b) persons acting on behalf of the Scottish Ministers in their capacity as an enforcement authority under that Act; and
> (c) constables or equivalent officers of any law enforcement authority.

It therefore follows that firms must maintain and keep all records of their work and due diligence documentation on their clients for a minimum period of five years. The firm must keep records in such a way so as to enable responses to be gi˙ clearly and quickly. See **4.3.2** for further guidance on record-keeping as ʳ AML Regulations.

3.7.4 Must take into account SRA risk assessment and Lˢ˙

Finally, reg.21(10) sets out:

> (10) In determining what is appropriate with regaʳ business, a relevant person–

ANTI-MONEY LAUNDERING

    (a)   must take into account its risk assessment under regulation 18(1); and
    (b)   may take into account any guidance which has been–
          (i)   issued by the FCA; or
          (ii)   issued by any other supervisory authority or appropriate body and approved by the Treasury.

The firm must therefore set its PCPs in accordance with the firm's AML risk assessment (see **3.3** for further guidance) and also the guidance as set out by the SRA and LSAG (see **5.1** for further guidance).

3.7.5 Training

Regulation 24 (as amended by MLR 2019) relates to training and reg.24(1) sets out the following:

24 Training

(1)   A relevant person must–

    (a)   take appropriate measures to ensure that its relevant employees and any agents it uses for the purposes of its business whose work is of a kind mentioned in paragraph (2) are–

          (i)   made aware of the law relating to money laundering and terrorist financing, and to the requirements of data protection, which are relevant to the implementation of these Regulations; and

          (ii)   regularly given training in how to recognise and deal with transactions and other activities or situations which may be related to money laundering or terrorist financing;

    (b)   maintain a record in writing of the measures taken under sub-paragraph (a), and in particular, of the training given to its relevant employees and to any agents it uses for the purposes of its business whose work is of a kind mentioned in paragraph (2).

Regulation 24(2) sets out that for the purposes of reg.24(1) a relevant employee or agent is someone whose work is relevant to the firm's compliance with the requirements or is otherwise capable of contributing to the identification, mitigation, prevention or detection of the risk of money laundering or terrorist financing in the firm.

Regulation 24(3) outlines that the measures that are appropriate under reg.24(1) should be determined taking into account the nature and size of the firm and the risks of money laundering occurring. Further, the firm should take into account any guidance provided by supervisory authorities (e.g. LSAG).

MLR 2019 amended reg.24 to include agents. The term 'agent' is undefined in the regulations but is very likely to mean that if a person works in the manner of an employee for a firm, they should be trained. The LSAG guidance now provides further direction on this aspect.

Training can take many different forms, and many different forms it should indeed take to be most effective. Some law firms will implement online training modules, and these can be effective and useful in large firms where face-to-face (physical or virtual) training may not be possible.

In the author's opinion, however, it cannot be the only method of training relied upon and every firm should consider, for example:

- producing guidance notes;
- providing summaries of AML stories (whether from the mainstream press or from the SRA or Solicitors Disciplinary Tribunal (SDT));
- attending team meetings;
- running drop-in sessions on AML, identification, source of funds and wealth and so on.

What must be remembered is that not everyone learns in the same way and variety is key – the more different ways in which training is given, the more effective it will be in reaching the most people in the firm.

Technically speaking, there may be some areas in the firm that do not need to receive training, for example, some practice areas such as litigation – however, no area of a law firm is impervious to money laundering, and in the spirit of collegiality every firm should consider ensuring that all members of staff are trained.

Frequency of training is down to each MLCO to decide. There is no prescribed frequency. In the author's view, money laundering is such a risk to practices that yearly training should take place, supplemented by the additional learning/training items outlined above.

Firms should not forget training for MLROs and MLCOs, and if necessary separate training for centralised CDD/risk teams.

The LSAG guidance provides further advice on training, and this should be visited.

CHAPTER 4

Client due diligence

4.1 CLIENT DUE DILIGENCE

The undertaking of due diligence is by far the biggest aspect of compliance with the Money Laundering, Terrorist Financing and Transfer of Funds (Information on the Payer) Regulations 2017, SI 2017/692 ('AML Regulations') faced by firms. This section will explore each aspect of due diligence as required under the regulations and where appropriate will reproduce the regulations. We will also explore where simplified due diligence can be applied, and where enhanced due diligence must be applied. Please note that there is more than one way to conduct due diligence and the contents of this section outline some suggestions but are not the only options available.

Many law firms confuse client due diligence (CDD) with identification documents (ID) but they are not the same. ID is certainly a part of CDD, but CDD comprises much more than ID, as is explored below. 'Know your client' (KYC) is another term for CDD.

Explained below are the five steps to CDD and their origins in the AML Regulations. The five steps are:

(a) identification and verification;
(b) client and matter risk assessment;
(c) understanding purpose and nature;
(d) source of funds and source of wealth; and
(e) ongoing monitoring and high-risk registers.

These steps should be conducted on a matter basis, i.e. when a new matter is taken on, and not only when a client is incepted in to the firm for the first time.

It is important for relevant persons to understand at the outset who their client is so as to understand against whom CDD should be undertaken. If a referring law firm is requesting/insisting they are the client, this needs to be carefully thought about and the Legal Sector Affinity Group (LSAG) now helpfully provides guidance in this area: 'Legal Sector Affinity Group Anti-money laundering guidance for the legal sector 2021', chapter 6 (**www.lawsociety.org.uk/en/topics/anti-money-laundering/anti-money-laundering-guidance**). In the author's opinion, if the service being provided is a subsidiary/subcontracting one to the referring law firm, then treating the law firm as the client will be ok, but the relevant person still needs to consider what CDD they need on the underlying client. For work that is more substantial in nature, such as a transaction, the underlying client of the referring law firm will be the client of the relevant person.

4.1.1 Step 1: identification and verification

4.1.1.1 Overview

Obtaining identification documentation is not about ticking boxes, and what is provided by a party must be read and considered carefully by the relevant person. Also, the relevant person should not ask for documents that they have no intention of reading. This does not mean that every single line of a lengthy document needs to be considered, but the relevant person should seek out at least the information that is needed in what is provided and then note that in a risk assessment.

Under AML Regulations, reg.27, a relevant person must apply CDD measures if they are establishing a business relationship; or are carrying out an occasional transaction that amounts to the transfer of funds within the meaning of art.3.9 of the funds transfer regulation exceeding 1,000 euros (the funds transfer regulation is Regulation 2015/847/EU of the European Parliament and of the Council of 20 May 2015 on information accompanying transfers of funds); or they suspect money laundering or terrorist financing; or they doubt the veracity or adequacy of documents or information previously obtained for the purposes of identification or verification.

Regulation 27(2) goes on to set out that those who are not high value dealers or casinos also must conduct CDD measures where a person carries out an occasional transaction that amounts to 15,000 euros or more whether in a single transaction or in a number of transactions that appear to be linked.

An occasional transaction is defined as a transaction which is not carried out as part of a business relationship. It follows therefore that law firms are unlikely to undertake occasional transactions. However, a law firm will establish business relationships with clients and therefore the AML Regulations bite.

Regulation 27(8) also sets out that the relevant person must apply CDD measures to existing clients on a risk-based approach or where that person becomes aware that the circumstances of the existing client relevant to the risk assessment of the customer has changed. It is therefore vital that a risk assessment is undertaken and ongoing monitoring is in place (see **4.1.2** and **4.1.5** respectively for more detail).

Regulation 27(9) sets out that when determining when it is appropriate to undertake CDD measures in relation to existing clients, the relevant person must take into account indications that the identity of the client has changed; any transactions which are not reasonably consistent with the relevant person's knowledge of the client; any change in the purpose or intended nature of the relevant

ANTI-MONEY LAUNDERING

person's relationship with the client; and any other matter which might affect the relevant person's assessment of the money laundering or terrorist financing risk.

Regulation 28 goes on to set out what CDD is needed. In this section we will concentrate only on the identification and verification of that identification.

Regulation 28(2)(a) sets out that the relevant person must identify the client unless the identity of the client is known to and has been verified already by the relevant person.

Regulation 28(2)(b) sets out that the relevant person must verify the client's identity unless this has already been done by the relevant person.

4.1.1.2 Individual person identification

The AML Regulations do not set out what should be obtained in order to identify an individual person client. LSAG provides some very useful guidance on this aspect and sets out that identity needs to be confirmed by using documentation or information obtained from a reliable source which is independent from the client (LSAG guidance, chapter 6).

Evidence of identity can include passports and photocard driving licences or other forms of confirmation including assurances from persons within the regulated sector or those in the firm who have dealt with the person for some time. Caution should be exercised, however, on relying on the confirmation of others as they may not have conducted appropriate checks themselves or may have accepted confirmation from others who may not have conducted appropriate checks or taken documentation which may not be deemed appropriate. It is always recommended that firms conduct their own due diligence and not rely on the assessment of others (see **4.3.1** for guidance on reliance).

Note that LSAG sets out that there is no provision in the AML Regulations allowing CDD to be waived on the basis of long-term relationships (para.6.2). Waivers of this kind can sometimes be requested when a solicitor is referring a family member or friend. Such waiver must be refused.

It is good practice to have either (i) one government document which verifies either name and address or name and date of birth or (ii) one government document which verifies the client's full name and another document which verifies their name and either their address or date of birth.

So under the first option, a passport or photocard driving licence will do; and under the second option some other form of government document which does not verify address or date of birth but name only plus one other document which verifies name and either address or date of birth.

The following may be useful sources of ID for those resident in the UK:

- current passport;
- birth certificate;
- marriage certificate;
- current photocard driver's licence;

- current European Economic Area (EEA) member state identity card;
- current identity card issued by the Electoral Office for Northern Ireland;
- residence permit issued by the Home Office;
- firearms certificate or shotgun licence;
- photographic registration on cards for self-employed individuals and partnerships in the construction industry;
- benefit book or original notification letter confirming the right to benefits;
- council tax bill;
- utility bill or statement, or a certificate from a utilities supplier confirming an arrangement to pay services on pre-payment terms;
- a cheque or electronic transfer drawn on an account in the name of the client with a credit or financial institution regulated for the purposes of money laundering;
- bank, building society or credit union statement or passbook containing current address;
- entry in a local or national telephone directory confirming name and address;
- confirmation from an electoral register that a person of that name lives at that address;
- a recent original mortgage statement from a recognised lender;
- legal professional's letter confirming recent house purchase or HM Land Registry confirmation of address;
- local council or housing association rent card or tenancy agreement;
- HM Revenue and Customs (HMRC) self-assessment statement or tax demand;
- house or motor insurance certificate;
- record of any home visit made by a relevant person;
- statement from a member of the practice or other person in the regulated sector who has known the client for a number of years attesting to their identity.

What is obtained should be based on the risk at hand, and generally speaking firms adopt the approach of obtaining photo ID and proof of address. This isn't always strictly necessary, but is good practice.

However, what is vital is that these documents are scrutinised. For example, if a client has engaged a firm to purchase a £1 million property and provides a bank statement as proof of address showing an income that could not support such a purchase, then questions need to be asked. Further, fee earners need to look out for proof of address that does not match a property being sold or does not make sense – for example, the client said they live in Manchester but the proof of address is in Devon. In some countries, proof of address may be hard to obtain because post is delivered to a post office (PO) box. In those cases, law firms should try to overcome this by obtaining other documents to satisfy the identity of the individual.

What is important is that obtaining proof of ID and address is not seen as a tick-box exercise and in any way proof that the client is not laundering money or is not committing fraud. Money launderers have addresses too, they live somewhere. What proof of ID and address does is to attempt to flush out those who may want to

ANTI-MONEY LAUNDERING

hide and provide the police an address to potentially raid – but it does not prevent money laundering 100 per cent on its own, far from it. The entire suite of CDD measures aims to do so.

When it comes to well-known individuals such as famous or ultra high net worth (UHNW) people, again a relevant person can adopt a risk-based approach. If, for example, Richard Branson were to instruct a firm, it is quite likely to be unnecessary to obtain a copy of his passport and proof of address, as the relevant person and firm will know who he is. More of concern will be ensuring that the person who is giving instructions (which is unlikely to be Richard Branson himself) is genuine and that their identity is known (we cover more on that below). For well-known individuals, the relevant person should document what they know and whether they have met the person. One suggested place for this documented knowledge is the client and matter risk assessment (see **4.1.2**).

Where a client is a regulated person, it is possible to confirm their identity via the regulator's register if it is appropriate.

4.1.1.3 Company identification

Regulation 28(3) sets out that where the client is a body corporate, the relevant person must obtain and verify the name of the body corporate; its company number and registration number; and the address of its registered office and if relevant its principal place of business. Further, the relevant person must take steps to determine and verify the law to which the company is subject and its constitution, and the full names of the board of directors (or if there is no board, the members of the equivalent management body) and other senior persons responsible for the operations of the body corporate. The regulations do not state that any ID documentation must be sought to verify a director's identity but many firms do this as a matter of good practice.

Regulation 28(4) goes on to set out that where a client is beneficially owned by another person, the relevant person must identify the beneficial owner; take reasonable steps to verify the identity of the beneficial owner so that the relevant person is satisfied that they know who the beneficial owner is; and if the beneficial owner is a legal person, trust, company, foundation or similar legal arrangement, to take reasonable measures to understand the ownership and control structure of that entity.

What the above means in practice is that the relevant person must secure documentation which provides the information needed in reg.28(3) including the information needed to determine whether there is a beneficial owner. Most firms will do this by obtaining relevant documentation from Companies House, such as the certificate of incorporation, details of the company's registration number, articles of association and registered office and filed audited accounts. The relevant person will also need to consult the 'people with significant control' (PSC) register held at Companies House, though this cannot be relied upon to confirm beneficial ownership (for further information, see **www.gov.uk/guidance/people-with-significant-control-pscs**).

Where the company is not in the UK, overseas registers (where possible) can be consulted – otherwise the client itself will need to be asked to provide the information needed.

For large companies, overseas or not, a good starting point is to ask the company to provide a structure chart showing how it is beneficially owned. By starting with a structure chart, the relevant person can determine what is needed in one go rather than asking for information in a piecemeal fashion which tends to frustrate clients. See below at **4.1.1.15** for some worked examples of what ID might be obtained.

For listed companies, reg.28(3) and (5) combined set out that the relevant person must obtain the name of the body corporate, company number or other registration number and address of its registered office if different from its principal place of business.

In the case of a listed company, the relevant person is not required to understand the law under which the company is governed, the names of its board of directors and senior persons who are responsible for management of the body, nor is the relevant person obligated to identify the beneficial ownership. The relevant person should obtain the information that they need from the relevant listing on the regulated market and record this. This could be by way of saving a screenshot of the relevant stock exchange website showing the company listing.

Not all regulated markets can be relied upon as being capable of providing sufficient ID, and this depends on the required disclosure obligations for that regulated market. LSAG sets out that for EEA markets, there is no requirement to check the market. However, for non-EEA markets, the relevant person needs to consider whether equivalent disclosure obligations are in place and the LSAG guidance suggests visiting the European Securities and Markets Authority website (**www.esma.europa.eu/**).

In terms of determining who is a beneficial owner of a company to determine whether identification measures have to be undertaken, the relevant person needs to consider reg.5(1), which sets out that a beneficial owner is an individual who exercises ultimate control over the management of the body corporate or an individual who ultimately owns or controls more than 25 per cent of the shares or voting rights or an individual who controls the company within the meaning of Companies Act 2006, Sched.1A, Part 1 (people with significant control); or if the individual was an undertaking, the body corporate would be a subsidiary undertaking of the individual under Companies Act 2006, s.1162 read with Sched.7 to that Act.

For those that are deemed beneficial owners of the company, they need to be identified and that identity verified. For individual persons, the process outlined above could be followed. The aim in following the beneficial ownership chain is to understand who sits as the ultimate beneficial owner and determine whether ID should be obtained on that person. ID is not needed on each layer of ownership which comprises another company. What is important here is that the approach must be proportionate and based on risk.

As noted above, reg.28(9) sets out that a relevant person cannot satisfy the requirements of identifying the beneficial owner of the corporate body by using solely the PSC register found at Companies House. So, whilst it must be consulted, it should not be relied upon on its own.

4.1.1.4 Inability to identify beneficial owner of body corporate

It is worth noting reg.28(6) and (7), which state the following:

(6) If the customer is a body corporate, and paragraph (7) applies, the relevant person may treat the senior person in that body corporate responsible for managing it as its beneficial owner.

(7) This paragraph applies if (and only if) the relevant person has exhausted all possible means of identifying the beneficial owner of the body corporate and–
   (a) has not succeeded in doing so, or
   (b) is not satisfied that the individual identified is in fact the beneficial owner.

Therefore, if the relevant person has done all that it can to identify the beneficial owner and has not been able to do so, it can rely on this regulation and treat the senior person in the body corporate responsible for managing the corporate as the beneficial owner.

The Money Laundering and Terrorist Financing (Amendment) Regulations 2019, SI 2019/1511 (MLR 2019) (implementing the Fifth EU Directive on Money Laundering (EU) 2018/843 (5AMLD)) added further to this regulation in that in these circumstances, the relevant person must take all reasonable measures to identify and verify the identity of the senior person and record in writing all actions and difficulties encountered in doing so. Therefore, MLR 2019 expanded the steps that need to be undertaken to utilise the benefit of this regulation.

Caution should be exercised when using this regulation, as not being able to identify the beneficial owner could be a red flag for something untoward happening, especially if there has been evasiveness, and in fact might raise suspicions for which a suspicious activity report (SAR) needs to be submitted.

4.1.1.5 PSC register discrepancy reporting requirement

MLR 2019 also added a further requirement under reg.30A which states that before establishing a business relationship with a company, limited liability partnership (LLP) or Scottish partnership, the relevant person must collect proof of registration or an excerpt of the relevant register for that corporate body (this will often be the PSC register). If the register is at odds with the information provided by the body, the relevant person will need to report the same to the Companies House. Law firms do not need to hunt out discrepancies or seek to ensure there are none, and legal professional privilege will apply. Reports should be made as soon as possible.

CLIENT DUE DILIGENCE

In practice, if discrepancies are found the firm or relevant person may well wish to raise them with the client and ask that they correct the anomaly and provide an explanation for it. To report without giving a client a chance to put the position right will undoubtedly damage client relationships. Should the client not put the register right, then the firm or relevant person has no choice but to report the matter to Companies House via its portal. It is recommended that a question is asked about discrepancies with the PSC register on the client and matter risk assessment.

4.1.1.6 Partnerships

A partnership, unless in Scotland, is not a separate legal entity and so relevant persons need to obtain identity information on its partners. This means identifying those partners as individuals as described above.

Where the partnership or unincorporated business is well known, reputable, has a long history and there is a substantial amount of public information about the partnership, its principals and controllers, then obtaining the name, registered address if any, trading address and nature of the business should be enough to identify it.

Further, LSAG suggests that for those partnerships that are not well known and are small, then ID measures should be applied to the individual partners, but where the partnership or unincorporated business is large, then it should be treated as a private company and ID carried out in that way (i.e. consider obtaining documentation for the partnership and those who own or control more than 25 per cent of it).

If the partnership is an LLP, LSAG suggests obtaining information as if the LLP was a company.

If the partnership is made up of regulated professionals (for example, solicitors or accountants), it is sufficient to confirm the existence of the partnership through a professional directory or search facility.

4.1.1.7 Trusts and estate administration

Conducting CDD on trusts can be time consuming and tricky. The first step is to identify who the client is. A trust is not a legal personality, and therefore it cannot be a firm's client. When advising in relation to a trust, the relevant person may be advising the settlor, the trustee(s), the protector(s) or one or more of the beneficiaries.

If the relevant person is advising on the set up of the trust, then the settlor will usually be the client and their identity should be verified. Source of funds and wealth being used to set up the trust will need to be considered (see **4.1.4**). If the settlor is not a natural person but instead an entity, then the appropriate identification measures need to be undertaken in relation to that entity.

If the relevant person is advising the settlor or trustee on the trust once the trust has been set up, the beneficial owner of the trust will need to be identified and their identity verified. In order to understand who the beneficial owner is, the trust deed is often needed.

Regulation 6(1) of the AML Regulations sets out that beneficial owner in relation to a trust means the settlor, the trustees and beneficiaries and where the individuals benefiting from the trust have not been determined, the class of persons in whose main interest the trust was set up and anyone who has control over the trust ('control' meaning power to dispose of trust property, vary the trust, add or remove a beneficiary or appoint or remove a trustee).

Beneficiaries whose interest has vested need to be identified. If the beneficiaries are a class that includes individuals who are not yet identified, e.g. grandchildren not yet born, then no identification documentation can be obtained and it will be enough for the relevant person to note the class of beneficiaries. Note, however, that in the case of a discretionary trust, if the relevant person does not note the names of the beneficiaries who are named in the trust deed or any associated document on the basis that their interest has not yet vested, the relevant person will need to seek regular updates on this aspect. It therefore may be better to obtain the names of the beneficiaries where possible and note the same.

Note that reg.30(7) requires the relevant person to establish and verify the identity of any beneficiary before payment is made to the beneficiary or the beneficiary exercises their vested rights in the trust, legal entity or legal arrangement.

In relation to acting in an estate administration, the client will be the personal representative of the deceased, and often therefore the executor. Identification and verification of that person's identity will be required. The relevant person may also want to obtain a copy of the death certificate and the grant of probate or letters of administration.

For further advice, see paras.6.14.12 and 6.14.16 of the LSAG guidance.

4.1.1.8 Charities

Charities may be registered or unregistered; excepted such as churches; or exempt such as museums. What due diligence is required will depend on what type of charity the client is.

If a charity is registered, then it is generally enough (in the absence of suspicion) to note the name, registration number and place of business of the charity from the registration directory. In England and Wales this would mean consideration of the Charity Commission's website (**www.gov.uk/government/organisations/charity-commission**). This is in effect a form of simplified due diligence (see **4.1.6**). Other countries may have a similar registration process and register. As with all categories of client, a charity/its persons should be checked for politically exposed person (PEP) status, sanctions and adverse media (see **4.2**).

CLIENT DUE DILIGENCE

If the charity is not registered, then what the relevant person requests in terms of identification and verification will depend on the business structure of the charity. If the charity is very well known, then the relevant person may decide that it does not need as much information as for a small unknown charity.

For further advice see para.6.14.15 of the LSAG guidance.

4.1.1.9 Clubs and associations

In order to carry out due diligence on these entities, the relevant person needs to verify that the club or association exists. This could be done via the entity's articles of association, recent audited accounts, statement from a bank and so on. The relevant person should have enough information to obtain and verify the full name, legal status, purpose, registered address and names of all office holders.

LSAG does not suggest that identification documentation is obtained for any specific individual within the club or association, and undoubtedly this would need to be on a risk-based approach.

For further advice see para.6.14.19 of the LSAG guidance.

4.1.1.10 Identification of other entities

There is a raft of other entities that could instruct a law firm – below are some with suggested identification measures that could be deployed:

- **Churches and places of worship** – The entity may have registered as a charity, in which case follow the guidance above. The entity can also apply for registration as a certified building of worship with the General Register Office which will issue the entity a certificate. Also, charitable status will be registered with HMRC. If the entity is not a registered charity, identification may therefore take place with reference to its General Register Office certificate or by enquiry with HMRC. Again, proportionality is key, and if the entity instructing the relevant person is well known, a note to that effect on the file together with the gathering of open-source information may be enough. For further advice see para.6.14.17 of the LSAG guidance.
- **Schools, colleges and universities** – These entities can be a number of different legal formations, and what identification measures are needed will depend on what they are. The Department for Education maintains a list of approved educational establishments, which should be consulted to assist in verifying the identity of an educational establishment (**https://get-information-schools.service.gov.uk/**). Again, if the establishment is very well known and there is enough open-source information about the entity, this may be enough to identify it. For further information see para.6.14.18 of the LSAG guidance.
- **Government agencies and councils** – Steps need to be taken to verify that the entity exists, and how far a relevant person needs to go in doing so will depend

on the risk of money laundering. Public domain information which confirms name of the entity; nature and status; address; names of key personnel such as directors or equivalent; name of the instructing person and their authority to instruct; and an extract from the official government website will be enough. PEP, sanction and adverse media checks may highlight some information which means that the relevant person should ask for more information from the client (see **4.2**). For further guidance see para.6.14.20 of the LSAG guidance.
- **Pension funds** – Under reg.37(3)(b)(iii) it is possible for pension, superannuation or similar schemes which satisfy certain conditions to qualify for simplified due diligence. That simplified due diligence may be seeing a copy of the page showing the name of the pension scheme or seeing the deed for the scheme.

4.1.1.11 Certification as a method of verification

Obtaining copies of documents that adequately identify the client is one method of verifying the client's identity. An additional method is certification. If the relevant person has not been able to meet (in person or virtually) the individual that they need to identify, the relevant person needs to consider whether to request that the identification documents are sent in copy form and those copies are certified by a regulated individual. It is preferable for those who are regulated to certify as they themselves have standards and codes to adhere to and may also need to adhere to the AML Regulations. Those that may be able to certify a copy of a person's ID are as follows (this list is not exhaustive):

- a qualified solicitor/barrister;
- a notary;
- a tax adviser;
- an accountant;
- an insolvency practitioner;
- an auditor;
- a credit or financial institution which is an authorised person;
- a consumer credit financial institution.

It is possible for the Post Office to certify also, but note that it is not regulated.

Suggested wording of the certification could be a statement that the document is 'Certified to be a true copy of the original seen by me' or where appropriate, 'This is a true likeness of [insert person's name]'. Note that the latter may be more preferable from a risk perspective as it means the document holder needs to be present.

The certification should also include:

- an official stamp of the person certifying;
- an indication of professional status, e.g. regulation number;
- signature and date;

CLIENT DUE DILIGENCE

- printed name of certifier;
- the occupation and address/telephone number.

There is nothing in the AML Regulations requiring documentation to be certified. However, many firms require copy documents to be certified by a regulated professional as part of their verification measures where they have not seen the original document or met the client.

With video conferencing becoming a more frequent method of communicating (especially during the COVID-19 pandemic), relevant persons should be encouraged to meet their client via that method if meeting physically face to face is not possible. Note, however, that this is not completely foolproof, and the relevant person will be unable to tell whether the client is in fact on the call completely alone. It therefore could be open to abuse, but it is just as good as or better than certification from another regulated professional that the client has simply popped in to see to obtain certification on their copy ID documentation.

Whether the relevant person or firm requests that the original certified (i.e. wet ink) copy is sent to the firm is a matter of risk-based approach. Given that law firms are becoming more electronic and possibly working more remotely during and after the COVID-19 pandemic, thought needs to be given as to whether this is requested and/or needed.

4.1.1.12 Electronic verification

It is possible to use electronic identification and verification methods to ID clients. The use of these tools can improve efficiency in the undertaking of ID and verification. There are many electronic identification providers, and if such methods are to be used firms need to consider whether electronic identification is to be used alone and in place of receiving ID documentation or in addition to that. Another aspect to consider is whether electronic identification and verification should/could replace the physical gathering of ID documents, and if so, when undertaking higher risk areas of work whether additional ID documentation is obtained.

LSAG has extensive coverage on the use of electronic tools for identifying clients, and firms who are considering using this method should consult chapter 7 of the guidance.

4.1.1.13 Identification of third parties acting on behalf of the client

Regulation 28(10) sets out that where a person purports to act on behalf of a client, the relevant person must verify that the person is authorised to act on behalf of the client, identify the person and verify the identity of the person and that verification needs to be independent of both the person being identified and the client.

The 2021 version of the LSAG guidance has helpfully expanded on this aspect of the AML Regulations and placed into guidance the practical approach to this regulation that most firms were taking (see para.6.6 of the guidance). This is that, where the third party quite clearly has apparent and ostensible authority to provide instructions, they should not be considered intermediaries, agents or representatives that require identification. An example might be the Head of Lending at a mainstream bank.

Identification will be needed where it is not clear or apparent and cannot be taken as being apparent that the third party has authority to act. This might be the situation, for example, where a grandchild is instructing a firm in the sale of their grandparent's house. Confirmation from the grandparent client as to the authority they are giving to the grandchild to instruct the firm and the grandchild's ID should be taken and verified.

4.1.1.14 The timing of verification of ID

All relevant persons want to know when verification has to be done by and how much work can be done before it has been completed.

Regulation 30 requires that the relevant person undertakes the verification of the identity of the client, anyone purporting to act on behalf of the client (see above) and any beneficial owner before establishing a business relationship or the carrying out of a transaction.

Regulation 30(3) goes on to state that as long as the verification is completed as soon as practicable after contact is first established, the verification measures may be completed during the establishment of the business relationship if that is necessary not to interrupt the normal conduct of business and there is little risk of money laundering or terrorist financing.

Regulation 31 sets out that where the relevant person is unable to carry out the due diligence measures, they must not carry out any transaction through a bank account with the client or on behalf of the client. Further, the relevant person must not establish a business relationship with the client or carry out a transaction with a client otherwise than through a bank account. The regulation then goes on to state that the relevant person must terminate any existing business relationship with the client and consider whether a SAR disclosure to the National Crime Agency (NCA) needs to be made (for guidance on SARs see **3.5**).

In practice, verification measures can take place during the very early stages of acting for a client; however, no transaction should be completed and as a matter of good practice no substantial work should be conducted (not least also because if the relevant person needs to cease acting, raising a bill and being paid becomes challenging).

All firms should consider putting into their policy what work is and is not allowed to happen before CDD has been completed, and also firms should consider whether there is a system flag or 'stop' that can be placed on files where CDD has not been completed to stop (or at least discourage) the relevant person from undertaking any further work.

CLIENT DUE DILIGENCE

4.1.1.15 *Practical examples of ID*

To illustrate what identification documentation a relevant person may wish to obtain to adequately verify the client, below are a few examples of what ID to gather for various client types. These examples are by way of illustration only, and as CDD is a risk-based assessment, other relevant persons or law firms may ask for more or less depending on the risk assessed.

INDIVIDUALS

For individual clients, identification documentation is relatively straightforward. For those clients who do not have the usual documentation – for example, because they are in a care home or without a permanent residence or a minor – creative thinking needs to be deployed. Most clients will be able to produce something which will help identify them, or the relevant person can ask for some form of documentation from those that care for or know the client. Examples might be a letter from a care home manager; a letter from someone who lives at the address where the client lives; a Home Office letter confirming immigration status; and so on. The bottom line is that the lack of availability of certain identification documentation needs to fit in to what the relevant person knows of the client. For example, it is highly likely that a refugee will not be able to provide proof of address, but very unlikely that someone selling a property could not.

The same analysis should apply when acting for the settlor of a trust or personal representative/executor of a deceased or identifying a beneficiary.

UK COMPANY

```
                    Honey Bees LLP
                       (UK LLP)
                    ┌─────────┴─────────┐
              Member:              Member:
          Queen Bee Ltd         Worker Bees Ltd
          (UK company)           (UK company)
         ┌──────┴──────┐        ┌──────┴──────┐
    Directors:     Shareholder:  Director:    Shareholder:
    Alfred Bee     Lucy Bee     Callum Bee    Callum Bee
    Lucy Bee        (100%)                     (100%)
```

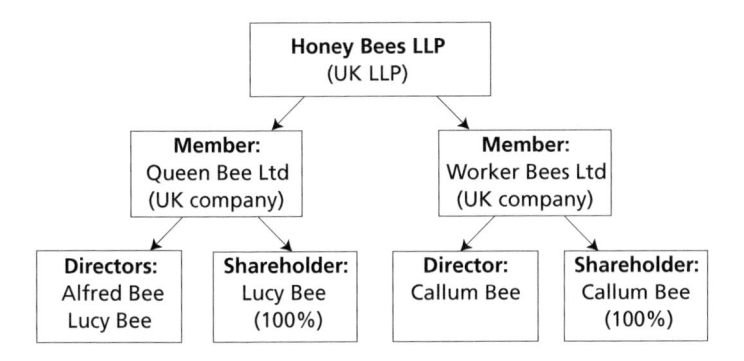

Figure 4.1 Honey Bees LLP

This entity is a UK LLP. The members of the LLP are UK-based companies, meaning all company documentation can be obtained from Companies House. The

ANTI-MONEY LAUNDERING

firm should consider requesting ID for Alfred Bee, Lucy Bee and Callum Bee (the latter two as beneficial owners).

```
                        Beehive Ltd
                        (UK company)
                       /            \
        Director:                    Shareholder:
        Umbrella Wasp Ltd            Hornet Ltd
        (UK company)                 (UK company)
         /        \                   /         \
 Directors:    Shareholders:     Director:    Shareholder:
 Belinda Bee   Belinda Bee (50%) Joe Bee      Joe Bee (100%)
 Delilah Bee   Delilah Bee (50%)
```

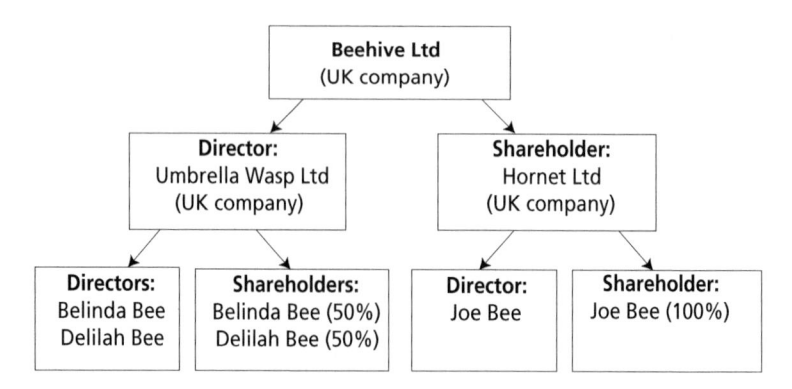

Figure 4.2 Beehive Ltd

This entity is a UK company and the director of Beehive Ltd is a UK-based company, therefore all company documentation can be obtained from Companies House. The firm should consider requesting identity documents for Belinda Bee and Delilah Bee. Further, the firm should consider requesting ID of Joe Bee as ultimate beneficial owner.

```
              NA Ltd
              (UK company limited
              by guarantee)
                   |
              Directors:
              Tim Turtle
              Belinda Bee
              Roger Heron
              Michael Philips
```

Figure 4.3 NA Ltd

This entity is a UK company limited by guarantee, meaning there are no shares/shareholders. Therefore, the firm should consider requesting ID for the directors. The regulations do not specify how many directors should be identified; however two may be reasonable and proportionate. The firm may also wish to consider whether it needs to identify those who control the entity if they are not the directors being identified.

CLIENT DUE DILIGENCE

INTERNATIONAL COMPANY

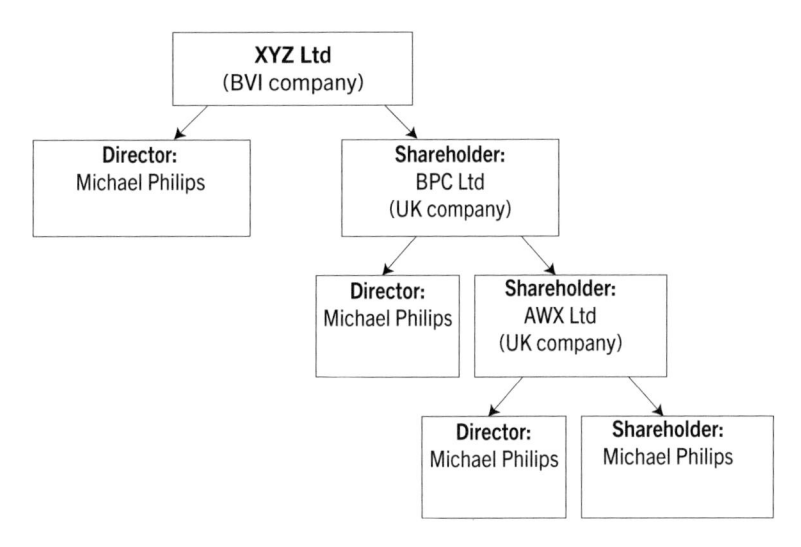

```
                    XYZ Ltd
                  (BVI company)
                   /         \
    Director:              Shareholder:
  Michael Philips            BPC Ltd
                           (UK company)
                            /        \
                   Director:      Shareholder:
                 Michael Philips     AWX Ltd
                                  (UK company)
                                   /        \
                            Director:    Shareholder:
                          Michael Philips  Michael Philips
```

Figure 4.4 XYZ Ltd

This entity is a non-UK company based in the British Virgin Islands (BVI). At the outset, the firm cannot obtain any documentation itself and should request a structure chart to enable the firm to understand the structure and determine on a risk-based approach what information is needed. When the firm is in receipt of the structure chart, it can see that Michael Philips is the sole director and the ultimate beneficial owner of the client entity. The firm should ask for company documentation (certificate of incorporation, memorandum and articles of association and the register of directors, or alternatively if the jurisdiction can provide a certificate of incumbency this would satisfy the company documentation requirement) for XYZ Ltd. Taking a risk-based approach, documentation for BPC Ltd and AWX Ltd is not required.

The firm should also consider requesting ID for Michael Philips.

ANTI-MONEY LAUNDERING

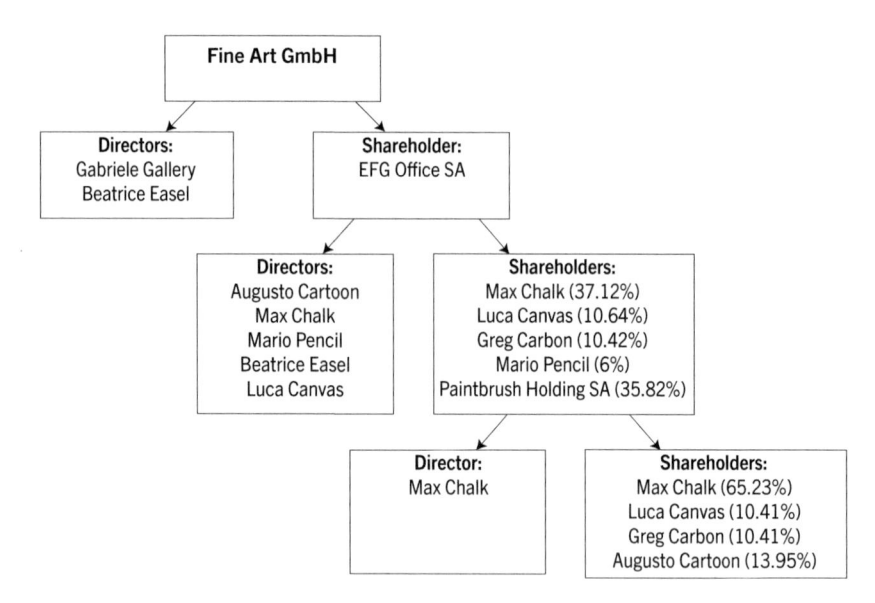

```
                    ┌─────────────────┐
                    │  Fine Art GmbH  │
                    └─────────────────┘
                     ↙               ↘
    ┌──────────────────┐      ┌──────────────────┐
    │  Directors:      │      │  Shareholder:    │
    │  Gabriele Gallery│      │  EFG Office SA   │
    │  Beatrice Easel  │      │                  │
    └──────────────────┘      └──────────────────┘
                                ↙              ↘
              ┌──────────────────────┐  ┌─────────────────────────────────┐
              │  Directors:          │  │  Shareholders:                  │
              │  Augusto Cartoon     │  │  Max Chalk (37.12%)             │
              │  Max Chalk           │  │  Luca Canvas (10.64%)           │
              │  Mario Pencil        │  │  Greg Carbon (10.42%)           │
              │  Beatrice Easel      │  │  Mario Pencil (6%)              │
              │  Luca Canvas         │  │  Paintbrush Holding SA (35.82%) │
              └──────────────────────┘  └─────────────────────────────────┘
                                           ↙                    ↘
                            ┌──────────────────┐   ┌─────────────────────────────┐
                            │  Director:       │   │  Shareholders:              │
                            │  Max Chalk       │   │  Max Chalk (65.23%)         │
                            │                  │   │  Luca Canvas (10.41%)       │
                            │                  │   │  Greg Carbon (10.41%)       │
                            │                  │   │  Augusto Cartoon (13.95%)   │
                            └──────────────────┘   └─────────────────────────────┘
```

Figure 4.5 Fine Art GmbH

This entity is a non-UK company based in Germany. At the outset, the firm cannot obtain any documentation itself and so should request a structure chart to enable it to understand the structure and understand what additional documentation it needs.

The firm should ask for company documentation (certificate of incorporation, memorandum and articles of association and the register of directors or alternatively if the jurisdiction can provide a certificate of incumbency this would satisfy the company documentation requirement) for Fine Art GmbH. From the documentation and with the assistance of the client, the above structure chart can be created if not provided by the client.

Taking a risk-based approach, documentation for EFG Office SA and Paintbrush Holding SA is not required.

The firm should consider requesting ID for Gabriele Gallery and Beatrice Easel as the two directors of the company client; and Max Chalk as the majority shareholder and ultimate beneficial owner.

CLIENT DUE DILIGENCE

TRUST

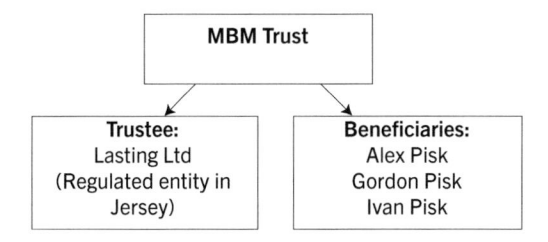

```
                    ┌─────────────┐
                    │  MBM Trust  │
                    └──────┬──────┘
              ┌────────────┴────────────┐
              ▼                         ▼
    ┌──────────────────┐     ┌──────────────────┐
    │    Trustee:      │     │  Beneficiaries:  │
    │   Lasting Ltd    │     │    Alex Pisk     │
    │ (Regulated entity in │     │   Gordon Pisk    │
    │     Jersey)      │     │    Ivan Pisk     │
    └──────────────────┘     └──────────────────┘
```

Figure 4.6 MBM Trust

The firm has been instructed by the trustees of a discretionary trust. Those trustees are Lasting Ltd which is regulated in Jersey. The firm can obtain evidence of Lasting Ltd's regulation from open sources. The firm will need to request the names of the beneficiaries under the trust.

CHARITY

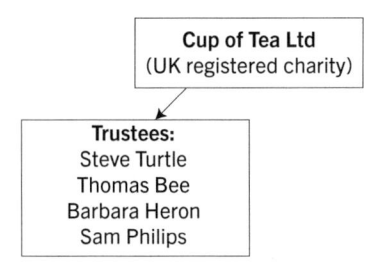

```
            ┌──────────────────────┐
            │    Cup of Tea Ltd    │
            │ (UK registered charity) │
            └──────────┬───────────┘
                       ▼
            ┌──────────────────────┐
            │      Trustees:       │
            │     Steve Turtle     │
            │     Thomas Bee       │
            │    Barbara Heron     │
            │     Sam Philips      │
            └──────────────────────┘
```

Figure 4.7 Cup of Tea Ltd

This entity is a UK registered charity, and therefore evidence of its regulated status can be obtained from the Charity Commission. As long as the work is not deemed high risk, this is all a firm will need to identify the client.

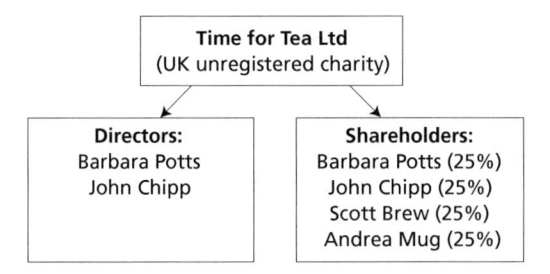

```
                    ┌──────────────────────┐
                    │    Time for Tea Ltd  │
                    │(UK unregistered charity)│
                    └──────────┬───────────┘
              ┌────────────────┴────────────────┐
              ▼                                 ▼
    ┌──────────────────┐           ┌──────────────────────┐
    │   Directors:     │           │    Shareholders:     │
    │  Barbara Potts   │           │ Barbara Potts (25%)  │
    │   John Chipp     │           │  John Chipp (25%)    │
    │                  │           │  Scott Brew (25%)    │
    │                  │           │  Andrea Mug (25%)    │
    └──────────────────┘           └──────────────────────┘
```

Figure 4.8 Time for Tea Ltd

ANTI-MONEY LAUNDERING

This entity is an unregistered charity, and therefore the firm needs to consider the type of business structure the charity resembles when deciding what ID requirements to apply. In this example, Time for Tea Ltd appears to be a UK company.

There are two directors and four shareholders all holding the same amount of shares. The firm should consider requesting identity documents for both directors and all shareholders.

4.1.2 Step 2: client and matter risk assessment

Part of a relevant person's due diligence on a client and matter is a risk assessment.

The essence of the AML Regulations is to conduct CDD on the basis of the AML risk assessed, and as such reference to assessing risk is peppered throughout the regulations.

Regulation 28(12) sets out that the way in which a relevant person complies with the requirement to undertake CDD measures and the extent of those measures must reflect the firm-wide AML risk assessment under reg.18(1) (see **3.3**) and the relevant person's assessment of the level of risk arising in the particular matter. The regulation sets out that what CDD is undertaken may differ from case to case.

It is important for relevant persons in the firm to understand the firm's firm-wide AML risk assessment, either by seeing it or a summary of it – or alternatively, if the client and matter risk assessment has been designed on the basis of the conclusions in the firm's firm-wide AML risk assessment (which it should), then the firm may decide that this is enough to satisfy the requirements of reg.28(12)(a)(i).

Regulation 28(13) goes on to state that when assessing the level of risk in a matter, the relevant person must take into account, amongst other things, the purpose of an account, transaction or business relationship; the level of assets to be deposited by a client or the size of the transaction undertaken by the client; and the regularity and duration of the business relationship. The firm may wish to place these items in the firm's client and matter risk assessment.

At **Appendix B6** is a template client and matter risk assessment which attempts to cover the AML risk indicators identified in the AML Regulations. These include client risk, geographical risk and transactional/matter risk.

Also in the template are other suggested additions that speak to risk more generally and are not AML-specific. The client and matter risk assessments are an opportunity for firms to concentrate fee earners' minds on all aspects of risk and not just money laundering risk. All client and matter risk assessments should be adapted and written to suit the firm within which they are undertaken, and firms may wish to create different question sets for different types of work.

The 2021 version of the LSAG guidance provides useful direction on client and matter risk assessments, and provides possible questions that an assessment could contain. Further, LSAG sets out a possible way of scoring the assessment which would require weighting to be applied. See paras.5.9–5.16 of the LSAG guidance. This can get very complicated and firms that wish to proceed in this way may want to engage an independent consultant to assist in designing such an assessment.

It is important to understand that the risk assessment should not be seen as a tick-box exercise for a relevant person to quickly get through to enable a file to be opened. In fact, controversially the author's opinion is that it is not often realistic or possible for a relevant person to fully answer a client and matter risk assessment before beginning some preliminary work, and if firms insist that it is completed before a file can be opened, then that firm may encourage a quick tick-box approach. That said, a timescale for completion does need to be given, with the understanding by relevant persons that the document needs to be revisited during the course of the matter and reviewed.

Ultimately what cannot be overemphasised is that risk assessments of a client and their matter must be documented to be compliant with reg.40 on record-keeping (see **4.3.2**) and further be available for regulators to see at any time. Non-compliance with the completion of risk assessments is viewed very dimly by the Solicitors Regulation Authority (SRA), and it will take disciplinary action for non-compliance.

4.1.3 Step 3: understanding purpose and nature

Feeding into the relevant person's client and matter risk assessment is the relevant person's need to understand the purpose and nature of the work being undertaken, as set out in reg.28(13). This means understanding what is to be done and why. If the relevant person understands the purpose and nature of the transaction, they will be able to spot when an AML flag arises. It is for this reason that understanding the purpose and nature of the matter at hand cannot be outsourced to a central team or a supervising partner who is not handling the work on a day-to-day basis. It is the fee earner conducting the work who needs to understand the purpose and nature of the work. That is not to say that others cannot understand it too, such as a supervising partner or client introducer, but it does not work for the conducting fee earner to delegate the assessment to those individuals.

Understanding purpose and nature of a transaction is also needed when applying 'enhanced' due diligence (EDD) measures as set out at reg.33 (see **4.1.7**).

The understanding of purpose and nature needs to feature in the client and matter risk assessment. See **Appendix B6** for a template.

4.1.4 Step 4: source of funds and source of wealth

4.1.4.1 Overview

When a matter is deemed to be of a higher risk such that EDD needs to be conducted, source of funds and source of wealth will need to be explored in the relevant matter.

Most if not all property work will be considered to be high risk with EDD measures applying, and therefore source of funds and source of wealth need to be understood.

ANTI-MONEY LAUNDERING

The first step is to understand what these terms mean.

'Source of funds' refers to where the monies for a transaction are coming from and how the monies got there; and 'source of wealth' is about the client's overall wealth. So, for example the deposit on a property purchase may come from a person's savings, which they can show by way of bank statements – that is their source of funds. Those savings were accumulated over a number of years from that person's salary, which they can evidence by showing their wage slips for, say, the last six months and a letter from their employer confirming their salary if that is not clear from the wage slips.

If a relevant person understands the source of funds and wealth on a transaction, there is a far less likely chance of money laundering taking place. What must not happen, however, is a tick-box exercise of obtaining bank statements which are then not looked at by the relevant person and/or do not in fact show the monies to be used for the transaction.

The question all fee earners ask about understanding source of funds and wealth is, how far to go. That is, it seems, the million dollar question, if you pardon the pun. Unfortunately, the answer is, 'it depends'.

How far to go depends on the matter at hand, and the fee earner needs to go far enough to be comfortable that what they are being told makes sense and that it stacks up, can weather scrutiny and that ultimately if a regulator or a crime enforcement agency were to ask the fee earner about it in the future, that fee earner would be comfortable with their investigations and the view they have taken. That may sound scary, but that is the bottom line. Fee earners need to understand that they are not required to be detectives and prove that all money is clean or not, but they are required to ask the appropriate level of questions depending on the risk factors at hand. Should it come to pass that there was in fact money laundering, but that all relevant questions were asked and the answers given made sense and it was reasonable to conclude that there was no evidence of money laundering, the fee earner will have undertaken all they are required to do under the regulations. There is no crystal-ball gazing required, and a sensible approach is needed.

To assist in determining what level of assessment of source of funds and wealth is needed, it might be best to think in terms of categories.

CATEGORY 1 – THE SOURCE OF FUNDS AND SOURCE OF WEALTH ARE WELL KNOWN

This could be when the relevant person acts for a well-known institution such as the NHS, a local authority, a bank or a well-known brand. In these cases, the source of both funds and wealth will be well understood, and what is known should be documented in the client and matter risk assessment or other designated place, and no further information should be required unless there are any money laundering concerns.

CLIENT DUE DILIGENCE

CATEGORY 2 – THE SOURCE OF WEALTH IS KNOWN, BUT THE RELEVANT PERSON DOES NOT KNOW THE SOURCE OF FUNDS

This could be when the relevant person is acting for an individual or a business whose wealth is well known or documented, such as a high net worth individual or a client well known to the firm. This could be a high net worth individual that the relevant person is purchasing a house for, or it could be a well-known restaurant or retailer, for example. In these instances, if the relevant person understands the source of wealth, then they do not need to ask anything more, but they do need to document what they know and why they did not ask for anything further in the client and matter risk assessment or designated place.

In matters like this, the relevant person needs to understand the source of funds (i.e., where the monies are coming from) and this needs to be asked of the client, and where necessary, proof provided. If monies are not coming from an account in the client's name, an explanation needs to be sought as to why, and further enquiries made if appropriate. For example, if the monies are coming from a third party that owes the client monies, the relevant person may want to ask about the loan arrangement, see proof of it and ask for ID information on the sender of the monies and about their source of funds and wealth on the basis that the monies that are sent to the firm might be monies that have been mixed with the sender's own monies and they could therefore be tainted. Further, PEP, sanction and adverse media checks should be conducted on the sender of the monies (see **4.2**).

If the sender is a company, then the relevant person may want to seek to verify that the company is likely to have those funds by looking at its audited accounts.

CATEGORY 3 – THE RELEVANT PERSON DOES NOT KNOW SOURCE OF EITHER FUNDS OR WEALTH AND/OR THE CLIENT IS A PEP OR FROM A HIGH-RISK THIRD COUNTRY

If the client does not fit into category 1 or 2 above, then they fit into this category. Further, if the client is a PEP or from a high-risk third country, they fit into this category (see **4.2.1** for more information on PEPs). Clients and matters will be in this category where the client is not a well-known high net worth individual or an institution, a business or a brand.

In these matters, the relevant person needs to ask about source of funds and source of wealth and ask for evidence for each.

4.1.4.2 Documentation that may be sought for proof of source of funds and source of wealth

Generally speaking, in most circumstances clients and matters will fall into category 3 for transactional work. In each matter, the relevant person will need to scrutinise what they are being told about source of funds and wealth and not accept it at face value.

ANTI-MONEY LAUNDERING

Table 4.1 shows a list of documents that could be asked for to evidence what is being told to the relevant person. Although it may feel uncomfortable for some relevant persons to ask this information, it goes without saying that embarrassment is not a defence to a money laundering offence, and most clients now understand the need to be asked this information.

Table 4.1 List of documents to evidence source of funds and source of wealth

Source of funds/source of wealth	Information/documentation that may be required
Employment income	• Nature of employer's business • Name and address of employer • Annual salary and bonuses for the last couple of years • Last three months' pay slips • Confirmation from employer of annual salary • Latest accounts, or tax declaration if self-employed
Savings/deposit	• Bank statements showing monies and bank statements showing where monies come from
Property sale	• Details of the property sold (e.g. address, date of sale, value of property sold) • Copy of contract of sale • Title deed from HM Land Registry
Sale of shares or other investment	• Copy of contract • Sale value of shares sold and how they were sold • Statement of account from agent • Transaction receipt/confirmation • Shareholder's certificate • Date of sale
Loan	• Loan agreement • Amount, date and purpose of loan • Name and address of lender • Details of any security
Company sale	• Copy of the contract of sale • Internet research of company registry • Name and address of company • Total sales price • Client's share participation • Nature of business • Date of sale and receipt of funds • Any media coverage
Company profits/dividends	• Copy of latest audited financial statements • Copy of latest management accounts • Board of directors' approval • Dividend distribution • Tax declaration form

CLIENT DUE DILIGENCE

Source of funds/source of wealth	Information/documentation that may be required
Inheritance	• Name of deceased • Date of death • Relationship to client • Date received • Total amount • Solicitor's details so facts can be checked
Gift	• Certified identification documents of donor • Date received • Total amount • Donor's relationship to client • Letter from donor explaining the reason for the gift and the source of donor's wealth
Maturity/surrender of life policy	• Amount received • Policy provider • Policy number/reference • Date of surrender
Other income sources	• Nature of income, amount, date received and from whom • Appropriate supporting documentation

4.1.4.3 Firm's policies

There are some policy decisions that need to be decided by each firm in relation to source of funds and wealth, as follows:

1. **Will the firm ask for a certain number of months' bank statements to prove funds and wealth?** Some firms ask for six months as standard.
2. **Will the firm ask for source of funds and wealth for the payment of fees and disbursements?** This is not necessary under the AML Regulations due to the adequate consideration defence. See **2.4.2**.
3. **Will the firm require ID documentation on third parties paying monies to the firm?** Source of funds and wealth should be asked about, but technically the regulations do not require the firm to undertake ID checks – though it is strongly recommended.
4. **When will source of funds and wealth be asked about?** Traditionally this has been left towards the end of the transaction when monies are about to be sent. However, this can cause transactional delays and upset from the client's side if evidence needs to be produced in a rush. Further, if a defence SAR needs to be made and completion is due in under seven working days (the time the NCA has to consider a SAR), then this will cause a delay to the transaction and put the fee earner and the firm in a very difficult spot. It is therefore far better to front load asking for source of funds and wealth information by asking for it early on and then refreshing understanding before completion. Also, this way, if the relevant person cannot get comfortable with the source of

ANTI-MONEY LAUNDERING

funds and wealth and needs to cease acting, little work will have been done and little wasted by way of costs (as the chances of being paid for work up to the point of ceasing to act are likely to be low).

5. **Will the analysis of source of funds and wealth be delegated to a central team?** This is not recommended, but there are some firms that have their central risk function undertake this analysis. The analysis of source of funds and wealth must be undertaken by the fee earner with conduct of the matter. Of course, a central risk team can assist, but that central risk team cannot decide whether what is being provided is enough information and makes sense in the context of what the relevant person is being told.

6. **Will the firm provide clients with a form to complete? And if it does, will that form provide a list of options for the client to select when confirming their source of funds and wealth?** There are two schools of thought here. One option would be to provide a comprehensive list to clients to choose from; another option would be not to do so in case it potentially feeds the client a convenient answer.

7. **Where will source of funds and wealth analysis be documented?** By providing a designated space for fee earners to document their analysis, the firm is encouraging recording of the analysis undertaken. Further, should the analysis need to be considered later, it will be found more easily. The template client and matter risk assessment found at **Appendix B6** has space allocated for the documentation of the assessment of source of funds and wealth.

4.1.4.4 Source of funds and source of wealth – practical examples

The following examples are all based on real estate matters that sit in category 3 outlined above. For non-real estate matters, such as corporate or trust matters, the principles are the same.

EXAMPLE 4.1 – Transaction: residential property purchase for £500k, two individuals, deposit £150k – category 3

In this case the clients are a young couple, unknown to the firm, who explained that they had saved the money for the deposit over a long period of time from their salaries. The fee earner should therefore ask for bank statements to see that the monies were being saved regularly from wages. The fee earner may also wish to ask for copies of the individuals' wage slips. One of the clients is a solicitor and so regulated. This fact does not mean the fee earner needs to ask fewer questions, but does give some comfort that the source of both funds and wealth is legitimate.

If the evidence before the fee earner verifies what the fee earner is being told, then no further information beyond the bank statements and wage slips is needed. The fee earner recorded this information in the client and matter risk assessment.

EXAMPLE 4.2 – Transaction: residential property purchase for £5 million, cash; client: 21 years old – category 3

This is a high value transaction for someone very young. The client came to the firm through their father, whom the firm also acts for. The purchase was to be funded by the client's father.

Upon investigation, the fee earner ascertained that the client's father is an art dealer, which places his activity in a high-risk category. Upon further investigation through open sources, the fee earner discovered that the father is listed on Forbes as being a billionaire and one of the richest art dealers in the world (this was further corroborated through other open sources on the internet).

The firm's risk team ran a PEP, sanctions and adverse media check, and no adverse results were found on either the client or his father.

Given the information ascertained from open sources, the fee earner did not consider that they needed more information as to the source of wealth of the father, who was paying for the purchase. In terms of source of funds, the fee earner asked the client to confirm which account the monies were coming from, and the client confirmed that the monies were coming from the father directly and details were provided. The fee earner decided that they did not need to see a copy of the bank accounts, as it was widely known that the father had monies as outlined above and it was not deemed necessary. The fee earner recorded this information in the client and matter risk assessment.

This is an example of a high-risk transaction (value, cash, property, funds emanating from art dealing) but where the funds were coming from a well-documented source.

EXAMPLE 4.3 – Transaction: residential purchase for £1.5 million for client whose mother is funding deposit of £200k – category 3

The fee earner when exploring source of funds and wealth was being offered an accountant's letter as comfort as to the mother's source of funds and wealth.

The purchase price was £1.5 million, and upon questioning the mother confirmed that £1.3 million of the purchase price was coming from the proceeds of a sale of a property on which another law firm acted. The mother confirmed that the remainder of the funds were coming from her personal monies, which had accumulated from her company which provided coaching advice. The fee earner obtained from the other law firm confirmation of the sale and was satisfied as to the monies coming from that property sale. The fee earner also considered the mother's company's accounts at Companies House, and could see that the turnover of the company was such that the payment of £200k could be made. No further information was sought and the fee earner recorded all this in the client and matter risk assessment.

EXAMPLE 4.4 – Transaction: residential purchase for £1.2 million; client will be paying £300k deposit from bonds, stocks and shares – category 3

In this matter the client's deposit was tied up in bonds, stocks and shares and he confirmed that he would liquidate these just before he needed to pay the deposit monies. The fee earner

ANTI-MONEY LAUNDERING

requested evidence of these bonds, stocks and shares being in the client's name and this was given. The fee earner did not need to ask the client for their bank statements, as the monies were not in the account at that time and so that would be unnecessary. The fee earner felt that what he was being told fitted with what he knew of the client and so no further information was requested prior to exchange. At exchange, the fee earner requested evidence of the bonds, stocks and shares having been liquidated and this was provided. The fee earner recorded all this in the client and matter risk assessment.

4.1.5 Step 5: ongoing monitoring and high-risk registers

AML Regulations, reg.28(11) sets out as follows:

> The relevant person must conduct ongoing monitoring of a business relationship, including–
>
> (a) scrutiny of transactions undertaken throughout the course of the relationship (including, where necessary, the source of funds) to ensure that the transactions are consistent with the relevant person's knowledge of the customer, the customer's business and risk profile;
>
> (b) undertaking reviews of existing records and keeping the documents or information obtained for the purpose of applying customer due diligence measures up-to-date.

Further, where EDD is undertaken as per reg.33 or reg.35, enhanced ongoing monitoring needs to take place. Records of ongoing monitoring of a client need to be maintained in accordance with reg.40.

CDD is not a one-off exercise at the beginning of a matter or when the client is first on-boarded – it is an ongoing exercise, and as such fee earners need to understand that they should monitor the transaction at hand for AML flags from start to end.

Some firms weave into their processes alerts to fee earners to assist in their ongoing monitoring. For example, at the point when monies are to be paid out, the firm's payment request form could ask the fee earner to confirm that they have considered and understand source of funds and wealth where appropriate, there are no money laundering concerns and if there are these have been reported to the money laundering reporting officer (MLRO) who has authorised for the payment to proceed.

Some firms also have processes where a further risk assessment or re-evaluation of the one completed is undertaken by the fee earner at certain intervals. Thought needs to be given as to what happens if that process is not undertaken and whether the file should be locked, time recording stopped and so on.

One other aspect of ongoing monitoring is the maintenance of a high-risk register. If a firm has a centralised risk and compliance team, this would normally be maintained by that team. Otherwise, this register could be maintained by the MLRO or the money laundering compliance officer (MLCO).

The purpose of this register is to record clients that the firm deems to be higher risk. This might be because they are a PEP, sanctioned and/or there is adverse media about them. Those who are on the register should be checked regularly, and at least

CLIENT DUE DILIGENCE

once a month and more frequently if necessary (perhaps dependent on work type and why they are on the register). When a client is placed on the register, the fee earner must be told. When checks are undertaken, the conducting fee earner should be informed of the outcome of those checks. There must be an open line of communication between those who maintain the high-risk register and the fee earner.

At **Appendix B7** is a template simple high-risk register and at **Appendix B8** a template ongoing monitoring form which could be used to record ongoing monitoring.

There are IT products that will continually monitor client names submitted by firms for PEP status, sanctions and adverse media. However, caution should be used when adding all of a firm's clients' names, as this will create many 'false positive' results that will then need to be considered. It may therefore be best to place only the names of those on the firm's high-risk register into such a product, at least to begin with.

4.1.6 Simplified due diligence and when it can be applied

AML Regulations, reg.37 allows simplified due diligence to be undertaken where a relevant person deems there to a low risk of money laundering and terrorist financing.

To determine whether there is a low risk of money laundering or terrorist financing, the relevant person needs to consider the firm-wide risk assessment carried out under the regulations, relevant information made available to them by their regulator (under regs.17(9) and 47) and any risk factors as set out in reg.37(3) and summarised below:

(a) *customer risk factors*, including whether the client is a public administration or a publicly owned enterprise; an individual resident in a geographical area of lower risk; a credit institution or financial institution which is subject to requirements in national legislation implementing the Fourth EU Directive on Money Laundering and is supervised for compliance; or a company whose securities are listed on a regulated market taking into account the location of that regulated market;

(b) *product, service, transaction or delivery channel risk factors*, including whether the product or service is a life insurance policy; a pension product; a financial product that provides appropriately defined and limited services to certain types of customer; a product where risks of money laundering and terrorist financing are managed by other factors; a child trust fund; or a junior ISA (see reg.37(3)(b) for further information); and

(c) *geographical risk factors* including whether the country where the client is resident, established or registered or in which it operates is in the United Kingdom; a third country which has effective systems to counter money laundering and terrorist financing; or a third country which credible sources confirm has a low level of corruption or other criminal activity.

Having taken these factors into account, the relevant person may decide to undertake simplified due diligence as opposed to standard due diligence.

The AML Regulations do not set out what needs to be undertaken when the simplified due diligence standard applies. Industry practice is that information about beneficial ownership is not required.

Generally speaking, regulated individuals and entities and those who are listed on the stock market will qualify for simplified due diligence so long as the aspects outlined at (a), (b) and (c) above are considered to mean the client and matter are low risk (note that these low-risk factors cannot be assumed, and need to be thought about, and that thought process documented in a client/matter risk assessment). This would mean that locating evidence of their regulated status via the relevant registry is enough to identify the client. An example may be being instructed by a mainstream bank in the UK regulated by the Financial Conduct Authority (FCA) in relation to a loan it is providing. Another example may be an overseas entity which is listed on a reputable stock exchange and again, as long as the other risk factors indicate the money laundering risk is low, evidence of their listed status should be enough.

LSAG rightly highlights that simplified due diligence should be kept under review and a higher standard applied if a relevant person doubts the truth of identification documents, if there is an obligation to apply enhanced due diligence (see below) or if there is a suspicion of money laundering (although if that arose, care would need to be taken not to 'tip off' (see **2.4.4**) when asking for further due diligence).

PEP, sanction and adverse media checks should still be undertaken (see **4.2**) and it is a good idea to factor simplified due diligence questions within the firm's client and matter risk assessment as one of the first items to be considered (see **Appendix B6** for template client and matter risk assessment).

4.1.7 Enhanced due diligence and when it should be applied

The Fifth EU Directive on Money Laundering (5AMLD) implemented by MLR 2019 has made some changes to when EDD needs to be undertaken and what EDD should be gathered. To understand the changes, firms should be careful to ensure that they are reading the latest version of the AML Regulations from 2017 as amended (ensuring 'latest available (Revised)' is displayed when viewing the legislation online at **www.legislation.gov.uk**).

AML Regulations, reg.33(1) sets out that a relevant person must apply EDD and enhanced ongoing monitoring in the following circumstances:

(a) where a high risk of money laundering has been identified;
(b) where the client or transaction is established in a high-risk third country unless reg.33(2) applies (note that this has been amended by MLR 2019 to

omit the words 'or transaction' and insert at the end 'or in relation to any relevant transaction where either of the parties to the transaction is established in a high-risk third country' – more commentary on this new amendment is set out below);
(c) in relation to correspondent relationships with a credit institution or financial institution in accordance with reg.34 – this does not apply to law firms;
(d) where the relevant person has determined that a client or potential client is a PEP, either directly or by association;
(e) where the relevant person has discovered that the client has provided false or stolen identification documentation or information and the relevant person proposes to continue to act;
(f) in any case where the transaction is complex or unusually large or there is an unusual pattern of transactions; or the transaction or transactions have no apparent economic or legal purpose (note that this was amended by MLR 2019 to change the emphasis from 'and' to 'or' in each of these situations – therefore, if any one of these situations applies, EDD needs to be considered);
(g) any other case which by its nature can present a higher risk of money laundering or terrorist financing.

A high-risk third country is a country which has been identified as so by the European Commission, and therefore relevant persons and firms need to ensure they keep up to date with this list. Further, MLR 2019 insert into the AML Regulations that a 'relevant transaction' for the purpose of reg.33(1)(b) means a transaction in relation to which the relevant person is required to apply CDD measures and being 'established in' a high-risk third country means in the case of a legal person, being incorporated or having its principal place of business in that country, or, in the case of a financial institution or a credit institution having its principal regulatory authority in that country and in the case of an individual being resident in that country but not merely having been born there.

Where AML Regulations, reg.33(1)(b) is satisfied, MLR 2019 insert a new reg.33(3A) that the following EDD measures must be undertaken:

(a) obtaining additional information on the customer and on the customer's beneficial owner;
(b) obtaining additional information on the intended nature of the business relationship;
(c) obtaining information on the source of funds and source of wealth of the customer and of the customer's beneficial owner;
(d) obtaining information on the reasons for the transactions;
(e) obtaining the approval of senior management for establishing or continuing the business relationship;
(f) conducting enhanced monitoring of the business relationship by increasing the number and timing of controls applied, and selecting patterns of transactions that need further examination.

AML Regulations, reg.33(4) sets out that where EDD is needed, as the criteria at reg.33(1)(f) have been met, the EDD should include: (a) as far as reasonably possible, examining the background and purpose of the transaction; and (b) increasing the degree and nature of monitoring of the business relationship in which the transaction is made to determine whether that transaction or that relationship appears to be suspicious.

Regulation 33(6) further sets out the risk factors that relevant persons must take into account when determining whether there is a high risk of money laundering or terrorist financing. These are categorised as follows:

(a) *Client risk factors* including:

- whether the business relationship is conducted in unusual circumstances;
- the client being resident in a geographical area of high risk;
- the client is a legal person or arrangement that is a vehicle for holding personal assets;
- the client is a company that has nominee shareholders or shares in bearer form;
- the client is a business that is cash intensive; or
- the corporate structure of the client is unusual or excessively complex given the nature of the company's business.

MLR 2019 amended this paragraph to add additional risk factors of the client being a beneficiary of a life insurance policy; or where the client is a third country national who is applying for residence in or citizenship of a state in exchange for transfers of capital, purchase of a property, government bonds or investment in corporate entities in that state.

Prior to the release of the 2021 LSAG guidance, a short note was issued to set out that in the view of those who write the LSAG guidance, whether the person is a beneficiary of a life insurance policy is only likely to be indicative of higher money laundering risk where the retainer bears direct relevance to the policy.

(b) *Product, service, transaction or delivery channel risk factors* including:

- whether the product involves private banking;
- the product or transaction is one which might favour anonymity;
- the matter involves non-face-to-face business relationships or transactions without certain safeguards such as electronic signatures (electronic signatures has been changed by MLR 2019 to be 'an electronic identification process which meets the conditions set out in regulation 28(19)');
- payments will be received from unknown or unassociated third parties;
- new products and new business practices are involved, including new delivery mechanisms or use of new technology; or
- the service involves provision of nominee directors or shareholders or shadow directors or the formation of companies in a third country.

MLR 2019 added a further risk factor to this paragraph to include where the transaction relates to oil, arms, precious metals, tobacco, cultural artefacts, ivory or other items related to protected species, or other items of archaeological, historical, culture or religious significance or of rare scientific value.

(c) *Geographical risk factors* including whether countries in the matter:

- are countries that have been identified by credible sources as not having effective systems to counter money laundering;
- are countries that have been identified by credible sources as having significant levels of corruption or other criminal activity;
- are countries subject to sanctions, embargos or similar measures;
- are countries providing funding or support for terrorism;
- are countries that have within them organisations that have been designated by the UK as proscribed organisations under the Terrorism Act 2000 or have been designated by other countries, international organisations or the European Union as terrorist organisations; or finally
- are countries that have been identified by credible sources as not implementing requirements to counter money laundering and terrorist financing.

AML Regulations, reg.33 sets out at (5) what EDD steps should be taken should the risk assessment by the relevant person deem EDD necessary, as follows:

(5) Depending on the requirements of the case, the enhanced customer due diligence measures required under paragraph (1) may also include, among other things–

(a) seeking additional independent, reliable sources to verify information provided or made available to the relevant person;
(b) taking additional measures to understand better the background, ownership and financial situation of the customer, and other parties to the transaction;
(c) taking further steps to be satisfied that the transaction is consistent with the purpose and intended nature of the business relationship;
(d) increasing the monitoring of the business relationship, including greater scrutiny of transactions.

As mentioned briefly above, MLR 2019 (reg.5(4)) changed AML Regulations, reg.33(1)(b) to set out that EDD needs to be applied when either party to a 'relevant transaction' is established in a high-risk third country. It goes without saying that firms will need to apply EDD measures when their client is in a high-risk country, whether that be a high-risk third country or not. However, the change in this regulation suggests that where the opposing party is in a high-risk third country, EDD should be applied. The challenge with this is that relevant persons are required to undertake due diligence on their clients and not opposing parties, and will often not know this level of detail about the opposing party.

Firms therefore need to consider whether they are undertaking a 'relevant transaction' as set out in reg.27. These are where the relevant person:

- establishes a business relationship – which firms would not be doing with the opposing party to a transaction;
- carries out an occasional transaction – which means a transaction which is not carried out as part of a business relationship, and again this does not seem to apply;
- suspects money laundering or terrorist financing – this could apply; or
- doubts the veracity of adequacy of ID documentation – which would not apply in the context of the opposing party.

The hope was that the 2021 version of the LSAG guidance would clarify this regulation. LSAG simply states that a relevant person will need to apply the EDD steps outlined in the regulations where the client or counterparty is established in a high-risk third country 'where you are undertaking an occasional transaction (within the meanings of R27(1)(b) and (2))' (para.6.18.2). LSAG sets out earlier in its guidance in relation to occasional transactions: 'Due to the ongoing duties a practice would have in most foreseeable circumstances this definition is not likely to apply to the relationship between a legal practice and a client for any transaction' (para.6.5).

It follows, in the author's opinion, that firms do not need to ask the opposing party whether they are established in a high-risk third country, or indeed carry out any due diligence on the opposing party. If, however, a suspicion of money laundering arises, then further risk analysis will be needed, and possibly a SAR made.

A firm's client and matter risk assessment needs to take into account all of the above areas of deemed risk under the regulations, including details of high-risk third countries, and at **Appendix B6** you will find a suggested template. There is no set and standard way of assessing risk, and each firm should adapt any risk assessment template to fit its firm and work type. Indeed, some firms may want to create different risk assessments for different types of work, put the risk assessment in an electronic format with a score, and so on.

The regulations require an assessment of whether a matter is complex or unusually large or represents an unusual pattern of transactions. This should be judged in the context of the firm's client base and transactions. What may be normal for a Silver Circle or Magic Circle law firm may not be for a regional or small firm.

An important part of considering whether EDD needs to be applied is also considering whether the client is a PEP. This is considered further at **4.2.1**.

4.2 POLITICALLY EXPOSED PERSONS (REGULATION 35), SANCTIONS AND ADVERSE MEDIA CHECKS

A vital part of CDD is checking clients for PEP status, checking to see whether the client is sanctioned and checking whether there exists any adverse media about the client which could give rise to a suspicion about money laundering.

There are online platforms where these checks can be conducted all at once. These platforms provide an efficient way of undertaking these checks. They do, however, come at cost and are not mandatory, with such checks being able to be conducted through open sources, albeit in a more manual and time-consuming way.

4.2.1 PEPs and regulation 35

AML Regulations, reg.35 sets out that a relevant person must have in place appropriate risk management systems and procedures to determine whether a client or beneficial owner is a PEP, or is a family member or known close associate of a PEP. The regulation goes on to set out that the relevant person must manage the risks arising from acting for PEPs.

PEP is defined by the AML Regulations under reg.35(12) as follows:

(12) In this regulation–
- (a) 'politically exposed person' or 'PEP' means an individual who is entrusted with prominent public functions, other than as a middle-ranking or more junior official;
- (b) 'family member' of a politically exposed person includes–
  - (i) a spouse or civil partner of the PEP;
  - (ii) children of the PEP and the spouses or civil partners of the PEP's children;
  - (iii) parents of the PEP;
- (c) 'known close associate' of a PEP means–
  - (i) an individual known to have joint beneficial ownership of a legal entity or a legal arrangement or any other close business relations with a PEP;
  - (ii) an individual who has sole beneficial ownership of a legal entity or a legal arrangement which is known to have been set up for the benefit of a PEP.

Regulation 35(14) goes on to state:

For the purposes of paragraphs (9), (11) and (12)(a), individuals entrusted with prominent public functions include–
- (a) heads of state, heads of government, ministers and deputy or assistant ministers;
- (b) members of parliament or of similar legislative bodies;
- (c) members of the governing bodies of political parties;
- (d) members of supreme courts, of constitutional courts or of any judicial body the decisions of which are not subject to further appeal except in exceptional circumstances;
- (e) members of courts of auditors or of the boards of central banks;
- (f) ambassadors, charges d'affaires and high-ranking officers in the armed forces;
- (g) members of the administrative, management or supervisory bodies of State-owned enterprises;
- (h) directors, deputy directors and members of the board or equivalent function of an international organisation.

The Financial Action Task Force's (FATF's) definition of a PEP – coined in 2003 and revised in its 2013 paper, 'FATF Guidance: Politically exposed persons (recommendations 12 and 22)' (June 2013, **www.fatf-gafi.org/media/fatf/documents/recommendations/guidance-pep-rec12-22.pdf** (para.11, reproduced with permission)) – is as follows:

- *Domestic PEPs:* individuals who are or have been entrusted domestically with prominent public functions, for example Heads of State or of government, senior politicians, senior government, judicial or military officials, senior executives of state owned corporations, important political party officials.

Note, however, that LSAG sets out that middle ranking and junior officials are not PEPs, and only those who truly hold prominent positions should be treated as PEPs with the definition not being applied to local government, more junior members of the civil service or military officials other than those holding the most senior ranks.

- *Foreign PEPs:* individuals who are or have been entrusted with prominent public functions by a foreign country, for example Heads of State or of government, senior politicians, senior government, judicial or military officials, senior executives of state-owned corporations, important political party officials.
- *International organisation PEPs:* persons who are or have been entrusted with a prominent function by an international organisation, refers to members of senior management or individuals who have been entrusted with equivalent functions, *i.e.* directors, deputy directors and members of the board or equivalent functions.
- *Family members* are individuals who are related to a PEP either directly (consanguinity [i.e. blood related]) or through marriage or similar (civil) forms of partnership.
- *Close associates* are individuals who are closely connected to a PEP, either socially or professionally.

The reason why PEP status matters is because there is the risk that those who are PEPs may be more susceptible to bribery, corruption and money laundering as a result of their position.

AML Regulations, reg.35(3) sets out that if a client or potential client is a PEP or a family member or known close associate of a PEP, the relevant person must assess the risk associated with that client and consider the extent of the EDD measures to be applied.

When considering the extent of EDD to be undertaken, reg.35(4) sets out that the relevant person must take into account information made available to it by regulators, including guidance such as the LSAG guidance.

Regulation 35(5) goes on to set out that the relevant person must have approval from senior management for establishing or continuing a business relationship with the PEP, take adequate measures to establish source of funds and wealth (see **4.1.4** for guidance) and conduct enhanced ongoing monitoring of that business relationship (see **4.1.7** for guidance on EDD in general). The PEP should also be placed on the firm's high-risk register as part of ongoing risk assessment measures (see **4.1.5**).

'Senior management' is defined under reg.3(1) as 'an officer or employee of the relevant person with sufficient knowledge of the relevant person's money laundering and terrorist financing risk exposure, and of sufficient authority, to take decisions affecting its risk exposure'.

In practice, senior management approval could come from the firm's MLRO or MLCO, and this should be a part of the firm's processes (either by way of a centralised function or by the fee earner seeking approval once they become aware they are acting for a PEP) and documented in the firm's AML policy (see **Appendix B5** for template policy). LSAG suggest that the senior management approval could be undertaken by a member of the board or equivalent senior management team, head of practice group or department, a senior or managing partner, MLRO or MLCO. What works will depend on the firm.

Regulation 35(9) sets out that where a client who was a PEP is no longer entrusted with a prominent public function, a relevant person must continue to apply EDD measures for a period of at least 12 months after the person to ceased to have that position, or for such longer period as the relevant person considers appropriate to address risk of money laundering or terrorist financing. There therefore needs to be an element of ongoing checking of the PEP status, either with the client or through open-source information. Note, however, that reg.35(10) sets out that paragraph (9) does not apply to those clients who were not PEPs within the meaning of reg.14(5) of the Money Laundering Regulations 2007, SI 2007/2157 when those regulations were in force and ceased to be entrusted with a prominent public function before the date of the 2017 AML Regulations coming into force.

If the client is a family member or a known associate of a PEP and that person is no longer a PEP, then reg.35(11) sets out that EDD measures can cease whether or not the time referred to in reg.35(9) has expired or not.

There is no set process for determining who is a PEP and who is not. As referenced above, there are web-based platforms that can be used to search for PEP status. These products employ people to create profiles on individuals and entities containing PEP, sanction and adverse media information. These are not 100 per cent foolproof, but as the information being gathered by such companies is public domain information they should be, in the author's opinion, as good as relevant persons undertaking the open-source information checks themselves.

An alternative or supplemental method is to ask a client whether they are or a beneficial owner is a PEP. This rather relies on honesty and further understanding of the definition of a PEP. Note that the SRA found that this method was used by firms, but that it should not be solely relied on (see **5.5.3**). If a firm is unable to afford a web-based platform, then a search of open-source information should be enough investigation of a client's PEP status – e.g. Google, LinkedIn, employer's website. Whatever is the firm's process, this should be documented in the firm's AML policy and be risk-based (i.e. for non-transactional work, a firm may decide not to undertake this check, although note the risk of passporting of the client from non-regulated work to regulated work).

ANTI-MONEY LAUNDERING

4.2.2 Sanctions

A firm's CDD should, on a risk-based approach, include checking for sanctions. A firm may decide to check clients for sanctions on matters where there is a high-risk jurisdictional element. Checks should be conducted against HM Treasury consolidated list, 'The UK sanctions list' (**www.gov.uk/government/publications/the-uk-sanctions-list**). This list will show UK sanctions – it does not, however, include international sanctions. Again, web-based platforms are able to check for sanctioned status of individuals and entities.

For further guidance on sanctions see **Chapter 8**.

4.2.3 Adverse media

Depending on the type of firm and the type of work that is undertaken, finding adverse media about a client may be a more frequent occurrence than finding that a client is a PEP or is sanctioned. There is no specific regulation within the AML Regulations requiring a firm to conduct adverse media checks. However, such checks should form part of a firm's risk-based CDD measures. Again, web-based platforms are able to provide adverse media information, but again those platforms will be gathering information from open sources which a relevant person will be able to do. Note, however, that some web-based platforms are able to access international news more easily due to having personnel based overseas profiling individuals. Conversely, web-based platforms each have their own definition of what is adverse which may not tally with the firm's view – for example, a firm may consider a freezing order to be adverse but the platform provider may not.

It is important to factor adverse media checks into a firm's checks, as adverse media can lead to suspicions about money laundering and the requirement to make a SAR (see **3.5**). If such information is in the public domain, then it is reasonable for regulators to expect relevant persons to have known about it. As such, checks on open sources should be conducted, and an internet search will be sufficient.

As with all checks, whether done centrally or by the fee earner, a record of the check and result should be made. See **Appendix B6** for a template client and matter risk assessment which includes a record of this check having been undertaken.

4.3 RELIANCE AND RECORD-KEEPING – REGULATIONS 39 AND 40

4.3.1 Reliance

AML Regulations, reg.39 allows a relevant person to rely on the CDD conducted by a third party who is required to undertake CDD under the regulations. However, the regulation is explicit that the relevant person remains liable for any failure in that CDD undertaken.

Regulation 39(2) goes on to state:

When a relevant person relies on the third party to apply customer due diligence measures or carry out any of the measures required by regulation 30A under paragraph (1) it–

(a) must immediately obtain from the third party all the information needed to satisfy the requirements of regulation 28(2) to (6) and (10) and regulation 30A in relation to the customer, customer's beneficial owner, or any person acting on behalf of the customer;

(b) must enter into arrangements with the third party which–

   (i) enable the relevant person to obtain from the third party immediately on request copies of any identification and verification data and any other relevant documentation on the identity of the customer, customer's beneficial owner, or any person acting on behalf of the customer;

   (ii) require the third party to retain copies of the data and documents referred to in paragraph (i) for the period referred to in regulation 40.

Therefore, the relevant person must obtain from the third party the name of the client and how it was verified (reg.28(2)); if the client is a company, the name of the senior person if the third party was unable to identify the beneficial owner and how that person's identity was verified (reg.28(6)); and where a third party is acting on behalf of the client, the name of that third party and how their identity was verified by the third party upon whom reliance is to be placed (reg.28(10)).

As a relevant person will remain liable for the CDD undertaken by the third party, it is important to seek an explanation of what CDD was deployed. Third parties that can be relied upon are not only those who are subject to the UK AML Regulations (such as credit or financial institutions, auditors, insolvency practitioners, other legal professionals) but also those in third countries (this includes countries in the EEA since Brexit) who are subject to equivalent anti-money laundering requirements.

It is, unfortunately in the author's experience, very common to find that no or very little CDD was taken by European law firms referring a client to a UK law firm. It is not enough, therefore, to ask a referring law firm to confirm that it has identified its client as per the EU anti-money laundering requirements and instead if reliance is to be placed on that referring law firm's CDD, the relevant person placing reliance must ask what CDD was done with a full explanation of what was found. An alternative to this is for the referring regulated entity/person to provide to the relevant person a copy of the CDD undertaken on the client at the time, of course with the client's permission. This way, the relevant person can make their own assessment and ask for more information if needed.

Reliance can only be used with agreement – i.e. those that are to be relied upon must consent.

Each law firm needs to decide for itself whether to allow relevant persons to rely on the CDD of others and whether the firm will allow reliance on the CDD it and/or its relevant persons have undertaken.

Many firms decline to allow reliance for fear that it creates liability. Allowing reliance was a common request after the fourth and fifth money laundering

ANTI-MONEY LAUNDERING

directives, as more businesses became regulated and were required to conduct CDD on their own clients, e.g. estate agents, letting agents, art dealers, casinos and so on.

In the author's view, allowing reliance on the firm's CDD should be avoided and instead an offer to produce the CDD gathered on the client with the client's consent could be made. Other regulated parties may ask what CDD was gathered on a client and with client consent this can be provided, but wording should be added to make it clear that reliance is not agreed. Suggested wording could be:

> Subject to obtaining our client's consent, we will provide you with a copy of the due diligence we hold on our file to assist your due diligence requirements under the Money Laundering Regulations. However, it is for you to form your own opinion of these documents.
>
> For the avoidance of doubt, [*name of firm*] does not consent to the application of Regulation 39 of The Money Laundering, Terrorist Financing and Transfer of Funds (Information on the Payer) Regulations 2017 amended by The Money Laundering and Terrorist Financing (Amendment) Regulations 2019 and you cannot place reliance on this firm's assessment.

4.3.2 Record-keeping

AML Regulations, reg.40 requires certain records to be kept for a certain period of time. These records are documents and information obtained by the relevant person to satisfy CDD requirements and sufficient supporting records in respect of the transaction which was the subject of CDD of ongoing monitoring to 'enable the transaction to be reconstructed' (reg.40(2)(b)).

Regulation 40(3) sets out that the period for which the information must be kept is five years, beginning on the date on which the relevant person knows or has reasonable grounds to believe:

(a) that the transaction is complete, for records relating to an occasional transaction; or
(b) that the business relationship has come to an end for records relating to–

    (i) any transaction which occurs as part of a business relationship, or
    (ii) customer due diligence measures taken in connection with that relationship.

Subparagraph (b) will be relevant to the work that law firms undertake. Regulation 40(4) sets out that for records held under reg.40(3)(b)(i), the relevant person will not be required to keep the records for more than 10 years.

Regulation 40(5) sets out that once the relevant period has expired the personal data obtained for the purposes of the regulations must be deleted save for in the following circumstances:

(a) the relevant person is required to retain records containing personal data–

    (i) by or under any enactment, or
    (ii) for the purposes of any court proceedings;

(b) the data subject has given consent to the retention of that data; or

(c) the relevant person has reasonable grounds for believing that records containing the personal data need to be retained for the purpose of legal proceedings.

The relevant person must therefore have sufficient processes and procedures in place to either delete the data at the relevant time or may instead seek the consent of the data subject to retain the data for longer than the regulations allow. This consent could be placed in the firm's engagement letter or terms of business. Please note, however, that consent to data retention for longer periods will likely need a positive confirmation and so this needs to be factored in.

If the relevant person does not seek such consent or consent is denied, then in all likelihood the firm will need to have a mechanism in place which seeks to destroy the CDD material before the file is destroyed, as the file is likely to be retained for longer. This is because in the event that the client instructed the relevant person for one piece of work, say a house purchase, and then the relationship ended, the material gathered under the regulations will need to be destroyed five years after but the firm will want to keep the file for at least six years and until the possibility of a negligence claim has elapsed. As such, the timescales are at odds with each other and so it is likely to be far simpler to seek the client's consent for a longer retention period.

It must be remembered that reg.40 is not simply about destruction. It is about retention of relevant records to be called upon to show compliance with the regulations and also to assist enforcement agencies in their investigations. Law firms should create a designated file space for due diligence gathering and analysis such as the client and matter risk assessment (see **4.1.2**) and also a place for filing due diligence for easy future access (such as a subfolder within the electronic file structure).

4.4 TRUSTEE OBLIGATIONS – REGULATIONS 44 AND 45

AML Regulations, regs.44 and 45 impose additional obligations on trustees of certain trusts to maintain accurate and up-to-date records relating to the trust's beneficial owners or potential beneficial owners and provide that information to law enforcement agencies when requested. This information must be provided to HMRC through its Trust Registration Service each year. The register is available to law enforcement agencies.

This aspect of the AML Regulations is particularly relevant where solicitors act as trustees. However, the requirements are complex and dealt with at a high level here. The LSAG guidance should be consulted for further information.

Trusts that are caught under these regulations are UK express trusts or a non-UK express trust which has a UK source of income or UK assets. Further, a taxable relevant trust (that is, a trust that has incurred a liability to pay UK tax) is caught by the regulations.

5AMLD widened the scope of trusts caught by the AML Regulations and the following additional trusts must provide information via the register:

- trusts that are UK express trusts, and are not already registered in the EEA or are an excepted type of trust;
- trusts that are express non-UK trusts with at least one trustee resident in the UK, are not already registered in the EEA or are an excepted type of trust, and where the trustees enter into a business relationship with a relevant person, or acquire an interest in UK land; and
- trusts that are express non-UK trusts which are not excepted under the legislation, with non-resident trustees who acquire an interest in UK land.

Trustees of these types of trusts, that were in existence before 9 February 2022, have until 10 March 2022 to register. For trusts created after this date, the trustee has 30 days from the trust being set up to register it; and in respect of changes to the trust's registration information, 30 days to change it.

5AMLD (via the Money Laundering and Terrorist Financing (Amendment) (EU Exit) Regulations 2020, SI 2020/991) adds a new Sched.3A to the AML Regulations to exclude the following types of trust from registration:

- a trust imposed or required by legislation;
- a trust created by, or in order to satisfy the terms of, a court or tribunal order;
- a trust holding assets under a registered pension scheme;
- a trust of a life insurance policy;
- a trust for charitable purposes, so long as it is registered as a charity in the UK, or is not required to be registered (England and Wales only);
- a trust holding assets with a value not exceeding £100;
- a trust effected by a will;
- a trust of jointly held property where the trustees and beneficiaries are the same persons;
- a trust created relating to financial markets;
- a trust created for the purposes of holding sums, assets or documents relating to professional services;
- a trust created by relevant supervised persons to hold client money;
- a trust created for the purpose of activities under the capital requirements directive ('the capital requirements directive' means Directive 2013/36/EU of the European Parliament and of the Council of 26 June 2013 on access to the activity of credit institutions and the prudential supervision of credit institutions and investment firms, amending Directive 2002/87/EC and repealing Directives 2006/48/EC and 2006/49/EC);
- a trust created for the purpose of enabling or protecting rights under a genuine commercial transaction;
- a trust created on the transfer or disposal of an asset solely for the purpose of holding legal title to that asset until the transfer or disposal becomes effective;
- a trust for bereaved minors;
- an 18–25 trust;
- a disabled person's trust;
- a trust for the maintenance of historic buildings;

CLIENT DUE DILIGENCE

- a personal injury trust;
- a share incentive plan trust;
- a share option scheme trust;
- a trust over a service charge account;
- a trust created to help a public authority carry out its functions.

The information that needs to be provided depends on the type of trust, but as a guide the HMRC registration service will need:

- Taxable trust:
  - the name and date of the trust;
  - information about the trust assets, including their value;
  - the place where the trust is resident/administered; and
  - identity information in respect of each of the beneficial owners of the trust, together with details of the nature and extent of their beneficial ownership.

- Non- taxable trust:
  - information about the beneficial owners of the trust.

4.5 NOTE ON POOLED CLIENT ACCOUNTS

As we explored in **4.1.6**, simplified due diligence can be applied under AML Regulations, reg.37. This also applies to a bank's application of simplified due diligence on its customers which open pooled client accounts on behalf of their clients.

Regulation 37(5) sets out:

> A relevant person may apply simplified customer due diligence measures where the customer is a person to whom paragraph (6) applies and the product is an account into which monies are pooled (the 'pooled account'), provided that–
>
> (a) the business relationship with the holder of the pooled account presents a low degree of risk of money laundering and terrorist financing; and
> (b) information on the identity of the persons on whose behalf monies are held in the pooled account is available, on request to the relevant person where the pooled account is held.

Regulation 37(6) sets out that it applies to those who are subject to the regulations under reg.8, which includes law firms.

Whereas under the Money Laundering Regulations 2007 there was an automatic application of simplified due diligence for pooled client accounts, there is now a requirement for banks to conduct an assessment on those to whom it gives access to pooled accounts and to only apply simplified due diligence where the risk of money laundering is deemed to be low.

It is possible that banks will ask their law firm clients for evidence of their policies, controls and procedures (PCPs) and for a copy of their firm-wide AML risk

ANTI-MONEY LAUNDERING

assessment. Law firms must therefore be ready to answer those questions and to do so adequately, or there is a risk of banking services being suspended or withdrawn.

The Joint Money Laundering Steering Group published guidance for those who need to assess the use of pooled client accounts (**https://jmlsg.org.uk/revisions/** under 'Part 1 Annex 5-V PCAs July 2020').

4.6 BENEFICIAL OWNERS, OFFICERS AND MANAGERS APPROVAL

AML Regulations, reg.26 requires approval from the SRA for beneficial owners, officers or managers, known as BOOMs. This approval needs to be obtained before a firm undertakes regulated activities.

Acting without this approval is serious and could lead to disciplinary action or worse: criminal prosecution and a prison sentence up to two years.

In deciding whether the firm has any BOOMs that need approval, it is important to understand the definitions of beneficial owners, officers and managers.

4.6.1 Beneficial owner

AML Regulations, reg.5 sets out the definition of 'beneficial owner' as follows:

(1) In these Regulations, 'beneficial owner', in relation to a body corporate which is not a company whose securities are listed on a regulated market, means–

    (a) any individual who exercises ultimate control over the management of the body corporate;

    (b) any individual who ultimately owns or controls (in each case whether directly or indirectly), including through bearer share holdings or by other means, more than 25% of the shares or voting rights in the body corporate; or

    (c) an individual who controls the body corporate.

(2) For the purposes of paragraph (1)(c), an individual controls a body corporate if–

    (a) the body corporate is a company or a limited liability partnership and that individual satisfies one or more of the conditions set out in Part 1 of Schedule 1A to the Companies Act 2006 (people with significant control over a company); or

    (b) the body corporate would be a subsidiary undertaking of the individual (if the individual was an undertaking) under section 1162 (parent and subsidiary undertakings) of the Companies Act 2006 read with Schedule 7 to that Act.

(3) In these Regulations, 'beneficial owner', in relation to a partnership (other than a limited liability partnership), means any individual who–

    (a) ultimately is entitled to or controls (in each case whether directly or indirectly) more than 25% share of the capital or profits of the partnership or more than 25% of the voting rights in the partnership;

    (b) satisfies one or more the conditions set out in Part 1 of Schedule 1 to the

CLIENT DUE DILIGENCE

Scottish Partnerships (Register of People with Significant Control) Regulations 2017 (references to people with significant control over an eligible Scottish partnership); or

(c) otherwise exercises ultimate control over the management of the partnership.

(4) In this regulation 'limited liability partnership' has the meaning given by the Limited Liability Partnerships Act 2000.

In terms of a law firm, a beneficial owner might be a partner (or non-partner) who exercises significant control by virtue of their role or a partner who owns more than 25 per cent of the firm.

4.6.2 Officer

'Officer' is defined under AML Regulations, reg.3 as:

(a) in relation to a body corporate, means–
   (i) a director, secretary, chief executive, member of the committee of management, or a person purporting to act in such a capacity, or
   (ii) an individual who is a controller of the body, or a person purporting to act as a controller;
(b) in relation to an unincorporated association, means any officer of the association or any member of its governing body, or a person purporting to act in such a capacity; and
(c) in relation to a partnership, means a partner, and any manager, secretary or similar officer of the partnership, or a person purporting to act in such a capacity;

Officers in a law firm setting could be a chief executive officer (CEO) or those who sit on boards or management committees.

4.6.3 Manager

'Manager' is also defined under AML Regulations, reg.3 as the following:

> in relation to a firm, means a person who has control, authority or responsibility for managing the business of that firm, and includes a nominated officer;

In a law firm, therefore, the MLRO will be a manager.

4.6.4 Application procedure

Application to the SRA must be made in the prescribed format and approval given before the individual who is to become a BOOM can take post if their post will bring them into the scope of the regulations. The applicant will give the SRA enough information for a criminal records check to be conducted, and provided no conviction of the offences under AML Regulations, Sched.3 has occurred, the SRA must approve.

Should a BOOM become convicted of a criminal offence listed under Sched.3, their approval will cease to be valid and those activities they were conducting that brought them within scope of the regulations must cease. The individual and firm should report the conviction to the SRA within 30 days of the conviction (if the person convicted is reporting) or from when they became aware (if the firm is reporting).

If a person ceases to be a BOOM, then the SRA must be notified within 14 days.

4.7 CLIENT DUE DILIGENCE CENTRALISATION AND DIFFERENT STANDARDS FOR NON-REGULATED AND REGULATED WORK

4.7.1 Centralisation

Some firms have the resources and money to centralise the gathering and/or checking of ID, PEP status, sanctions and adverse media information, high-risk register maintenance and so on.

There are many good reasons to centralise these tasks, such as ensuring consistency, ensuring all checks are done and the ID gathered is right. It is also easier to adopt risk-based approaches to ID where you have one, two or more highly trained people in a central team, rather than a number of fee earners trying to make such decisions.

However, there is a downside to centralising, that the SRA is keen to see does not happen, and that is the perception by fee earners that if the task of gathering ID is done by a central team then the fee earner has nothing to do with the process, nor has any responsibility. This is simply not the case, and is a very dangerous position to take.

It is not possible to outsource one's responsibility under the AML Regulations, and fee earners who think they are doing this are leaving themselves very vulnerable to criticism and prosecution by the SRA, and worse, law enforcement agencies. Most certainly a fee earner's defence to allegations of failure to follow the requirements under the regulations should never, ever be 'The risk team do that, I don't' or 'I don't know anything/much about this client, the risk team on-boarded them, that is their job not mine'.

When law firms do decide to centralise, they must first make it absolutely clear that the responsibility still lies with the fee earner with conduct of the matter and the centralised team is assisting that fee earner in fulfilling their duties. Secondly, to enable the fee earner to take responsibility and understand who their clients are and whether any concerns or suspicions have arisen during the gathering of ID the fee earner should be copied in to all emails between the central team and the client. Additionally, if resource allows it, the central team could provide the fee earner with a report at the end of its gathering of information with all the information provided, the structure of the client if a company and an analysis of what is missing if anything.

Some firms also centralise the gathering and signing off of source of funds and wealth. It is the author's opinion that whilst it is possible for the information to be gathered by a central team, it must never be signed off by the central team as adequate, as the central team is not the team who has ultimate responsibility for assessing, analysing and signing off of the source of funds and wealth. Further, a central team is very unlikely to be able to understand the nature of the client or matter in the way the fee earner should, and in the author's opinion it should not be asked to.

Put simply, fee earners cannot ever be detached from the CDD process required when undertaking work for a client.

4.7.2 Imposing different standards for non-regulated and regulated work

It is possible for firms to adopt different standards of CDD required for non-regulated and regulated work. For example, for non-regulated work (for example, litigation and wills) the firm may simply wish to check the client for sanctions and adverse media and record their name, address and date of birth.

However, many firms adopt the same CDD requirements on client matters regardless of whether the work is non-regulated or regulated. The reason for this is because clients can passport from non-regulated to regulated work, and also systems do not need to be too sophisticated so as to spot when this happens and more CDD is required.

If a firm is considering asking for less information on clients who instruct the firm in relation to non-regulated work, or a firm already does this, the firm needs to consider this in the light of the AML Regulations' definition of 'tax adviser'.

Tax advisers are considered to be in-scope of the AML Regulations, and therefore need to comply with the CDD requirements. As a result of 5AMLD (which came into force on 10 January 2020) the definition of tax adviser was widened so that it is now (AML Regulations, reg.11(d)):

> a firm or sole practitioner who by way of business provides material aid, or assistance or advice, in connection with the tax affairs of other persons, whether provided directly or through a third party, when providing such services.

The SRA has written a guidance note 'Tax adviser guidance' on this new widened definition (**www.sra.org.uk/globalassets/documents/solicitors/tax-adviser-guidance.pdf?version=4aade6**) and this sets out the following under the heading 'Controls for those providing tax adviser services':

> Recognising tax adviser services that are in scope can be challenging because this is so broadly defined in the regulations. Services that are normally out of scope may, with a subtle change, be brought within scope. For example, employment law would generally be seen as out of scope. But advising on the tax implications of a settlement between the employer and employee could draw the matter into scope.
>
> Being able to determine when this happens, and when you may need to apply the requirements in the regulations is very important so that you are able to appropriately risk

assess the client and undertake fully compliant customer due diligence. Failure to do so might mean you are risking facilitating money laundering and might be opening yourself to criminal sanctions and disciplinary action. This can also help mitigate against the risk of committing an offence under the Proceeds of Crime Act (2002) or Terrorism Act (2000).

You might choose to protect against this risk by applying AML-compliant onboarding procedures (client and matter risk assessments, customer due diligence etc) for all clients, whether the service you are asked to provide is in scope or not. This can help mitigate the risk of, subsequently providing your client with a service where the regulations apply (also known as 'passporting'), without maintaining AML compliance.

If you decide not to treat all work as being in scope, you need to take steps to 'police the boundary' between non-regulated and regulated work. This would require you to create policies, procedures and controls to allow the identification of where these changes might occur and train relevant staff to recognise where they need to begin applying AML-compliant procedures or to seek advice or assistance from others within the organisation.

If you are offering both in-scope and out-of-scope services and do not apply AML-compliant procedures for all clients, you should consider explaining to new clients which services you cannot provide without first completing AML-compliant due diligence. This could be in your terms of engagement and client care letters. See the table below for areas of legal service where this is likely to occur.

The SRA guidance has a table which sets out how work that was out of the scope of the regulations might now be in scope, and firms should consider this table if they already adopt a different CDD standard for non-regulated work or are considering doing so.

If a firm does decide to adopt a different CDD standard for non-regulated work, it must consider the following:

- How will the firm pick up when a client moves from non-regulated work to regulated work for the first time, so that the correct level of CDD is undertaken?
- Will fee earners understand the definition of 'tax adviser' sufficiently to spot when the non-regulated work then becomes regulated? And what are the chances of them informing a centralised CDD gathering team or obtaining the required CDD?
- If further CDD is required due to a client passporting to regulated work or the work being conducted becoming regulated due to the definition of tax adviser, how challenging will it be to gather CDD? Will the client be upset?
- Is it possible that non-regulated work will become regulated before or during a key milestone or date, such as a settlement, mediation or a court hearing? If likely, will work have to cease until full CDD can be gathered? What effect will that have on the work, and is it possible that it will lead to complaints and negligence claims?

Careful thought needs to be given to whether to treat non-regulated work differently for the purposes of CDD, or whether one standard across the board should apply.

CHAPTER 5

Guidance, reviews, visits, regulations and compliance

5.1 LEGAL SECTOR AFFINITY GROUP GUIDANCE AND SOLICITORS REGULATION AUTHORITY GUIDANCE

Peppered throughout the Money Laundering, Terrorist Financing and Transfer of Funds (Information on the Payer) Regulations 2017, SI 2017/692 ('AML Regulations') is reference to relevant persons taking into account regulatory guidance. In the case of Solicitors Regulation Authority (SRA) regulated entities, this will mean taking into account the Legal Sector Affinity Group (LSAG), 'Anti-money laundering guidance for the legal sector 2021' (**www.lawsociety.org.uk/en/topics/anti-money-laundering/anti-money-laundering-guidance**).

The LSAG document is guidance approved by HM Treasury and applies to all independent legal professionals. The LSAG guidance is co-authored by the Law Society, the SRA and the Bar Standards Board (BSB), amongst others.

A new version of the LSAG guidance was released on 20 January 2021, and as at the time of writing was yet to receive Treasury approval. It is hoped, however, that it will not change significantly from that which is current drafted.

As the AML Regulations require relevant persons to understand and take into account this guidance, there is no substitute for reading it from beginning to end. There is no way around this, unfortunately, and firms would do well to provide their money laundering reporting officer (MLRO), money laundering compliance officer (MLCO) and any central risk team a bound and laminated copy for their regular and frequent reference.

The SRA also has a page on its website titled 'Money laundering', which is full of anti-money laundering (AML) resources (**www.sra.org.uk/solicitors/resources/money-laundering/money-laundering/**). Correctly, the SRA directs the reader to the LSAG for guidance. The SRA has also, however, produced further guidance: 'Anti-money laundering: what tax advisers need to know' on providing tax advice (16 February 2021, **www.sra.org.uk/sra/news/events/on-demand-events/aml-tax-advisers/**); and 'Trust and company service provider guidance' (updated 18 March 2021, **www.sra.org.uk/solicitors/resources/money-laundering/money-laundering/trust-company-service-provider-guidance/**). The SRA has also

ANTI-MONEY LAUNDERING

reported the outcomes of the various thematic reviews it has conducted (see **5.5** for further information); and has published four relevant 'warning notices' (these are explored at **5.3**).

Whilst law firms regulated by the SRA are not required to follow Joint Money Laundering Steering Group (JMLSG) guidance, it is useful guidance to consult if LSAG or further SRA guidance is not clear. The JMLSG is a private sector body that is made up of the leading UK trade associations in the financial services industry. Its current members include:

- Association for Financial Markets in Europe (AFME);
- Association of British Credit Unions Limited (ABCUL);
- Association of British Insurers (ABI);
- Association of Foreign Banks (AFB);
- British Venture Capital Association (BVCA);
- Building Societies Association (BSA);
- Electronic Money Association (EMA);
- European Venues and Intermediaries Association (EVIA);
- Finance & Leasing Association (FLA);
- Investment Association (IA);
- Loan Market Association (LMA);
- Personal Investment Management and Financial Advice Association (PIMFA);
- Tax Incentivised Savings Association (TISA);
- UK Finance (UKF).

When consulting the LSAG guidance or any other guidance in relation to a specific matter, a note should be made to show that the guidance was considered and the outcome of that consideration.

5.2 LAW SOCIETY OF ENGLAND AND WALES GUIDANCE

The Law Society has a plethora of guidance which can be found on its website and which is of great use for law firms. These guidance pieces are not summarised here as they are too numerous, but instead here is a useful list:

- 'AML compliance for small firms – part one: conducting an AML risk assessment' (16 December 2019, **www.lawsociety.org.uk/topics/anti-money-laundering/aml-compliance-for-small-firms-conducting-a-risk-assessment**);
- 'AML compliance for small firms – part two: policies, controls and procedures' (16 December 2019, **www.lawsociety.org.uk/Topics/Anti-money-laundering/Guides/aml-compliance-for-small-firms-policies-controls-and-procedures**);
- 'AML compliance for small firms – part three: customer due diligence and warning signs' (16 December 2019, **www.lawsociety.org.uk/Topics/Anti-money-laundering/Guides/aml-compliance-for-small-firms-customer-due-diligence-and-red-flags**);

GUIDANCE, REVIEWS, VISITS, REGULATIONS AND COMPLIANCE

- 'Anti-money laundering guidance for the legal sector' (20 January 2021, **www.lawsociety.org.uk/topics/anti-money-laundering/anti-money-laundering-guidance**);
- 'Anti-money laundering in the property market' (9 September 2019, **www.lawsociety.org.uk/topics/property/anti-money-laundering-in-property**);
- 'Anti-money laundering risk assessments' (20 January 2020, **www.lawsociety.org.uk/topics/anti-money-laundering/anti-money-laundering-risk-assessments**);
- 'Customer due diligence' (20 January 2020, **www.lawsociety.org.uk/topics/anti-money-laundering/customer-due-diligence**);
- 'Anti-money laundering after Brexit' (1 April 2021, **www.lawsociety.org.uk/topics/brexit/anti-money-laundering-after-brexit**);
- 'Global AML guidance' (10 January 2020, **www.lawsociety.org.uk/topics/anti-money-laundering/global-aml-guidance**);
- 'Internal money laundering reporting' (12 January 2020, **www.lawsociety.org.uk/topics/anti-money-laundering/internal-money-laundering-reporting**);
- 'LSAG Advisory Note: COVID-19 and preventing money laundering and terrorist financing in legal practices' (27 April 2020, **www.lawsociety.org.uk/topics/anti-money-laundering/lsag-advisory-note-covid-19-and-preventing-money-laundering**);
- 'Money laundering warning signs' (20 January 2020, **www.lawsociety.org.uk/topics/anti-money-laundering/money-laundering-warning-signs**);
- 'Mortgage fraud guidance' (21 October 2019, **www.lawsociety.org.uk/topics/property/mortgage-fraud-guidance**);
- 'Politically exposed persons' (19 December 2019, **www.lawsociety.org.uk/topics/anti-money-laundering/peps**);
- 'Property fraud' (9 September 2019, **www.lawsociety.org.uk/topics/property/property-fraud**);
- 'Quick guide to the Money Laundering Regulations 2017' (7 July 2021, **www.lawsociety.org.uk/topics/anti-money-laundering/quick-guide-to-the-mlrs**);
- 'Suspicious activity reports' (3 June 2021, **www.lawsociety.org.uk/topics/anti-money-laundering/suspicious-activity-reports**);
- 'Tipping off a client' (21 January 2020, **www.lawsociety.org.uk/topics/anti-money-laundering/tipping-off-a-client**);
- 'UK sanctions regime' (20 January 2020, **www.lawsociety.org.uk/topics/anti-money-laundering/sanctions-guide**);
- 'House competitions' (13 January 2020, **www.lawsociety.org.uk/topics/property/house-competitions**);
- 'Responding to a financial crime investigation' (22 January 2020, **www.lawsociety.org.uk/topics/anti-money-laundering/responding-to-a-financial-crime-investigation**).

ANTI-MONEY LAUNDERING

Further, the Law Society also has the following 'questions and answers' guidance:

- 'A client's exchanged contracts with a cash buyer who refuses to share the source of funds. What should I do?' (**www.lawsociety.org.uk/Contact-or-visit-us/Helplines/Practice-advice-service/Q-and-As/A-cash-buyer-refuses-to-share-the-source-of-funds-what-should-the-mlro-do**);
- 'Can I accept my client's £20,000 cash deposit?' (**www.lawsociety.org.uk/Contact-or-visit-us/Helplines/Practice-advice-service/Q-and-As/Can-I-accept-my-clients-20000-cash-deposit**);
- 'Is outlining our reporting obligations in client care letters "tipping off"?' (**www.lawsociety.org.uk/Contact-or-visit-us/Helplines/Practice-advice-service/Q-and-As/Is-outlining-our-reporting-obligations-in-client-care-letters-tipping-off**);
- 'My client is a possible sanctions match. What should I do?' (**www.lawsociety.org.uk/contact-or-visit-us/helplines/practice-advice-service/q-and-as/my-client-is-a-possible-sanctions-match-what-should-i-do**);
- 'Practice advice Q&As' (**www.lawsociety.org.uk/Topics/Anti-money-laundering/Q-and-A/practice-advice-questions-answers-january-2021** and **www.lawsociety.org.uk/Topics/Anti-money-laundering/Q-and-A/practice-advice-questions-answers-may-2021**);
- 'Should I carry out an AML risk assessment on every new regulated matter?' (**www.lawsociety.org.uk/contact-or-visit-us/helplines/practice-advice-service/q-and-as/should-i-carry-out-an-aml-risk-assessment-on-every-new-regulated-matter**);
- 'Should we quote our account number on bills?' (**www.lawsociety.org.uk/contact-or-visit-us/helplines/practice-advice-service/q-and-as/should-we-quote-our-account-number-on-bills**).

5.3 SRA WARNING NOTICES

From time to time the SRA issues what it terms a 'warning notice'. Although these notices are not an extension to the SRA Standards and Regulations, they do serve as guidance that the SRA expects firms to follow, and the SRA will use them when prosecuting what it considers to be misconduct.

It is important therefore to stay on top of the SRA warning notices. Unfortunately, the SRA website does not have a designated space for warning notices and to find them a search on the term 'warning notice' needs to be placed into the SRA website search engine. Once a warning notice has been amended or archived, the old version no longer appears on the website. This is regrettable, as often conduct from the past is reconsidered and when doing so a firm cannot know what warning notices were in place at the time. The SRA too has a habit of reviewing conduct in the past through the lens of today, and it is important for firms to recognise that they can only act in accordance with what was required of them at the time of the conduct

GUIDANCE, REVIEWS, VISITS, REGULATIONS AND COMPLIANCE

in question. To that end firms may wish to print and/or save a copy centrally in case the warning notice changes or disappears. If you ask nicely, sometimes the SRA will send you an archived warning notice – but to ask, you need to know it existed!

There are four warning notices that are relevant to AML. Below is a short summary of each of these warning notices.

5.3.1 Warning notice: Money laundering and terrorist financing

The SRA's 'Warning notice: Money laundering and terrorist financing' was first published on 8 December 2014 and updated 25 November 2019 (though as indicated above, unless firms retained the old version it is not possible to see what has been amended with any certainty) (**www.sra.org.uk/solicitors/guidance/money-laundering-terrorist-financing/**).

The purpose of this warning notice is to highlight warning signs which relevant persons should be aware of and which may require the relevant person to take action to avoid committing a criminal offence or breaching requirements under the SRA Standards and Regulations.

The reason for the warning notice was the SRA's concern that some firms were not complying with the AML Regulations by failing to have adequate systems and controls in place to prevent, detect and report money laundering. This concern followed on from the Financial Action Task Force's (FATF's) report of 2013 highlighting 42 'red flag indicators' and vulnerabilities in the legal profession to money laundering ('FATF report: Money laundering and terrorist financing – vulnerabilities of legal professionals', June 2013, **www.fatf-gafi.org/media/fatf/documents/reports/ML%20and%20TF%20vulnerabilities%20legal%20professionals.pdf**).

Being aware of these flags will assist relevant persons in applying a risk-based approach to meeting obligations under the AML Regulations – and further, if such flags are present in dealings with a client this may lead to further reporting internally to the firm's MLRO, and by the MLRO to the National Crime Agency (NCA).

The warning notice goes on to set out the warning signs highlighted by FATF as follows:

If the client:

- Is secretive or evasive about who they are, the reason for the transaction, or the source of funds.
- Uses an intermediary, or does not appear to be directing the transaction, or appears to be disguising the real client.
- Avoids personal contact without good reason.
- Refuses to provide information or documentation or the documentation provided is suspicious.
- Has criminal associations.
- Has an unusual level of knowledge about money laundering processes.
- Does not appear to have a business association with the other parties but appears to be connected to them.

If the source of funds is unusual, such as:

- Large cash payments.
- Unexplained payments from a third party.
- Large private funding that does not fit the business or personal profile of the payer.
- Loans from non-institutional lenders.
- Use of corporate assets to fund private expenditure of individuals.
- Use of multiple accounts or foreign accounts.

If the transaction has unusual features, such as:

- Size, nature, frequency or manner of execution.
- Early repayment of mortgages/loans.
- Short repayment periods for borrowing.
- An excessively high value is placed on assets/securities.
- It is potentially loss making.
- Involving unnecessarily complicated structures or steps in transaction.
- Repetitive instructions involving common features/parties or back to back transactions with assets rapidly changing value.
- The transaction is unusual for the client, type of business or age of the business.
- Unexplained urgency, requests for short cuts or changes to the transaction particularly at last minute.
- Use of a Power of Attorney in unusual circumstances.
- No obvious commercial purpose to the transaction.
- Instructions to retain documents or to hold money in your client account.
- Abandoning transaction and/or requests to make payments to third parties or back to source.
- Monies passing directly between the parties.
- Litigation which is settled too easily or quickly and with little involvement by you.

If the instructions are unusual for your business such as:

- Outside your or your firm's area of expertise or normal business, or if client is not local to you and there is no explanation as to why a firm in your locality has been chosen.
- Willingness of client to pay high fees.
- Unexplained changes to legal advisers.
- Your client appears unconcerned or lacks knowledge about the transaction.

If there are geographical concerns such as:

- Unexplained connections with and movement of monies between other jurisdictions.
- Connections with jurisdictions which are subject to sanctions or are suspect because drug production, terrorism or corruption is prevalent, or there is a lack of money laundering regulation.

The SRA ends its warning notice by setting out that it expects firms and individuals to comply with the AML Regulations and to be aware of and act properly upon warning signs that a transaction may be suspicious.

To ensure adherence to this warning notice, firms would do well to make sure that appropriate warning signs are set out in the firm's client and matter risk assessment (see **4.1.2** for guidance and **Appendix B6** for a template), are considered as part of the firm-wide AML risk assessment (see **3.3** for guidance and **Appendix B1** for a template) and are covered off in the firm's AML policy (see **Appendix B5** for a template).

5.3.2 Warning notice: Compliance with the money laundering regulations – firm risk assessment

The SRA's 'Warning notice: Compliance with the money laundering regulations – firm risk assessment' was first published on 7 May 2019 and updated on 25 November 2019 (**www.sra.org.uk/solicitors/guidance/compliance-money-laundering-regulations-firm-risk-assessment/**).

This warning notice arises out of the SRA's concern that law firms were not complying with the requirement to undertake a firm-wide AML risk assessment in accordance with AML Regulations, reg.18 and further to the SRA's various thematic reviews. See **3.3** for guidance on firm-wide risk assessments; and at **5.5** is an exploration of the various thematic reviews that the SRA has undertaken.

In its warning notice, the SRA sets out that preventing money laundering is a high priority for it and that 'solicitors and law firms are in a position of privilege and act as gatekeepers to assets and markets that are tempting to criminals, so we expect the profession to take proactive action to avoid enabling financial crime'.

The SRA says in its notice that many firms have still not conducted a compliant firm-wide AML risk assessment, and of the 400 risk assessments that the SRA asked to see (see **5.5.2**), the SRA has taken regulatory action on around 20 per cent. The warning notice also sets out that the SRA has seen broad use of templates and some with prepopulated specimen text. In some cases, near identical risk assessments were submitted by different firms. The SRA considers this use of templates concerning, and expect assessments to be relevant to the firm.

The SRA also sets out in its warning notice that some assessments it has seen do not take into account the risks that the AML Regulations require firms to consider, such as high-risk jurisdictions, transactions or delivery method of services. Further, the SRA sets out in the warning notice that some firms do not understand their responsibilities when dealing with politically exposed persons (PEPs) (see **4.2.1** for guidance on PEPs), with some firms setting out that they do not provide services to PEPs but not putting in procedures to identify PEPs.

Finally, the SRA set out in its notice that:

> Failure to have a money laundering risk assessment in place for your firm is a significant breach of the money laundering regulations. We will take robust enforcement action where firms do not have one in place, where it is not sufficient to meet their responsibilities or where breaches are not rectified immediately.

5.3.3 Warning notice: Improper use of client account as a banking facility

The SRA's 'Warning notice: Improper use of client account as a banking facility' was first published on 18 December 2014 and updated 25 November 2019 (**www.sra.org.uk/solicitors/guidance/improper-client-account-banking-facility/**). The notice is designed to highlight some of the issues with law firms allowing their client account to be used as a banking facility.

Rule 3.3 of the SRA Accounts Rules sets out that:

> You must not use a client account to provide banking facilities to clients or third parties. Payments into, and transfers or withdrawals from a client account must be in respect of the delivery by you of regulated services.

Regulated services are defined as 'the legal and other professional services that you provide that are regulated by the SRA and includes, where appropriate, acting as a trustee or as the holder of a specified office or appointment'.

There has been a plethora of Solicitors Disciplinary Tribunal (SDT) cases on the non-banking rule, and the warning notice names *Fuglers LLP* v. *SRA* [2014] EWHC 179 (Admin); *Patel, Premji Naram Patel* v. *SRA* [2012] EWHC 3373 (Admin); and *Zambia (Attorney General of Zambia)* v. *Meer Care & Desai* [2008] EWCA Civ 1007 – and there are, of course, more.

The warning notice sets out that courts have confirmed that operating a banking facility for clients that is divorced from any legal or other professional work is objectionable. Law firms are not regulated as banks to provide such facilities, and should therefore only receive monies where there is a proper connection between the funds and the delivery of regulated services. The notice goes on to state that it is not enough that there is an underlying transaction if the firm or individual is not providing regulated legal services. This explains why the equivalent old rule 14.5 of the SRA Accounts Rules varied slightly in that money coming through the client account must relate to an underlying transaction *or* to a service forming part of normal regulated activities. The phrase 'underlying transaction' has now been removed from the rule because it is not enough that there is an underlying transaction alone, and the firm or individual must be providing regulated services in relation to it.

The notice goes on to set out that there must be a proper connection between the monies being paid and the regulated services. There is an acknowledgement in the warning notice (as there was in prior iterations of the notice) that historically some solicitors held funds for clients to make routine outgoing payments where the client was a long-term private client or a client based abroad. The SRA's view is that with the ability to bank from anywhere in the world, it considers that 'allowing client account to be used in this way is no longer justifiable and a breach of rule 3.3'.

Note that the terminology suggests that it was once upon a time justifiable and so should a firm discover historical payments that would today offend rule 3.3, careful thought needs to be given as to when those payments were made and whether they were in fact a breach of the rule at the time and out of step with any SRA guidance at that time (which is why it is important to try to maintain a copy of guidance as and when it is published, as once it is replaced or updated by the SRA it disappears from its website). This analysis will help the compliance officer for legal practice (COLP) and compliance officer for finance and administration (COFA) determine whether a report to the SRA needs to be made.

The notice highlights the risk of a client asking for funds to be paid through a client account to avoid their obligations under insolvency laws – but more importantly for the purposes of this book, the warning notice provides some details as to the risk of money laundering when monies are passed through a client account when devoid of any connection to the provision of regulated services.

The notice outlines that complying with rule 3.3 offers an important 'first line of defence' against clients or others who seek to use a firm's client account to launder money. Further, the warning notice sets out that the SRA considers it a breach of rule 3.3 for a law firm to make transfers between ledgers of different clients or companies without evidence of the purpose or legal basis for such transfers such as board resolutions or contracts. The SRA sets out that if behaving in such a way would make tracing money more difficult this would be of significant concern to the SRA. Firms should read into this that disciplinary action is likely to follow.

The warning notice sets out that rule 3.3 exists independently of the AML Regulations and it is no defence to a breach of rule 3.3 that no money laundering actually occurred. The notice goes on to set out that in fact such arguments indicate a lack of insight into the reasons for rule 3.3 and the risks that it addresses. The SRA usefully provides some examples to illustrate its thought process, and these are reproduced below:

- Rule 3.3 and the [AML Regulations] are to a large extent preventative provisions, intended to make it more difficult for people to use regulated businesses for improper purposes but also to deter law firms from helping such people.
- Any impropriety may be distant from the movement of money through a client account. In a classic laundering process, the movement through a client account may be the third or fourth stage of laundering the proceeds of a distant crime. But every stage contributes to the effectiveness of the laundering process.
- There are many potential forms of impropriety as well as money laundering. The Fuglers' case [*Fuglers LLP* v. *SRA* [2014] EWHC 179 (Admin)] is one example in an insolvency context but there are many others such as hiding assets improperly in commercial or matrimonial disputes. You should also be aware of the risks in allowing your client account to be used to add credibility to questionable investment schemes.
- Movement of money through client account is attractive to those with an improper purpose:
  - Attempts by law enforcement or opposing litigants to obtain information may be blocked by a claim to privilege, even though the claim to privilege may be unsustainable on proper analysis with access to the documents.
  - It largely circumvents the sophisticated risk systems used by banks.
  - Solicitors, particularly in smaller firms, with a close relationship to an important client may be vulnerable to pressure to avoid making suspicious activity reports.

ANTI-MONEY LAUNDERING

The warning notice ends by setting out that law firms and individuals should be prepared to justify any decision to hold or move client monies, and that failure to have proper regard to the warning notice is likely to lead to disciplinary action.

5.3.4 Warning notice: Money laundering and terrorist financing suspicious activity reports

The SRA's 'Warning notice: Money laundering and terrorist financing suspicious activity reports' was first published on 8 December 2014 and updated 25 November 2019 (**www.sra.org.uk/solicitors/guidance/money-laundering-terrorist-financing-suspicious-activity-reports/**).

The warning notice sets out that the SRA is concerned that firms have inadequate systems and controls to prevent, detect and report money laundering. The notice goes on to state that the NCA 'recently' produced analysis of the SARs it receives for consent to proceed (known as defence against money laundering (DAML) SARs) and considered them to be of poor quality. The notice sets out that the NCA confirmed that from 1 October 2014, DAML SARs that do not contain reasons for suspicion or a statement regarding criminal property will be closed by the NCA on receipt.

The SRA sets out in the notice that it expects all relevant persons to have regard to the SRA Standards and Regulations (in particular para.7.1 of the Code of Conduct for Solicitors, RELs and RFLs and para.3.1 of the Code of Conduct for Firms), to comply with the AML Regulations, the Proceeds of Crime Act (POCA) 2002, the Terrorism Act (TA) 2000 and further NCA guidance in relation to the submission of 'consent' SARs.

The warning notice goes on to summarise the NCA's comments about what SARs from solicitors lack, as follows:

1. The information or other matter that gives grounds for knowledge, suspicion or belief
2. A description of the property that is known, suspected or believed to be criminal property, terrorist property or derived from terrorist property
3. A description of the prohibited act for which consent is sought
4. If known, the identity of the person or persons known or suspected to be involved in money laundering or who committed or attempted to commit an offence under any of sections 15 to 18 of TACT [Terrorism Act] 2000
5. If known, the whereabouts of the property that is known or suspected to be criminal property, terrorist property or derived from terrorist property

Finally, the SRA comments that 'failure to comply with this warning notice may lead to disciplinary action, criminal prosecution or both'.

Full guidance on SARs can be found at **3.5**.

5.4 OPBAS AND ITS REVIEW OF THE SRA

To understand, in part, the SRA's approach to its AML supervision of law firms, you need to understand who is supervising the SRA.

Housed within the Financial Conduct Authority (FCA) office, the Office for Professional Body Anti-Money Laundering Supervision (OPBAS) was set up in 2018 with the aim of improving the supervision of the implementation of AML measures by regulators of those they regulate. OPBAS does not therefore oversee what those who are regulated do, but rather is there to supervise the regulators. The watchers have now become the watched.

OPBAS oversees not only the SRA, but also many other legal and accountancy regulators.

In a speech delivered by OPBAS's Director of Specialist Supervision, Alison Barker, 'Money laundering and supervising trusted professionals' (12 March 2019, **www.fca.org.uk/news/speeches/alison-barker-speech-on-opbas-at-rusi**), she set out that during a comprehensive review of regulators by OPBAS and FCA ('Anti-money laundering supervision by the legal and accountancy professional body supervisors: Themes from the 2018 OPBAS anti-money laundering supervisory assessments' (March 2019, **www.fca.org.uk/publication/opbas/themes-2018-opbas-anti-money-laundering-supervisory-assessments.pdf**)), two main issues stood out.

The first issue related to poor standards of supervision by regulators. OPBAS reported in its review that 23 per cent of regulators under its watch had no form of supervision in the AML space, and 18 per cent had not identified who they needed to supervise. They also found that over 90 per cent hadn't fully developed a risk-based approach and were not collecting the data they needed to analyse who their riskiest members were.

OPBAS also reported that in its view supervision was often under-resourced, and that supervision was seen as an 'add-on' and not a core function, meaning it was not on the agenda.

In terms of enforcement action, OPBAS found that 'only' 50 per cent of professional bodies issued fines for AML failings and the year before its review it was 27 per cent. In the speech, OPBAS commented that this was 'hard to believe, given the high-risk activities of lawyers and accountants'. Interestingly OPBAS reported that some bodies within the accountancy sector informed OPBAS that they feared members would leave if they took regulatory action against them.

The second issue that OPBAS says it found was a lack of intelligence sharing. OPBAS reported that supervisors all have a responsibility to 'pool intelligence and put the picture together' and reported that as at February 2018, 40 per cent of supervisory bodies were members of the main intelligence sharing networks; as at the date of its report in 2019 this had risen to 48 per cent. In OPBAS's view, membership needs to be 100 per cent. OPBAS further reported that some supervisors had no resource allocated to intelligence sharing and some have no systematic

ANTI-MONEY LAUNDERING

approach to sharing, and there was evidence in the review that suspicious activity reports (SARs) should have been made but weren't.

OPBAS also found that in all bodies but two, the process for handling whistleblowing was inadequate; and 56 per cent of those reviewed had no whistleblowing policy in place. As can be seen in **Chapter 9**, whistleblowing can provide vital reporting of issues and therefore it is crucial to get whistleblowing policies and procedures in place.

In her speech, the Director of Specialist Supervision set out that OPBAS wants to see the following:

- risk-based supervision of the professions, i.e. focused on the riskiest types of business or clients like tax, conveyancing, company formation;
- supervision which is properly resourced;
- leadership from the top with a programme regularly discussed;
- robust enforcement outcomes;
- professional bodies to recognise the risk that members can be vulnerable to facilitating money laundering and a positive uptake in intelligence sharing.

In a report published by the SRA Board, 'Office for Professional Body anti-money laundering (AML) Supervision (OPBAS) findings and next steps' (24 October 2018, **www.sra.org.uk/globalassets/documents/sra/board-meetings/2018/board-item-opbas-24-10-2018.pdf?version=4a1abd**), the SRA noted that OPBAS visited the SRA in July and September 2018 and it provided to OPBAS over 1,000 pages of documents and further 39 SRA people were interviewed by OPBAS. The SRA Board report sets out that OPBAS 'found very little room for improvement' and had identified three areas for change:

1. The first was the methodology used by the SRA to risk assess firms for AML compliance and that this should include the likelihood of firms being used for money laundering rather than the chances of the SRA receiving an AML report and that the methodology should take into account the firm's steps to mitigate money laundering.
2. The second area for improvement was that the SRA's supervisory regime should include an examination and assessment of the firm's AML risk mitigation, i.e. by way of visits by the SRA.
3. The third area highlighted by OPBAS was that there was potential for conflicting advice from the SRA and the Law Society, and that agreement should be reached as to who has responsibility for these queries.

The SRA Board report set out the following action plan:

- The SRA will change the methodology used to assess a firm's AML risk to include the use of the SRA's existing model plus 'a more traditional model based on human intelligence that takes account of our likely risk based on

GUIDANCE, REVIEWS, VISITS, REGULATIONS AND COMPLIANCE

factors we will feed in from the SRA sectoral risk assessment and the government national risk assessment' (para.9). The methodology will also include how the firm is mitigating its risk of money laundering occurring.
- The SRA set out that it does already undertake assessment of firm's policies, controls and procedures (PCPs) but that it does not make an assessment of their effectiveness or feed the outcome back into the SRA's risk assessment on the firm. The SRA stated that it will introduce a risk rating which allows the SRA to formally assess a firm's PCPs. To enable this to happen, the SRA set out that it will expand its question set when it visits firms and firms will be rated as 'compliant', 'partially compliant' or 'non-compliant'. Note that at **5.7** there is an outline of what is asked at these visits taken from the author's experience which occurred after the SRA's report confirming an expansion of the question set and so as at the time of writing, this outline of the SRA's AML visit is accurate to the best of the author's knowledge.
- In terms of providing clear advice from one provider, the SRA said that it is discussing this with the Law Society.

You can see from the OPBAS report and the SRA response to it how the SRA has adapted its supervisory approach to AML in those that it regulates, and this involves mainly a change in how it chooses firms by way of risk assessment, an increase in the number of firms that it visits and a more thorough visit. The SRA has also created a dedicated AML team.

5.5 SRA THEMATIC REVIEWS, OUTCOMES AND WHAT IS NEXT

The SRA is a supervisory authority under the AML Regulations and therefore has a vital role in checking that those it regulates are complying with the regulatory requirements. It does this by conducting periodic reviews with increasing frequency. Below is an outline of the most recent reviews that the SRA has conducted, the learnings from each and what is next for the SRA in this regulatory area.

5.5.1 Thematic review of trust and company service providers

As the creation and administration of trusts and companies on behalf of clients is considered one of the legal service areas at higher risk of money laundering – where beneficial ownership and control of the assets can be obscured, structures can be complicated and opaque and further such entities can be used for avoiding tax – the SRA conducted a thematic review of firms that provide these services during 2018 (**www.sra.org.uk/sra/how-we-work/reports/aml-thematic-review**).

The SRA quite rightly notes in its report following its review, however, that such vehicles can be used legitimately, but that this legitimacy is why criminals may use such vehicles to add a sheen of respectability.

During its review, the SRA visited 59 firms and met with their MLROs and MLCOs. The SRA also reviewed 115 files from these firms.

In general terms, the review found that most law firms that carry out trust and company services were meeting the requirements under the regulations. The SRA set out in its report that it found no evidence of actual money laundering – however, there was a significant minority of firms that were not taking enough steps under the regulations.

In relation to the requirement to have a firm-wide AML risk assessment, the SRA found that in 24 of the firms the assessment did not cover areas required under the regulations; 20 were not able to show that they had addressed trust and company services as part of the assessment; and four did not have a firm-wide risk assessment at all.

One-quarter of the firms did not have an adequate process to manage risks around acting for PEPs; and the file reviews showed that on 21 occasions firms were not conducting ongoing due diligence and keeping the same up to date, which the SRA notes is particularly important for trusts and company services work where the beneficial ownership of a client can change. The SRA did note in the report, however, that 15 firms turned down work on the basis that clients were being evasive.

In terms of training, the SRA reported that most firms provided specific training about trust and company work, but that seven firms did not provide training about beneficial ownership and five firms had been referred for disciplinary action owing to their training or lack thereof.

The SRA reported that of those 59 firms visited, only 10 had submitted SARs in the prior two years and that this tallies with the NCA's view that law firms are not being proactive enough in looking to identify suspicious activity and then reporting it.

Overall, as a result of the review, 26 of the 59 firms were referred for disciplinary action – that is a staggering 55 per cent.

Further as a result of the review, the SRA published a warning notice in relation to firm-wide risk assessments (see **5.3** for further information), wrote to 400 firms asking them to produce their firm-wide risk assessment (see below) and set up a new dedicated AML team within the SRA to increase its monitoring of compliance with the regulations.

This thematic review, therefore, highlighted that some firms did not fully understand the requirements of the AML Regulations or were reckless with regard to them.

5.5.2 Review of 400 firm-wide AML risk assessments

Following on from the SRA's 2018 thematic review, in March 2019 the SRA wrote to 400 firms and asked to be sent their firm-wide AML risk assessments. The SRA reported that 21 per cent (83) of those assessments were not compliant in the following ways (**www.sra.org.uk/solicitors/guidance/firm-risk-assessments**):

GUIDANCE, REVIEWS, VISITS, REGULATIONS AND COMPLIANCE

- 40 firms did not send a firm-wide risk assessment, instead sending something else, though the SRA noted that maybe once they realised, they might have corrected that mistake given the opportunity; and
- 43 firms did not address one or more of the AML Regulations, reg.18 criteria.

The SRA also reported that 135 of the assessments were dated after its request to see the assessment had been sent. One might argue that at least the firms were being honest. The SRA recognises that some of those assessments may have been updates of earlier risk assessments, but that some may have been newly created – suggesting that the firms did not have an assessment before the request was made.

The SRA further reported that when it considered the type of work that the firm did, the assessment was not appropriate to the size of the firm, the services that it offered and the geographical area it operated in.

The SRA also noted that generally speaking, risk assessments based on a template (of which there were 64 per cent – although how it knew this is hard to say) were of lower quality, and as echoed in this book, if a template is to be used then it needs to be tailored to fit the firm.

5.5.3 2019/20 AML thematic review

On 25 November 2020, the SRA published its findings from visits it conducted in 74 firms from September 2019 to October 2020 (**www.sra.org.uk/sra/how-we-work/reports/anti-money-laundering-visits-2019-2020**). The SRA calls this series of visits its rolling programme of reviews. For more detail about what this review/visit entails, see **5.7**.

The firms that were reviewed ranged in size from three fee earners to over 500 fee earners, and over half of those reviewed had more than 50 fee earners. Twenty-five firms had their head office in London, six in Wales and the remainder spread across England.

The SRA sets out in its report that the reviews entailed meeting the firm's MLRO and MLCO and discussing their approach to AML by way of policies and processes. Further, two fee earners were chosen on the day of the visit and two files for each were reviewed.

During these visits, the Fifth EU Directive on Money Laundering (EU) 2018/843 (5AMLD) came into force and so the SRA sets out in its report that it updated its questions – and it further adapted its review during the COVID-19 pandemic.

The SRA's report sets out its findings in 10 key areas, which are summarised below.

5.5.3.1 Audits

Of the 74 firms, 18 firms had undertaken both an internal and external audit and 14 had not conducted an audit at all, with four of those not aware of the requirement to have an independent audit conducted. The SRA found that there was a tendency to assume that an external audit was automatically compliant, but that was not in fact what the SRA found. Of the firms, 21 relied on an accreditation scheme as a method of external audit, when that did not address AML compliance at all. The SRA found that 41 firms had conducted an internal audit, but that these were not always compliant with the requirements of reg.21. In some firms, the SRA found that audits were undertaken by the MLRO/MLCO or compliance department, and that the audit was not therefore independent. The SRA noted that when audits had taken place the action usually taken was to recommend improvements on existing measures at the firms.

The SRA sets out in its report that only the very smallest practices will not be appropriate for an independent audit, and all other practices must establish an independent audit function. If firms do not consider that they need an independent audit, then they need to justify this. The SRA considers that having more than one office, having fee earners focus on a particular area of regulated work and where partners are responsible for others' compliance with the regulations, would indicate that an independent audit was needed.

In terms of independence, the SRA sets out that a firm does not have to engage a specialist agency or consultancy, but that those who are responsible for maintaining the AML compliant framework in the firm should not be the ones auditing. Given that in order to audit properly the auditor needs to fully understand the regulations, it is hard to see who in a firm other than the MLRO or MLCO would be an appropriate person to audit. The SRA suggests that perhaps the auditor could be someone in the firm who does not carry out regulated work, the MLRO from another firm by way of reciprocal arrangement or an office manager who does not undertake a fee earning role. How realistic these suggestions are is unclear.

The audit itself must look at the firm's policies, controls and procedures (PCPs) and assess whether they meet the regulatory requirements and make recommendations for improvement. **Appendix B9** contains a template audit document which might be used.

Although the AML Regulations do not specify the frequency of audits, the SRA suggests that an audit should take place when there is a regulatory change; following revision of the firm's PCPs; following any other major change at the firm (for example, a merger); or at regular intervals depending on the size and nature of the firm, and that for some an annual basis may be appropriate.

Conducting a thorough AML audit annually may just be too much, in the author's opinion. However, one option may be to have a form of external audit which is thorough with a full review of the firm's PCPs, file reviews and fee earner interviews say every three years and every other year a more low-level form of review by an internal person even if that person is the firm's MLRO or MLCO or both. An external independent yearly audit will no doubt be costly and may not be necessary.

In terms of good practice versus bad practice in the SRA's view, there are some handy tips in the SRA's report. As evidence of good practice, including new joiners to the firm as part of the audit, and conducting file reviews annually and on an ad hoc basis were applauded. In terms of areas for improvement, the SRA noted that some firms carried out simple reviews of policies without trying to understand their effectiveness, and further some firms had in fact failed to implement recommendations in a timely way.

5.5.3.2 Due diligence

The SRA looked at standard client due diligence (CDD) measures as well as simplified due diligence and PEP processes. The SRA found that in 39 matters (some 53 per cent) there was insufficient client ID and that it was deficient for a range of reasons. These reasons included: the client being known to a partner in the firm but this not being documented on the file and the party not being known to the individual conducting the work; expired ID being accepted; ID collected on only one of several joint clients; ID not being found when stored on other files; the fee earner who assumed that the central compliance team had gathered the ID; and ID not being accessible to the fee earner who was conducting the work.

Interestingly, 67 per cent of firms confirmed to the SRA that they did not use simplified due diligence even though their own policy allowed for it.

Even more interesting, only six firms (eight per cent) relied on ID provided by others under reg.39 (see **4.3.1**). In these cases, reliance was used for overseas clients and where the referral had come from a regulated person.

Eleven per cent of firms had no written policy on PEPs, although most of those had a process in place to identify PEPs. To identify PEPs, eight firms relied on a declaration given by the client, 41 firms used electronic search methods and 10 firms used both.

Overall, 91 per cent of firms confirmed that they had turned away work because of the AML risk posed, and several of the firms reviewed set out that they imposed enhanced due diligence (EDD) measures in line with the firm's policy, and as a result the client had ceased to contact them.

The SRA found that in 15 matters EDD should have been implemented but was not, and notes that in one case there was an Iranian PEP dealing with a number of offshore jurisdictions and the firm's own notes set out that EDD was not needed.

The SRA report notes that collecting passports, driving licences and utility bills is one way of collecting CDD on a client, and that if a client cannot produce this evidence then there are other methods that can be deployed, but the SRA does not say what they are.

The SRA noted that many firms have a centralised compliance team that collects CDD information and whilst there is nothing wrong with that approach, the SRA considers that the fee earner must, as a minimum, understand this information and have access to it.

The SRA reported that electronic search methods and self-declarations are both valid methods of identifying PEPs, but that each had its limitations. The SRA holds the view that electronic search methods may not pick up on PEPs that are PEPs by association or family membership. It is important, in the author's view, to check with the electronic search provider what level of PEP will come up, and in the

ANTI-MONEY LAUNDERING

author's experience most reputable companies will flag PEPs by association or family membership, and it is certainly worth making sure. Of course, client declarations as to PEP status are only good if the client is honest and they understand what is being asked.

The SRA notes in its report that PEP policies should be realistic and that it may not be realistic to take the view that the firm will not act for PEPs at all. The SRA also sets out that as a minimum it expects the firm when acting for a PEP to keep a written record of PEP clients and for regular meetings between the MLCO/MLRO and fee earners acting for PEPs to take place. This is, in the author's opinion, wholly unrealistic for any large firm which may act for hundreds of PEPs at any one time, especially as the definition of PEP includes those by association or family membership. If a firm were to consider this to be unachievable, then (in the author's opinion) an alternative would be to take a risk-based approach as to which fee earners the MLCO/MLRO should meet regularly to monitor their matters, and a firm may decide this should be for PEPs where there is also adverse media about the PEP.

The SRA in its report notes as good practice:

- firms being creative when obtaining conventional CDD documents is not possible;
- storing CDD centrally so it can be used on multiple client matters;
- systems that prevent billing until CDD is completed;
- using more than one method for identifying PEPs;
- keeping in touch with fee earners who act for PEPs; and
- appreciating the risks posed by using simplified due diligence and using that method with caution.

The SRA noted that areas for improvement include:

- fee earners not having access to CDD;
- an outdated view of what a PEP is; and
- an assumption that PEPs would not instruct the firm.

5.5.3.3 Electronic verification

The SRA found that 85 per cent of those who were reviewed used an electronic verification system and that 25 different providers were used. Eleven firms used more than one electronic verifier, and some even used three. The SRA casts doubt on some of these systems, however, and noted that one system determined property title and not in fact identity. Some firms used this method for certain types of work, for individual clients or on an ad hoc basis.

The SRA notes that the use of electronic verification alone will not be sufficient to ensure compliance and that firms should check that the provider is fit for purpose.

The SRA advises firms to use electronic verification on the basis of risk and to not over-rely on electronic verification.

GUIDANCE, REVIEWS, VISITS, REGULATIONS AND COMPLIANCE

5.5.3.4 Matter risk assessments

In 29 per cent of the files that the SRA reviewed there was no matter risk assessment. The SRA also reported that whilst in some cases an analysis had been carried out, there was no conclusion as to the matter risk level, making it difficult for the firm to know whether EDD should be carried out. It seems also that some of the risk assessments were woefully inadequate as they simply asked whether the client was a PEP or not; and further, in one firm the fee earner thought that the electronic verification system considered the risk for them.

The SRA also found that the matter risk assessment sometimes conflicted with the firm-wide risk assessment – for example, where the firm-wide risk assessment set out that all conveyancing matters are considered high-risk but the matter risk assessment did not say so.

The SRA states in the report that it expects firms to make sure that fee earners understand the need to carry out matter risk assessments, and also understand when EDD is required.

The SRA confirms that in its view, making risk assessments part of file opening is good practice, and also that the assessment is clear when EDD is required. The SRA also notes that some firms had set up files so that they cannot be worked on or billed unless a risk assessment had been completed. Care needs to be taken, however, to ensure that the risk assessment is carefully thought through and does not become a form-filling exercise. The SRA notes that requiring the matter risk assessment to be revisited at certain milestone points was good practice.

The SRA recommend that fee earners understand the firm's firm-wide AML risk assessment. Depending on how a firm has conducted that assessment, it may be quite a complicated document to read and therefore firms should consider releasing a summary of the document for fee earners to read once a year and as and when it is reviewed and changed.

5.5.3.5 MLCOs and their roles

In 76 per cent of the firms the SRA visited, unsurprisingly the MLCO and MLRO were the same person. In relation to employee screening, eight MLCOs were unsure what measures were undertaken and the SRA reported that in some cases the MLCO did not consider this to be a part of their role.

In the firms visited, 10 MLCOs and 10 MLROs had not received training specifically about their roles. In eight of these cases both roles were held by the same person. The SRA reported that it appeared that some MLCOs did not fully understand their overarching responsibility for compliance with the AML Regulations and were not fully engaged.

The SRA announced in the report that it will be conducting a thematic review into the roles of the MLCOs and MLROs which will also consider the training and experience that those roles need and what makes a good role-holder.

ANTI-MONEY LAUNDERING

Regulation 21 provides that an MLCO must be appointed having regard to the size and nature of the firm. The SRA sets out that with the exception of sole practices with no staff, it expects all firms to appoint an MLCO. This might be a challenging pill to swallow for those firms that conduct solely unregulated work such as litigation.

The SRA also sets out that the MLCO will be the main point of contact with the SRA on any AML matter, and further the MLCOs must understand that their role includes responsibilities under screening, training, auditing and compliance by the MLRO with their obligations under POCA 2002 if the role-holders are different. The MLCO must also have oversight of all the firm's processes and procedures.

The SRA considers as good practice appointing a proactive and empowered MLCO who can hold fellow senior managers to account. Areas for improvement the SRA notes are:

- not allowing the MLCO to abdicate their duties to the MLRO who is not accountable for overall compliance; and
- further overloading the MLCO with different roles leaving them with insufficient capacity to fulfil their duties under the regulations.

5.5.3.6 Sanctions

Of the firms visited by the SRA, 57 ran sanctions checks on all new clients and of those 39 also ran checks on existing clients. Seven firms did not run sanctions checks at all, and when pressed for a reason some took the view that sanctioned individuals would not instruct the firm. Four firms chose only to check conveyancing clients for sanctions. The SRA report states that it is, of course, dangerous to assume that sanctioned entities would not instruct a particular firm, and also firms should not see sanction-checking as a one-time activity.

5.5.3.7 Source of funds

Of the files that the SRA reviewed, 21 per cent did not have adequate evidence of source of funds. The SRA found that in some cases this was because the fee earner did not understand the requirements or made an assumption about the client's means. Some firms confirmed that they would not seek information on source of funds until later on in the transaction. The SRA reported that several firms provided clients with a source of funds form with their client care documents and that this provided a useful basis for the fee earner to then analyse what requests for information and questions to ask of the client. However, in one case the SRA sets out that the fee earner obtained bank statements but simply filed them without reading them.

The SRA says that it expects source of funds to be evidenced on the file and this is not limited to transactional work; it also applies to other types of work such as setting up a trust.

The SRA's view is that it is best to get evidence about source of funds early on in a transaction so that any report to the NCA can be made in a timely manner and so as to cause less disruption to the transaction, and further as the source of funds is an integral part of the matter risk assessment.

The SRA considers it good practice to apply the same standards to all clients regardless of personal knowledge, gathering as much evidence as needed to be sure of source of funds and managing the client's expectations at the outset by setting out what information will be required. The SRA notes that areas for improvement are:

- assumptions about a client's source of wealth based on anecdotes and perceptions rather than evidence;
- where gathering of evidence is undertaken but the evidence is not then read.

It is well worth creating a space where fee earners can easily record source of funds and wealth, and this could be in the client/matter risk assessment.

Note that the SRA's report does not distinguish between source of funds and source of wealth, but these are in fact two separate things and both need to be considered (see **4.1.4**).

5.5.3.8 Staff screening

For pre-employment checks, the SRA found that 97 per cent of firms undertook these, with the most basic check being checking the Law Society or SRA databases. More comprehensively, 36 firms were found to also undertake qualification checks, check regulatory history, take references and also conduct a Disclosure and Barring Service (DBS) check (criminal records bureau check against criminal records). Some firms only carried out DBS checks on those who were required to have one under the Law Society's Conveyancing Quality Scheme (CQS). Other checks included electronic verification, credit check and social media checks.

For in-employment checks, 78 per cent of firms were carrying out some form of check; 88 per cent of firms did not conduct any regulatory check once fee earners were employed; 38 per cent of firms used appraisals for the knowledge and integrity aspect of screening; and 16 per cent of firms placed reliance on annual self-declarations.

The SRA states in the report that it expects the following checks to be conducted to be compliant with reg.21(2):

1. On appointment

    - Skills, knowledge, and expertise:
        - qualification checks (seeing original certificates);
        - validating practising status via the SRA Solicitors Register (**www.sra.org.uk/consumers/register/**) or applicable regulator.
    - Conduct and integrity:
        - taking up references;

    - checking disciplinary history via the SRA Solicitors Register or applicable regulator;
    - adverse media checks via search engines;
    - e-verification, if available.

2. During employment (annually)
   - Skills, knowledge, and expertise:
     - annual competence declaration;
     - appraisal procedure.
   - Conduct and integrity:
     - adverse media checks via search engines;
     - checking disciplinary history via the SRA Solicitors Register or applicable regulator or emailing: contactcentre@sra.org.uk;
     - e-verification, if available.

The SRA states that firms will also need to consider whether to conduct DBS checks as part of their risk-based approach. The SRA sets out that seeking a self-declaration is not on its own a sufficient method of screening and it cites the SDT case of *SRA v. Podger* (12065-2020) as an example where a solicitor had failed to declare his drugs conviction to his firm or to the SRA.

The SRA goes on to state that those who limit their in-employment checks to those required by the CQS are in danger of viewing money laundering as something which affects conveyancing only.

The SRA considers that good practice is using multiple methods of screening, and screening on an ongoing basis – and further, that relying on independent sources rather than personal knowledge is better. The SRA also sees as good practice using existing methods of screening, such as appraisals. The SRA's view is that there is improvement to be made in the MLCOs' understanding of screening.

5.5.3.9 SARs

As part of the review the SRA asked MLROs how many internal SARs they had received within the firm and how many had turned into SARs to the NCA (both within the prior two years).

The SRA noted that some firms recorded every query made of an MLRO as an internal SAR (when that cannot be the case).

The SRA reported the following numbers for internal SARs:

- 16 MLROs received 0;
- 32 MLROs received 1–10;
- 19 MLROs received 11–49;
- seven MLROs received more than 50 (the highest single total was 412 – presumably that firm recorded every approach to the MLRO made).

The SRA reported the following numbers for SARs to the NCA:

- 25 firms had submitted 0;
- 43 firms had submitted 1–10;
- six firms had submitted 11–50 (50 was the highest number).

Unfortunately, the SRA does not set out in its report what the conversion rate of internal to external SARs is, though it does note that most fee earners that they interviewed correctly understood that they should speak to the MLRO if they develop suspicion. The SRA does report that some fee earners said that they would seek out their line manager or supervising partner for discussion before approaching the firm's MLRO, and that this was welcomed, but that firms need to make sure staff understand that reporting to the MLRO is the only way to protect their position.

Where firms require internal SARs to be in a specified form, the firm needs to consider whether this is off-putting and to ensure the firm has a culture where staff feel able to speak to the MLRO to discuss AML concerns.

The SRA is also of the view that maintaining internal SAR records will help the MLRO spot trends and may assist in any defence should criminal proceedings occur.

The SRA considers it good practice to appoint a deputy MLRO, and have a MLRO who is visible and approachable. Further, the SRA suggests using examples of internal and external SARs in training; the author would suggest real-life examples from the firm are best.

5.5.3.10 Training

Of the firms reviewed, 85 per cent had provided training in the year leading up to their visit. Four firms had never provided firm-wide training – three of those had focused on key fee earners, and one firm was relatively new and had training planned. Most firms used more than one method of training, and many (84 per cent) opted for online training. Many firms also gave AML training to non-fee earning staff including receptionists, administrative and finance staff. One firm even went as far as training its delivery drivers and warehouse workers. The SRA does not consider that AML training should be limited to fee earning staff alone; it should include all those who play a role in detecting and preventing money laundering.

Although the AML Regulations do not state how frequently training should be conducted, the SRA suggests that training should be provided regularly and perhaps annually, provided to new starters as soon as practical and provided on any changes to the regulations. The SRA sets out that training should be geared to the learner, and generic training meant for fee earners is not likely to be relevant for certain other members of staff such as receptionists.

As good practice the SRA confirms that using more than one method of training is advisable and using methods that test knowledge is best. The SRA suggests that infrequent training which allows AML knowledge to become out of date is an area for improvement for firms.

ANTI-MONEY LAUNDERING

5.5.4 SRA's next steps and actions with firms

The SRA reported that over half of the firms reviewed needed some form of engagement and remedial action, which included amending the firm's AML policy, specific corrective actions on files reviewed or a formal review of all open files for AML compliance.

Twelve firms were issued with written guidance, and a further nine firms were referred to the AML Investigations Team for further investigation which may lead to disciplinary action.

5.6 WHAT ARE THE SRA'S PLANS FOR 2021 AND BEYOND?

All firms should ensure that they are aware of what is on the SRA agenda at the present time and in future years so that they can ensure compliance in the areas of the SRA's focus and be ready for any queries raised by the SRA or visits.

In order to understand the focus of the SRA, one needs to look at the SRA's business plan, 'Risk Outlook' and any other information it may provide at events such as the COLP/COFA conference.

5.6.1 SRA business plan 2020/21

The SRA consulted (for the first time) on its draft business plan for 2020/21 mid-way through 2020 (the consultation documents are available at: **www.sra.org.uk/sra/consultations/consultation-listing/business-plan-2020-21/**).

The SRA business plan sets out the 'SRA corporate strategy 2020 to 2013' (**www.sra.org.uk/sra/corporate-strategy/**). This strategy was published in March 2020 and forms the basis of the SRA's overall business plan. It sets out the following objectives:

- **Objective one** – We will set and maintain high professional standards for solicitors and law firms as the public would expect and ensure we provide an equally high level of operational service.
- **Objective two** – We will actively support the adoption of legal technology and other innovation that helps to meet the needs of the public, business community, regulated entities and the economy.
- **Objective three** – We will continually build our understanding of emerging opportunities and challenges for the legal sector and our role in effectively regulating it.

It is against the backdrop of these objectives that the SRA business plan is built.

The SRA's overall budget for its business plan is approximately £71 million, with objective one taking the lion's share of the budget at 92 per cent, and objectives two and three coming in at four per cent each.

The SRA sets out its ambition:

GUIDANCE, REVIEWS, VISITS, REGULATIONS AND COMPLIANCE

Our ambition is to be a progressive and relevant regulator, able to anticipate and respond with agility to emerging opportunities and challenges for the legal sector in England and Wales.

This will be built on the foundation of doing our core work well – the public protection and setting and maintaining of high standards for the profession that has to be the priority for effective regulation – and delivering excellent service.

To achieve this, it says it will be anticipatory, evidence and intelligence driven, responsive, collaborative, agile and authoritative.

5.6.2 SRA Risk Outlook 2020/2021

The SRA published its Risk Outlook for 2020/2021 on 23 November 2020 (**www.sra.org.uk/risk/risk-outlook/**). The SRA has been publishing a Risk Outlook each year for some time, and it provides insight into what the SRA considers are the risks that the SRA and firms should be considering.

In the foreword to the Risk Outlook, the SRA highlights that the Outlook is published against the backdrop of COVID-19, which has undoubtedly brought many challenges to many firms not only from a revenue perspective but also in the need to adapt quickly to remote working which has, as the Outlook comments, exacerbated already existing risks.

In terms of using the Risk Outlook, the SRA's view is that it should be used by firms to develop and update their own risk assessments. The Outlook:

- sets out the SRA's views on the priority risks in the legal market so firms can reflect on how they affect the firm's work;
- reminds firms of some of their legal and regulatory obligations in relation to these risks;
- suggests how firms can manage risks and avoid harm to the public, the rule of law and the proper administration of justice;
- includes resources that firms can refer to; and
- highlights potential changes and planned actions for the risks, including forthcoming regulatory and legislative changes, where applicable.

The SRA advises that, when considering the Risk Outlook, firms should recognise how the risks apply to their firm, consider any other risks that are specific to the firm and decide what actions should be taken to control risks and monitor the work that is being undertaken.

In terms of the risks that are outlined in the Risk Outlook, it is worth noting that these risks are not new and have been on prior years' Risk Outlooks.

Although the SRA correctly states that the Risk Outlook is not guidance and is a tool to raise awareness, firms need to understand that the Risk Outlook is an instrument which is used to focus the SRA's attention for the coming year and firms are expected to know about it, understand it and act accordingly.

ANTI-MONEY LAUNDERING

5.6.3 The SRA's AML agenda for 2021 and beyond

Taking the above into account, therefore, at the top of the SRA's agenda is the prevention of money laundering and adherence to the AML Regulations.

The SRA sets out in the Risk Outlook that firms that conduct conveyancing work, handle consumers' money and create and manage trusts and company structures are most at risk of money laundering. Further, the SRA points out that high net worth individuals from overseas may seek to exploit the investor visa scheme and use solicitors to make UK investments using criminal proceeds. The SRA's view is that solicitors working in the London property market are at high risk of being used in this way.

The SRA notes that due to the COVID-19 lockdowns, some firms may have found it more challenging to carry out CDD needed as per the regulations. The SRA Risk Outlook highlights the increasing risk of vendor fraud, where a fraudster sells a property without the consent or knowledge of the owners.

The Outlook sets out that firms must understand their obligations under the money laundering regulations and sanctions legislation. Further, firms who are within scope of the regulations must have a written and compliant firm-wide risk assessment, maintain policies, controls and procedures, train staff, obtain an independent audit, monitor transactions, report suspicions appropriately and so on.

As per the draft SRA business plan, AML compliance will continue to be a priority for the SRA and it plans to conduct AML visits on what it deems to be high-risk firms on a three-year rolling basis alongside sampling lower risk firms. The SRA is also planning to undertake a thematic review into tax advice given to clients. So, expect visits to continue.

Unsurprisingly, the topic of AML featured in the SRA's COLP/COFA conference in November 2020, where the SRA confirmed that it planned on undertaking a thematic review of the roles of MLRO and MLCO. It also plans to ask firms for their firm-wide risk assessments to review on a rolling basis (after it requested firm-wide AML risk assessments from 400 firms in 2018, see **5.5.2**).

The SRA's focus on AML will not wane. It will undoubtedly continue beyond 2021 and some may say particularly in the light of the continuing pressure on the SRA from OPBAS. As long as there is money laundering and law firms are seen as targets for money launderers, the SRA will continue to ensure that those it regulates will remain as compliant as possible in this space.

5.7 SRA VISITS – WHAT TO EXPECT AND HOW TO HANDLE THEM

As part of the SRA's programme of supervision of AML compliance across law firms, the SRA can, at any time, visit and audit a law firm. Further, in the SRA's business plan for 2020/21, AML compliance remains a top priority for the SRA with no sign of that changing. This business plan outlines an intention to conduct AML visits on what the SRA deems to be high-risk firms on a three-year rolling basis

GUIDANCE, REVIEWS, VISITS, REGULATIONS AND COMPLIANCE

alongside sampling lower risk firms. SRA visits are therefore here to stay, and stay for a long time, and hence firms should be aware of what to expect during visits and how to handle them.

To that end, in this section we explore what happens before, during and after the SRA's visit and tips for how a law firm may prepare in readiness for such a visit. The visit format that is outlined below was correct as at 2020 and if you are reading this much later it may have changed. During the COVID-19 pandemic these visits continued, but were of course conducted remotely.

5.7.1 Prior to your visit

The SRA will contact the firm to inform it that it has been selected for a review and set out whether the firm has been selected for any particular reason. In all likelihood the firm will have been selected using a risk matrix that the SRA uses to deem the firm high risk. The SRA may give the firm a selection of dates to choose from for the visit, and depending on how confident the firm feels, the firm may be wise to select the date furthest away to enable as much preparation as possible.

The SRA will explain in a letter what will be required during the visit and how long the visit will last. Generally speaking, the visit may last half a day, depending on the size of the firm and therefore cannot be held out as a 'deep dive' exercise. This can of course work both ways in terms of its advantages and disadvantages. It is advantageous as the SRA will not be looking at many files and seeing many people. It is disadvantageous if it picks a file which does not meet the standards in terms of evidencing compliance, or it picks two fee earners and both are very nervous or, worse, not able to answer AML questions and the SRA is not at the firm long enough to appreciate that this is not a true reflection of the firm as a whole.

The letter should explain who the SRA wants to interview, and normally this will be the MLRO and MLCO. Further, the letter will explain how many fee earners undertaking regulated work the SRA wants to interview and how the interviewees will be selected. Selection will be by way of a list of all relevant fee earners being supplied by the firm to the SRA one week before the visit, and then the SRA will narrow that list down to a dozen fee earners a day or so before the visit. The timings here are tight and it may be wise to inform fee earners in advance that they may be up for selection for an interview with the SRA – but perhaps it is unwise to tell fee earners exactly when the SRA will be visiting, in case there is a mass holiday request for that day.

The SRA will also explain in the letter that it would like access to two files for each fee earner, and the firm will therefore need to provide a list of files for the selected fee earners for the SRA to choose from on the day of the visit. It is likely that the SRA will pick files that have matter descriptions that pique its interest, for example because of the location of a property if that location signifies an expensive address.

The letter will also explain that the firm needs to provide the following on the day of the visit:

(a) any policies and information held by the firm demonstrating its approach to AML/countering the financing of terrorism (CFT);
(b) either physical or electronic access to the CDD, time recording and risk assessment records for two of each fee earner's selected files;
(c) the firm's AML/CFT training records;
(d) records of any internal SARs made by staff to the firm's MLRO, and the MLRO's decision, in each case, during the past two years;
(e) records relating to any SARs made to the NCA by the MLRO during the past two years.

The SRA may ask that this bundle of information is sent electronically and will not take the bundle away. It is best to check this before creating multiple bundles. Of course, if the visit is virtual then electronic bundles are likely to be requested.

5.7.2 During the visit

During the visit, the MLRO and MLCO are likely to be asked the following:

- Have the AML/CTF policies and procedures been communicated across the firm, and if so how?
- How does the firm screen new and existing employees?
- When did the firm last audit its policies, procedures and controls (PCPs)? Did the firm have an internal or external audit? (Note that the SRA does not normally request to see the audit. The MLCO may decide, however, to share this with the SRA to show the controls the firm has implemented to tackle AML compliance.)
- Does the firm have an AML risk assessment covering the areas it should such as (i) areas identified by the SRA risk assessment; (ii) clients; (iii) products and services; (iv) types of transactions; (v) delivery channels?
- Has the firm turned work away in the light of the AML risk?
- Is the firm's AML policy based on the firm's risk assessment and does it take the LSAG guidance into account?
- Does the policy set out how to identify and scrutinise complex or unusual transactions or transactions that have no apparent legal or economic purpose?
- Does the firm use simplified CDD, and if so when?
- How are sanctions lists checked?
- How long does the firm keep CDD records for?
- Is there a written policy on PEPs and does this include senior management approval to act for PEPs? How are PEPs identified?
- Who has received training in the firm? Are relevant people trained on AML, terrorist financing, data protection and recognising and reporting suspicious activities?
- When was training last delivered? Have the relevant people completed it?

GUIDANCE, REVIEWS, VISITS, REGULATIONS AND COMPLIANCE

- How many internal SARs have been made to the MLRO, and how many of those have been reported to the NCA? What is the conversion rate?
- Has a defence been refused by the NCA?

Of the fee earners, the SRA is likely to ask the following:

- Do they know who the MLRO is? Who is it?
- Do they know how to identify suspicious activity? What would they do if they suspected money laundering?
- Do they understand their responsibilities under the AML Regulations?
- In relation to each file, the fee earner may be asked to explain:
  - what the retainer is about;
  - who the client is;
  - what does the fee earner know about the client;
  - any suspicious activity;

  and asked to produce:

  - the risk assessment;
  - documentary evidence of ID, source of funds and wealth and any analysis.

5.7.3 After the interview with MLRO/MLCO and fee earners

The SRA may be happy to provide a short debrief, and where necessary will give feedback on any issues it has seen or ask the firm to clarify aspects of compliance. It may not do this, however, and may simply leave after the interviews. It is worth remembering that the SRA visit is not designed to provide an appraisal of the firm's AML procedures, and so the firm should not expect one.

5.7.4 After the visit

The SRA will write a letter confirming the outcome of the visit, any corrective action and recommendations. It will also inform the firm whether any further action is going to be taken. This letter should come around six to eight weeks after the visit, but it may depend on the issues found as to when the outcome is known. Presumably if the SRA considers serious breaches are occurring, it will act quickly.

5.7.5 How to get prepared

Below are a series of steps that firms can take to ensure readiness for an SRA AML visit:

1. Make sure the firm-wide AML risk assessment is complete, covers all the areas it needs to and is up to date. When it is reviewed, the firm should document that it has done so.

ANTI-MONEY LAUNDERING

2. Decide how the firm will screen new and existing employees if not already decided, and document this in the firm's AML policy.
3. Make sure the AML policy is up to date, taking into account the LSAG guidance, and make sure that the policy states this.
4. Remind all fee earners of the regulatory requirement that each client and matter must have a risk assessment undertaken and ask that they ensure that all their risk assessments are up to date. Note that the SRA takes this aspect very seriously.
5. Make sure that fee earners appreciate the requirement to understand and obtain evidence of source of funds and wealth, and that this must be documented on the file. Now is the time to start ensuring that this is being done.
6. If the firm's internal and external SARs are not up to date, now is the time to make sure they are. If the firm does not have a method of recording such reports, internal or external, it should devise one as soon as possible and start using it. The firm must be ready to provide the numbers of internal and external reports to the SRA and also what the conversion rate of internal to external reports is.
7. Make sure that if the firm has a central on-boarding team, fee earners understand that their overall AML obligations are not delegated to that team. The SRA is keen to make sure this is understood, and the firm does not want fee earners saying otherwise.
8. If the firm has not trained in a while, it should get some training out. That could be via an online module; face-to-face sessions (in person or virtual); attendance at team meetings; guidance notes; and/or the use of stories of what has happened in the firm or outside the firm (such as SDT cases) to illustrate compliance. There are many ways to train and not all people take information in the same way.
9. The firm should undertake, if it has not done so already, an internal or external audit of the firm's AML policies, procedures and controls.
10. The firm should make sure it is up to date on its implementation of 5AMLD/MLR 2019.

5.8 6AMLD AND BREXIT REGULATIONS

EU member states were required to implement the Sixth EU Money Laundering Directive (Directive (EU) 2018/1673 of the European Parliament and of the Council of 23 October 2018 on combating money laundering by criminal law) (6AMLD) into national laws by 3 June 2021. The UK decided to opt out of implementing 6AMLD, as it will have left the EU by this time and the vast majority of the requirements under 6AMLD were already enshrined in UK legislation. However, one aspect of 6AMLD that is not part of UK legislation is the introduction of corporate liability for failure to prevent money laundering. This will not form part of

GUIDANCE, REVIEWS, VISITS, REGULATIONS AND COMPLIANCE

the UK's AML legalisation, and arguably there has hence already begun a divergence between EU and UK AML legislation. Note, however, that the principle of corporate criminal liability exists under UK law already.

As the UK has now left the EU, some changes to the current regulations needed to be made. To that end, the Money Laundering and Transfer of Funds (Information) (Amendment) (EU Exit) Regulations 2019, SI 2019/253 came into force when the UK left the EU (1 January 2021).

The effect of these regulations is that the definition of a 'third country' has changed, so that a third country is one that is outside the UK and not outside the EEA. The effect is that transactions and business relationships involving EU clients will be subject to the same considerations as those that apply to third countries. However, EU countries are generally not high risk and so the EDD measures for high-risk third countries do not apply. Where applicable, changes made by the exit regulations have been incorporated into this chapter.

The UK will remain a member of FATF (see **2.2**) and as such will continue to meet FATF's guidelines and recommendations.

Now that the UK has left the EU it will not transpose into UK law future AML directives. It remains to be seen whether the UK will bring its AML legislation into line with the EU as and when new directives are issued to EU countries. Those under the EU AML legislation will see the UK as a third country, and as such will only be prepared to treat the UK as having measures equivalent to those of the EU if the UK continues to keep up with the EU's changes to AML legislation. Too much divergence will threaten how robust the EU considers the UK's AML legislation to be, and indeed vice versa.

Those who advise law firms on AML, are MLROs/MLCOs or just have a particular interest in AML legislation may well wish to continue to keep up with EU AML directives to foresee what the UK might do with its legislation – assuming that it follows and does not in fact lead in this space.

5.9   FIRMS AND SOLICITORS – DISCIPLINARY ACTION

There are very few criminal prosecutions of solicitors for money laundering offences or failure to follow the requirements of the money laundering regulations. However, firms should not let that provide some form of comfort or sign to relax. Criminal prosecutions are a real prospect, and the SRA prosecutes regulatory breaches on a regular basis, as the cases below show. These cases have not been picked as a way of singling out these firms or individuals – there were firms who were sanctioned for AML breaches before these firms and individuals, and sadly there will be more after.

5.9.1 Taylor Vinters LLP

The SRA reached a regulatory settlement agreement with Taylor Vinters LLP (TV) on 28 August 2020 in relation to breaches of the AML Regulations resulting in a fine of £19,200 (**www.sra.org.uk/consumers/solicitor-check/560892/**).

In this matter, TV acted on 161 matters for 88 clients who were overseas nationals purchasing off-plan properties in London. The firm received around £16.8 million into client account for first and second stage deposits. Personnel at the firm had met around half of these clients.

In 43 of the matters, the firm had received deposit funds before due diligence was fully completed. In 27 of these matters, third parties had deposited funds into the client account.

TV stated that its client account details had been provided to clients without its knowledge, and that when this was discovered it asked clients to cease sending any more funds.

In 41 of the 43 matters, TV was able to complete the CDD successfully following the receipt of funds into its client account. For two matters which related to the same client, the firm was unable to complete due diligence as the client was uncontactable and the monies were ultimately paid to charity with the SRA's permission.

TV noted all the matters as high risk but enquired about the client's source of funds and wealth on a 'exception basis', when it deemed it to be appropriate.

In the light of the above, the SRA concluded and the firm agreed that it had failed to conduct due diligence before receipt of monies; failed to conduct ongoing monitoring including source of funds checks; and failed to conduct enhanced ongoing monitoring.

The firm agreed to the breaches as put by the SRA and agreed a fine of £19,200.

The fine itself is not a significant sum and this is because the firm did not invite the clients to send monies before due diligence was completed, and further the firm co-operated.

5.9.2 Seatons Law Limited

The SRA reached a regulatory settlement agreement with Seatons Law Limited (Seatons) on 20 November 2020 in relation to breaches of the AML Regulations resulting in a fine of £14,000 (**www.sra.org.uk/consumers/solicitor-check/592206/**).

The matters for which Seatons found itself before the SRA related to a series of transactions transferring properties from a donor of a power of attorney, and in some instances instructions through a third party.

The SRA found that the firm had failed to allocate the correct risk ratings to matters; failed to obtain adequate ID documentation; breached its own policies around certification of ID documentation; failed to conduct ongoing monitoring;

GUIDANCE, REVIEWS, VISITS, REGULATIONS AND COMPLIANCE

failed to conduct adequate source of funds investigations; and failed to act upon red flag indicators. The firm also accepted that it did not have at the time an adequate AML policy.

Again, the fine of £14,000 is not significant and this was because the firm assisted the SRA with its investigations, made early admissions and corrections and is committed to ensuring the issues do not arise again.

5.9.3 Child & Child partner

In 2019 a partner of law firm Child & Child was fined £45,000 by the SDT for failing to carry out any searches on clients who were daughters of a central Asian head of state who set up companies in the British Virgin Islands to manage two properties in Knightsbridge, London worth nearly £60 million (**www.lawgazette.co.uk/law/panama-papers-solicitor-fined-45000-/5068873.article**).

Failing to undertake these checks meant that the partner did not know that the clients were PEPs, although their connection to their father should have been enough to know this. As such, the partner did not undertake EDD.

To make matters worse, the partner was the firm's MLRO!

In contrast to the two cases above, this fine is more significant and against an individual. This will no doubt have been because the matter went to the SDT and was not settled by agreement.

5.9.4 Alexander Dobrovinsky and Partners LLP partner

A partner at this firm was suspended for nine months for a number of AML Regulations failures after an agreed outcome with the SRA was reached in July 2020 (**www.sra.org.uk/consumers/solicitor-check/355242/**). Further, the partner is unable to be a manager, an owner or a partner in a firm, hold or receive client money or be a COLP/COFA for two years after the suspension is concluded.

The partner's client base was in Russia and the Ukraine, and the partner admitted that she had not conducted EDD measures including source of funds and wealth checks when red flag indicators were present; had breached the SRA Accounts Rules; and also did not have an adequate AML policy in place and no firm-wide risk assessment. The partner's reasoning for having no firm-wide risk assessment or risk assessment on clients' matters was because 'they knew 99% of their clients who were family or friends'.

The firm had already been rebuked and fined in 2015.

5.9.5 Clyde & Co and partners

In 2017, Clyde & Co and three of its partners were fined a total of £80,000 between them (which was then one of the largest fines ever handed down by the SDT) for allowing the client account to be used as a banking facility in 2013 which breached the SRA Accounts Rules and the money laundering regulations in place at the time,

ANTI-MONEY LAUNDERING

including failing to carry out adequate CDD; failing to conduct EDD when a higher risk of money laundering had been identified; failing to cease to act for a client when due diligence procedures could not be applied properly; and relying on a third party's CDD without the consent of that third party.

5.9.6 Solicitor who was described as a 'puppet'

A solicitor was found in November 2020 by the SDT to have been chosen by clients to be their 'puppet' in high value international transactions and acted as their banker (despite denials) (**www.sra.org.uk/consumers/solicitor-check/471104/**).

It was reported that incredibly the solicitor said he would do the same again if the opportunity arose, having described the fees generated from the transactions as a one-off opportunity (they amounted to 10 per cent of his firm's turnover).

The tribunal found that the solicitor had not carried out due diligence of his clients or checked source of funds. Further, the solicitor was found on a separate transaction to pay over sale proceeds to a third party with no underlying legal transaction connected. The SDT did not consider the solicitor to be dishonest, but found that he had failed to follow rules and had made poor decisions.

The solicitor was suspended from practice indefinitely.

5.10 AML COMPLIANCE – WHERE DO I START?

As acknowledged at the beginning of Part II, AML is by far the most complicated and costly area of compliance in financial crime prevention, and possibly in all aspects of law firm compliance. What is important to remember is that this is a marathon and not a sprint. It takes time (sometimes a long time) to get AML compliance in a law firm to where it should be. There are some quick wins, and there are some aspects which will take time and effort to embed.

Knowing where to start is key, and below is a list of key areas to tackle (taken from the January 2021 version of the LSAG guidance).

5.10.1 AML governance

1. All current beneficial owners, officers and managers must be approved by their supervisory authority in accordance with reg.26. (See **4.6**.)
2. Practices must appoint an MLRO. The practice must notify the SRA of this appointment within 14 days of the date of the appointment. (See **4.6** and **3.7.2**.)
3. Where appropriate, the firm should appoint an MLCO. The practice must notify the SRA of this appointment within 14 days of the date of the appointment. (See **3.4** and **3.7.1**.)
4. Delegation by the MLCO of the operational aspects of AML compliance must be documented. (See **3.4** and **3.7.1**.)

5. The AML duties/responsibilities of all partners and employees of the practice should be adequately documented. (See **3.6**.)
6. The AML policies, controls and procedures (PCPs) of the practice must be approved by the practice's senior management (and/or board). This approval must be documented. (See **3.6**.)
7. The board (or equivalent) must monitor and manage compliance with AML PCPs. Board discussions and decisions regarding AML compliance must be documented. (See **3.6**.)
8. All practices must allocate adequate and competent resources to the management of money laundering/terrorist financing (ML/TF) risks.
9. Procedures (including robust, easily accessible record-keeping) must be in place to ensure comprehensive and timely reporting and submissions to relevant supervisory authorities. (See **3.5**.)

5.10.2 Practice-wide risk assessment[1]

10. Practices must have a written, up-to-date practice-level risk assessment in place, in line with reg.18 requirements. (See **3.3**.)
11. Practices must use this risk assessment to directly inform their AML PCPs. (See **3.6**.)

5.10.3 Client/matter level risk assessment

Practices must have:

12. Client and matter level ML/TF risk assessment procedures that include a requirement to undertake a written risk assessment on each new client and matter/retainer particularly where the matter is non-repetitive. (See **4.1.2**.)
13. A documented procedure for the application of client/matter level risk assessment outcomes to the due diligence undertaken on any particular client/matter. (See **3.6**.)

5.10.4 AML policies, controls and procedures

The practice must have clearly documented PCPs based on its practice-wide risk assessment which include:

14. The AML governance arrangements of the practice. (See **3.6**.)

---

[1] 'Practice-wide risk assessment' is the term used in the LSAG guidance. We use 'firm-wide risk assessment' elsewhere in this book.

ANTI-MONEY LAUNDERING

5.10.5 Client due diligence

The practice must have clearly documented PCPs based on its practice-wide risk assessment which include:

15. CDD procedures (including procedures to identify the ownership and control structures of non-natural persons). (See **4.1**.)
16. Identification and verification (ID&V) procedures relating to natural persons (this includes ID&V procedures in relation to the ultimate beneficial owners of non-natural clients, and those purporting to act on behalf of a client). (See **4.1.1**.)
17. Procedures to facilitate a clear understanding of the client's source of wealth and funds in relation to a transaction, and the level of evidence required, in line with the risk profile of the client/matter. (See **4.1.4**.)
18. Procedures to facilitate reporting of discrepancies between beneficial ownership information obtained through due diligence checks and what is held on the Companies House register. (See **4.1.1.15**.)
19. EDD procedures – including the provision of adequate controls to manage higher risk clients/transactions, and measures to establish source of funds/source of wealth where appropriate. (See **4.1.7**.)
20. The practice's position on the use and application of simplified due diligence. (See **4.1.6**.)
21. The timing of any due diligence procedures. (See **4.1.1.14**.)
22. The practice's position on the use of reg.39 reliance and any related procedures. (See **4.3.1**.)
23. The ongoing monitoring of clients and their matters. (See **4.1.5**.)
24. The identification of instances where it is required or appropriate to reapply or renew CDD or EDD on a client.
25. Dealing with the return of unsolicited or apparently accidentally deposited funds.
26. Identification and scrutiny of any complex or unusually large transactions, or an unusual pattern of transactions, or those which serve no apparent economic or legal purpose. (See **3.6** generally.)
27. Any additional measures to prevent products/transactions that support anonymity being used for ML/TF. (See **3.6**.)
28. Identification of PEPs, their relatives or close associates and the control of any associated risks. (See **4.2**.)

5.10.6 Suspicious activity reporting

29. The practice must have procedures setting out how, and in what circumstances, an internal disclosure should be submitted to the nominated officer (MLRO). (See **3.6** for PCPs and **3.5** for SARs.)

5.10.7 Technology

The practice must have clearly documented PCPs based on its practice-wide risk assessment which include:

30. Measures taken when new technology is adopted to protect against ML or TF risks. (See **3.6**.)
31. Where practices use electronic identification and verification (EID&V) tools they should document the role of the tool, the data sources it uses, and in what circumstances (clients/matters) it is appropriate to use the solution. (See **4.1.1.12**.)

5.10.8 Training

The practice must have clearly documented PCPs based on its practice-wide risk assessment which include:

32. Measures deployed to ensure AML relevant training of partners, staff and agents, including the maintenance of records relating to such training. (See **3.7.5**.)
33. Procedures for the communication of PCPs to partners and staff. (See **3.7.5** for training and communication.)

5.10.9 Internal controls

Where appropriate to the size and nature of the practice:

34. The practice must conduct an independent audit of the adequacy and effectiveness of its AML PCPs. (See **3.7.1**.)
35. The practice must undertake screening of relevant employees – both at pre-employment stage and on an ongoing basis. (See **3.7.1**.)

5.10.10 Record-keeping

36. The practice must have procedures relating to record-keeping and related data protection matters. (See **4.3.2**.)

5.10.11 High-level AML compliance actions

37. Taking this up to a higher level, the firm needs to consider the following as a starting point:
    - firm-wide risk assessment;
    - AML/CTF policy that covers all that is required from the list above

including CDD requirements; reliance; record-keeping; what suspicion looks like; who to report suspicions to; screening of employees; training; and more;
- client and matter risk assessments;
- training roll-out to all relevant staff, and specific training for the MLRO/MLCO;
- independent audit (which can help with a gap analysis of the above).

PART III

Criminal finances and investigations

CHAPTER 6

Criminal Finances Act 2017 and tax evasion

This chapter sets out the requirements of the Criminal Finances Act (CFA) 2017 ('the Act') and how to ensure compliance.

6.1 BACKGROUND TO THE CRIMINAL FINANCES ACT 2017

As set out in HM Revenue and Customs (HMRC) guidance 'Tackling tax evasion: Government guidance for the corporate offences of failure to prevent the criminal facilitation of tax evasion' ('Tackling tax evasion 2017') (1 September 2017, **www.gov.uk/government/publications/corporate-offences-for-failing-to-prevent-criminal-facilitation-of-tax-evasion**) the government is of the view that relevant bodies should be criminally liable where they fail to prevent those who act for them or on their behalf from criminally facilitating tax evasion.

The government guidance explains that prior to CFA 2017, attributing criminal liability to a business required prosecutors to show that senior members were involved in and aware of the illegal activity. This made it difficult for prosecutors to prove their case against large multinational businesses where decision-making was not always at board level or where certain decision-making was deliberately not conducted at board level to ensure that those sitting on the board were protected from any liability. Further, the guidance sets out that common law may have acted to discourage internal reporting of any suspected illegal tax activity to senior members of the business, as to do so would mean the senior members would be required to act or the business would find itself liable.

The effect of the legal position prior to CFA 2017, therefore, was to create an environment of businesses who were not incentivised to challenge illegal tax activity head-on.

To tackle this position, CFA 2017 created a new offence where a relevant body fails to prevent an associated person from criminally facilitating the evasion of tax where that tax is evaded in the UK or abroad. The aim of this offence is to overcome the difficulties in attributing criminal liability for the acts of a relevant body's employees, agents or those who provide services on the relevant body's behalf.

CRIMINAL FINANCES AND INVESTIGATIONS

CFA 2017 itself does not alter what activity is criminal, but rather addresses who is to be held accountable for it by focusing on failure to prevent the act from happening.

The government guidance goes on to state that if a relevant business can demonstrate that it has put in place a system of reasonable measures that identifies and mitigates its tax evasion and yet a criminal act does in fact take place, it is unlikely that prosecution will occur. What is clear is that doing nothing, taking no steps at all, is not negotiable in order for the relevant body to have a hope of a reasonable defence.

6.2 OUTLINE OF THE CRIMINAL FINANCES ACT 2017

CFA 2017 came into force on 30 September 2017 and created a criminal offence for any relevant body that fails to prevent the criminal facilitation of tax evasion by associated persons (these terms are defined below). The offence (outlined in Part 3 of the Act) is not so much about tax law, and as noted above it does not change the scope of what is a crime, but the Act is more focused on behaviours which are dishonest and the failure to prevent.

A 'relevant body' is an incorporated body such as companies and partnerships (s.44(2)). The offences under the Act cannot be committed by individuals, though individuals may commit offences under different legislation. Note that where there is a UK tax facilitation offence, it does not matter where the relevant body was incorporated or based, or whether the associated person performs the facilitation of the criminal act in the UK or overseas.

At the Act's core, an entity is in the frame if it fails to prevent tax evasion by its associated persons. If there is tax evasion by the associated persons, the entity's defence is that it did all it could to prevent it from happening. Therefore, entities need to do their best to ensure compliance so as to use those compliance steps as a defence.

The offence of tax evasion will be committed where an associated person (s.45(5)):

(a) is knowingly concerned in, or takes steps with a view to, the fraudulent evasion of tax by another person; or
(b) aids, abets, counsels or procures the commission of a UK tax evasion offence by another person; or
(c) is involved in the commission of an offence consisting of being knowingly concerned in, or taking steps with a view to, the fraudulent evasion of tax.

There are three stages to the offence under the Act:

(a) the criminal evasion of UK tax, i.e. the underlying tax evasion offence by taking steps with a view to or being knowingly concerned in the evasion of tax even if tax was not in fact evaded (this could be by way of common law

CRIMINAL FINANCES ACT 2017 AND TAX EVASION

offence of cheating the public revenue, or one of a range of statutory offences such as fraudulently evading VAT or income tax);
(b) the criminal facilitation of this offence by a person associated with the relevant body. The associated person must deliberately and dishonestly facilitate the taxpayer evading tax. If the associated person is found to have accidentally or negligently facilitated tax evasion, then no offence will be committed by the relevant body;
(c) the relevant body failing to prevent the associated person from committing that facilitation. This is a strict liability offence and if stages (a) and (b) have occurred then stage (c) is deemed to have taken place unless the relevant body can demonstrate it has put in place reasonable prevention measures.

As well as a UK offence, there is also a foreign offence (s.46). This offence is the same as the UK offence described above, but the tax evaded is non-UK tax. The relevant body in question must have sufficient nexus to the UK and be incorporated under UK law, be carrying on a business or part of a business in the UK or be a relevant body whose associated person is located within the UK at the time of the criminal act.

As well as the tax evasion being a criminal offence in the non-UK jurisdiction, it must also be an offence in the UK for it to be considered an offence under CFA 2017. Further, the non-UK jurisdiction must have an equivalent offence of criminal facilitation of tax evasion and the associated person's act would have been a crime in the UK had it occurred there.

Relevant bodies do not therefore need to understand what acts would be a criminal act in different jurisdictions unless the act being undertaken would be criminal in the UK. There is therefore no need to be well versed in tax evasion offences across the world. If the act is lawful in the UK but illegal in the non-UK jurisdiction, there can be no offence under CFA 2017.

Note that it is no prerequisite for bringing a prosecution under the Act for a conviction of the taxpayer to have taken place, though the prosecution would have to show beyond all reasonable doubt that the taxpayer level offence had been committed.

6.3 ASSOCIATED PERSONS

A really important element of this legislation is the associated person.
A 'person associated with a relevant body' is defined (s.44(4)) as a person who is:

(a) an employee of the relevant body who is acting in the capacity of an employee (in the case of a law firm, this would include partners and consultants);
(b) an agent of the body who is acting in their capacity as an agent; or
(c) any other person who performs services for and on behalf of the body who is acting in the capacity of a person performing such services.

A person acting in the capacity of an employee of the firm is an easy concept to understand – but agents can be a little trickier.

Those who act as agents may be experts that the body instructs, including counsel. These parties may therefore be construed as being associated persons. In the case of a law firm, most if not all such persons will be regulated persons and so will be subject to their own regulators' requirements and CFA 2017. A firm may therefore decide to consider these associated persons as being low risk.

However, if a firm were instructing a non-regulated person to provide a service which may cause them to be seen as an associated person, and they are providing advice which may include tax advice or be in a position which could afford the opportunity to commit a tax evasion offence, the firm needs to consider the risks of that instruction and whether it needs to ask some questions about the adherence to CFA 2017 by the person being instructed.

6.4 INVESTIGATIONS AND PENALTIES

Investigations in relation to the UK tax offence will be undertaken by HMRC and prosecutions brought by the Crown Prosecution Service (CPS). Investigation as to a foreign tax offence is undertaken by the Serious Fraud Office (SFO) or the National Crime Agency (NCA) and prosecutions brought by the SFO or the CPS.

Penalties for an offence under CFA 2017 are unlimited financial penalties and ancillary orders such as confiscation orders or prevention orders. Of course, the consequences do not stop there. A conviction will undoubtedly bring intense interest from regulators and bring reputational damage.

To mitigate penalties, early self-reporting is encouraged and is also seen in itself to be a reasonable measure put in place to prevent further criminal acts from occurring.

It is possible to reach an agreement with prosecutors under the supervision of a judge to allow a prosecution to be suspended for a defined period providing certain conditions are met by the relevant body. This can include the body making full reparation for the criminal behaviour without being convicted. These agreements (known as 'deferred prosecution agreements') must be considered by a judge to be in the interests of justice, fair, reasonable and proportionate.

6.5 PROSECUTIONS TO DATE AND HMRC RESEARCH

There have, at the time of writing, been no prosecutions by HMRC under CFA 2017, though it is thought investigations are underway. Such investigations may be due in part to the research that was undertaken and explored below.

HMRC commissioned research in late 2018 to understand the impact of the implementation of CFA 2017 and the resulting corporate criminal offences. This research, titled 'Evaluation of corporate behaviour change in response to the corporate criminal offences' (March 2019, **www.gov.uk/government/**

publications/evaluation-of-corporate-behaviour-change-in-response-to-the-corporate-criminal-offences) had the following objectives (para.1.2):

(a) to examine companies' and partnerships' awareness of the new corporate criminal offences; and
(b) to examine the extent to which the introduction of corporate criminal offences has resulted in changes to the culture and behaviour of companies and partnerships.

The researchers focused on a representative sample of UK companies and partnerships across all sectors of the economy, selected at random. Research was conducted by way of telephone interviews of 1,002 businesses, with the interviews lasting on average 12 minutes.

The research found that on average 25 per cent of businesses had heard of CFA 2017 and this figure rose with the size of the business. Therefore, a staggering 75 per cent of businesses had never heard of the Act and the offences it created. When asked whether the business understood what the new Act meant for their business, the finance and insurance sectors with 42 per cent and 33 per cent respectively confirmed that they did understand (para.2.1).

When asked how relevant the Act was to their business, 32 per cent confirmed their view that the Act was relevant to 'at least some extent', and 9 per cent believed that it was relevant 'to a great extent' (para.2.2). Again, the research found that larger businesses were more likely to be aware of the Act's relevance to their business (especially if they were multinational businesses) than smaller UK businesses.

In terms of changes made, 20 per cent of those surveyed had made changes because of the Act and 11 per cent were planning changes. However, the majority (64 per cent) had not made or did not plan to make any changes (para.2.2). Again, larger businesses were found either to have made changes or planned to make changes.

In terms of conducting a risk assessment (see below for guidance), at the time of the research 24 per cent of businesses had assessed the risk of being exposed to the facilitation of tax, again with larger business more likely to have assessed this risk.

The researchers found that around 60 per cent of businesses had not formally documented risk related to the facilitation of tax evasion, although larger businesses are more likely to have documented their risk assessment. The research showed that 70 per cent of businesses confirmed that they were not looking to make any changes in the next 12 months to their risk assessment procedures regarding the facilitation of tax evasion (para.3.1). Those who had heard of the Act and those who felt it was relevant to their business were also more likely to have formalised periodic review processes with documented findings.

Researchers asked whether businesses had undertaken any internal reviews into whether criminal facilitation of tax evasion had occurred, with 11 per cent confirming that they had done so. Those in the professional/administrative, information and communication and finance and insurance sectors were found most likely to have undertaken such a review.

The research found that just over 10 per cent of businesses required third parties such as subcontractors, suppliers or customers to adhere to procedures aimed at preventing the facilitation of tax evasion (para.3.3). Only two per cent of businesses said they had stopped working with third parties or discontinued a service, as a result of a risk assessment related to the facilitation of tax evasion.

In terms of procedures adopted to prevent the facilitation of tax evasion, over half of the businesses surveyed had such a procedure with larger businesses more likely. Financial and insurance sector businesses were more likely to have such procedures as well as those who are multinational.

The most common procedure in place related to due diligence on specific transactions or customers, prospective/existing employees or board members responsible for managing risks relating to facilitation of tax evasion. Around 35 per cent of those surveyed confirmed that any such procedures had been put in place at least partly due to the Act. When asked about future changes, 26 per cent of businesses stated that they intended to make changes in the following 12 months, with 20 per cent stating this was partly or wholly because of the Act (para.4.1).

In terms of raising awareness in the business, only eight per cent of businesses had undertaken internal or external training, and again training was more prevalent in larger businesses (para.5.1). Of those, around 60 per cent confirmed that awareness raising had occurred because of the Act. Of those surveyed, 19 per cent confirmed that they intended to undertake awareness activities in the following 12 months.

In relation to top level commitment, the research found that 30 per cent of businesses confirmed they had board members or senior directors with specific responsibility for risk detection and monitoring the prevention of the facilitation of tax evasion, and 20 per cent had appointed a senior figure or champion (para.5.2).

The research therefore highlighted that as at late 2018, business adoption of the steps required by CFA 2017 – and indeed the level of understanding of the Act itself – was relatively low.

Therefore, whilst there have been no prosecutions under the Act thus far, they could be yet to come.

6.6 UNEXPLAINED WEALTH ORDERS

6.6.1 Overview

Further to the insertion of POCA 2002, Part 8, ss.362A–362T, CFA 2017, s.1 introduced for the first time the concept of an unexplained wealth order (UWO). This is a form of court order which compels the recipient to explain their wealth. A UWO can be applied for by the National Crime Agency, Crown Prosecution Service, Her Majesty's Revenue and Customs, Financial Conduct Authority and the

Serious Fraud Office. For a UWO to be granted, the court must be satisfied that there are reasonable grounds to suspect that the known sources of the individual's income would not be enough to enable them to acquire the property that they hold (and the property value exceeds £50,000) and that either the individual is a politically exposed person (PEP) or there is a reasonable suspicion that they are involved in serious crime.

Persons who fail to account for their wealth under one of these orders are liable to have assets seized.

UWOs are interesting as a concept, as the burden for proving the source of the wealth falls to the individual holding the wealth as opposed to authorities who have suspicions about it.

6.6.2 Examples

UWOs are still relatively new, infrequently used and not always successful.

6.6.2.1 First UWO

Once notable case is that of *Hajiyeva* v. *National Crime Agency* [2020] EWCA Civ 108, the recipient of the first UWO to be made.

Mrs Hajiyeva was married to Jahangir Hajiyev, the former chairman of the International Bank of Azerbaijan. Mr Hajiyev had been accused of embezzling public funds amounting to around 125 million euro. Mr Hajiyev was convicted and sentenced in Azerbaijan for 15 years, and it is thought that his criminal activity led to more than $9 billion of the financial turnover of Azerbaijan being laundered.

Mrs Hajiyeva, through this case, became famous for her spending in UK luxury department store Harrods, which came to around £16 million between 2006 and 2016. She also owned a five-bedroom house in Knightsbridge, a golf club in Ascot and a private jet. Given her husband's conviction, unsurprisingly the authorities wanted to understand where Mrs Hajiyeva's wealth came from, and a UWO was made in 2018.

Mrs Hajiyeva appealed the court order on the basis that it had been granted by the judge on the back of her husband's conviction, which she said had been obtained unfairly. Secondly, she also argued that the definition of PEP under the Proceeds of Crime Act (POCA) 2002 required the person to be entrusted with a prominent public function imposed by the state.

The Court of Appeal rejected both of Mrs Hajiyeva's arguments. In relation to the first, it found that the NCA did not rely solely on the conviction of her husband to obtain a UWO against her; it had also relied on the fact that his income from employment and business ventures would not have enabled him to buy the property he had. In relation to Mrs Hajiyeva's argument about the definition of a PEP, the court rejected the notion that a prominent public function needed to have been granted by the state. Further, the court found that as the bank in which Mr Hajiyev a prominent position was a state-owned enterprise, he fell within the definition of a PEP and therefore as his wife, Mrs Hajiyeva was also a PEP.

Interestingly, Mrs Hajiyeva also argued that the UWO offended the rules of self-incrimination and also spousal privilege – statements made under a UWO cannot be used in evidence against the giver of the statement in a criminal prosecution. This protection is, however, limited to prosecutions in the UK, and Mrs Hajiyeva argued that the statement she would give could be used against her in Azerbaijan. The court found that the prospects of Mrs Hajiyeva being prosecuted in the UK or Azerbaijan was low, and further that the statutory scheme giving rise to UWOs has impliedly revoked spousal privilege.

As at early 2020, Mrs Hajiyeva's UWO was therefore in place and she is required to comply with it.

6.6.2.2 UWO implemented through to its end

For a UWO that has been successfully implemented through to its end, we have the case of Mansoor Mahmood Hussain, a Leeds businessman who in August 2020 handed over 45 properties and other assets with a combined value of around £9.8 million. Mr Hussain is alleged to have associated with gangsters, a murderer and drug trafficker. Though he was never convicted of a crime, enough suspicion was raised as to how Mr Hussain obtained his wealth (and for which he paid no income tax in some years) to enable the court to grant a UWO.

Although on the face of it, it may appear that Mr Hussain has got away without prosecution, the settlement with the NCA has ultimately saved a small fortune in taxpayers' money and does not close the door on future prosecutions – though Mr Hussain's response to the UWO cannot be used against him.

6.6.2.3 Unsuccessful cases

Not all UWOs (of which there have been a little more than a handful) have been successful, however. The NCA lost its case in *NCA v. Baker* [2020] EWHC 822 (Admin) concerning three UWOs made without notice in May 2019 relating to properties worth £80 million.

Mr Baker was a solicitor specialising in trusts and tax planning and was also the president of charitable foundations that were the registered owners of the properties in question. The UWOs were obtained on the basis that the monies that had been used to purchase the properties were in fact the laundered proceeds of crime stemming from criminal conduct of a deceased Kazakhstan national, Rakhat Aliyev.

Mr Baker challenged the UWOs on three bases:

(a) that the NCA had made errors of law in its application of the statutory framework requirements for UWOs;

(b) that there was material non-disclosure at the ex parte hearing by the NCA and that the NCA had made inadequate enquiries; and
(c) that additional information that had come to light since the orders were made demonstrated that the UWOs were sought on a basis that was flawed.

The High Court discharged the UWOs on the basis of the above, and went on to set out that the fact that property is held through complex offshore structures or trusts does not necessarily mean that the structures are being used for the purposes of laundering money.

Overall, a UWO is a powerful tool for the NCA and is one that is likely to be used more often.

6.7 ACCOUNT FREEZING ORDERS

Further to the insertion of POCA 2002, Part 5, s.303Z, CFA 2017, s.16 created the ability for enforcement officers to apply to a magistrate for an account freezing order (AFO). These orders freeze funds held in bank accounts and building societies.

To obtain an AFO, the enforcement officer must have reasonable grounds to suspect that money (of which there must be more than £1,000 held in the account in question) held is 'recoverable property' (on the balance of probabilities the monies were obtained through unlawful conduct) or intended for use in unlawful conduct. No criminal conviction is required.

The *Financial Times* reported in its article 'HMRC profits by new powers to crack down on illicit finance' (May 2020, **www.ft.com/content/bc4128d8-8bd7-4088-aae6-8d7686e26fda**) that HMRC had frozen 166 bank and building society accounts via AFOs in the 2019/2020 tax year preventing access to or withdrawals from £19.5 million which it suspected had resulted from criminal conduct. This was an increase for HMRC who in the prior year had obtained orders to freeze 60 accounts totalling £8 million. According to the *Financial Times* article, the reason for the increase is the ease with which an AFO can be obtained due to the lower threshold required, i.e. reasonable grounds to suspect monies have been obtained by unlawful conduct. Further, because AFOs may be obtained via the magistrates' court as opposed to a UWO obtained via the High Court, they are less costly to achieve.

Once an account has been frozen, the monies contained in it can be subject to a forfeiture order if the court is satisfied that the monies are recoverable or were intended to be used in unlawful conduct.

An account forfeiture notice can also be issued, and this will set out the monies to be taken and the period of time available for objection. If no objection is raised, then an order is made. The order is capable of appeal for 30 days after being made.

6.8 IMPLEMENTING COMPLIANCE

To achieve compliance with CFA 2017, one of the first steps is to consider the guidance provided by HMRC ('Tackling tax evasion 2017' – see **6.1**) and for a shorter read the Law Society's practice note 'Criminal Finances Act 2017' (27 January 2020, **www.lawsociety.org.uk/topics/tax/criminal-finances-act-2017#sub-menu-dy5**).

HMRC indicated that, while it did not expect businesses to have had everything in place by the time of the Act coming into force on 30 September 2017, it did expect businesses to have taken some steps towards compliance and have a plan of action. We are now a few years on from the implementation of the Act and compliance should already be in place. Whether you are complying for the first time or revisiting your compliance, below are the steps that should be taken.

In all steps, remember to write down your plans, processes and methodology for production to the SRA or HMRC or other body should they conduct further research or investigate your firm.

6.8.1 Step one – risk assessment

The first step is to conduct a firm-wide risk assessment to enable your firm to inform itself how these risks can be mitigated. There is no set risk assessment to complete and you should tailor it to your own firm dependent on size, type of work conducted and clients. See **Appendix C1** for a template.

In accordance with HMRC guidance, the assessment should cover commonly encountered risks which it sets out are (pp.17–18):

(a) **Country risk** – Where there are high levels of secrecy or use as a tax shelter.
(b) **Sectoral risk** – Such as financial services, tax advisory and legal sectors.
(c) **Transaction risk** – Such as complex tax planning involving high levels of secrecy or transactions involving PEPs.
(d) **Business opportunity risk** – These might arise in high value projects or with projects involving many parties, jurisdictions and intermediaries.
(e) **Business partnership risk** – Some relationships may involve higher risk, for example, the use of intermediaries where they are based in jurisdictions with lower levels of transparency and disclosure. Further, the HMRC guidance sets out that a risk here is entering into a business partnership with organisations that have no fraud prevention procedures or are known to have deficiencies in their fraud procedures.
(f) **Product risk** – Certain products and services may have a higher risk of misuse by either clients or associated persons.
(g) **Customer risk** – The HMRC guidance sets out that if a business has a particular risk related to customers or products it is highly likely to indicate that there is a risk of criminal facilitation of tax evasion by an associated person.

CRIMINAL FINANCES ACT 2017 AND TAX EVASION

The firm needs to translate these risks into questions that it poses to itself in the form of a risk assessment.

The HMRC guidance also sets out that the risk assessment should consider the extent to which the relevant body's internal structures or procedures may themselves add to the level of risk. For example (p.20):

- deficiencies in employee training, skills and knowledge;
- a bonus culture that rewards excessive risk taking;
- lack of clarity on the organisation's policies on, and procedures for, the provision of high-risk services and products;
- deficiencies in the organisation's submission of suspicious activity reports (SARs);
- lack of clear financial controls or whistleblowing procedures;
- lack of clear messaging from top-level management on refusing to engage in tax fraud.

Below are sets of questions that you may wish to consider and then score accordingly (either by way of low, medium or high risk; or by reference to whether the situation would arise, be that never, rarely, sometimes or often; or by way of a traffic-light scoring system; and so on). This is a small sample set of questions to kick-start the process – firms will need to add more to suit their business.

1. Clients:
    - Does the firm act for clients whom the firm has reason to suspect of tax evasion in the past or present?
    - Does the firm act for clients who may pose particular tax evasion risk? For example, because they are cash-based, have assets in higher risk jurisdictions or hold assets through complex or obscure ownership structures.
    - Does the firm act for PEPs? And does the firm have proper procedures in place around the discovery of source of funds and wealth?

2. Services:
    - Does the firm advise clients on tax?
    - Does the firm assist in creating corporate or tax structures which may be used to facilitate tax evasion?
    - Does the firm act on matters connected to tax havens?
    - Does the firm set up structures to minimise tax?

3. Employees:
    - Does the firm have a lack of supervision anywhere?
    - Does the firm ensure that appropriate checks are carried out before employment?
    - Is there a culture of compliance in the firm and can it be better?
    - Do any employees display an ignorant attitude to compliance?

CRIMINAL FINANCES AND INVESTIGATIONS

- Do employees receive training on tax evasion?

4. Firm risk:
    - Does the firm contract with suppliers who may pose a high tax evasion risk due to their work or geographical location?
    - Does the firm have in place a procurement process to minimise the risk of being associated with a business that engages in tax evasion?

The Law Society practice note 'Criminal Finances Act 2017' provides further detail on the risk assessment and so further guidance can be found there.

After analysing the risk assessment, the firm needs to draw up a plan of any changes that need to be made and obtain approval of these changes and the risk assessment from senior management. These changes might include an amendment to the firm's client and matter risk assessment template; how to vet third parties/ suppliers; how and who to train; whether a new anti-tax evasion question forms part of your firm's file review/audit process; and so on.

6.8.2 Step two – policy implementation

The firm will need a documented 'anti-tax evasion policy'. See **Appendix C2** for a template policy.

As with the risk assessment, there is no set template to use and it should be tailored to your own firm. The policy will need to set out:

- what CFA 2017 says;
- what the commitment of the firm is, i.e. to do business ethically and in accordance with its obligations under regulations and relevant laws;
- what the firm expects of its staff/employees and external people (this could include how the firm will treat the vetting of those the firm instructs such as counsel – remember that a risk-based approach can be adopted and so if the firm is instructing regulated persons the firm may wish to consider the risk to be low; however, if the firm is instructing non-regulated persons, the risk may be higher and so questions may need to be asked about their own policies, procedures and controls);
- what the facilitation of tax evasion is, how the firm's staff/employees can unwittingly become involved, and how they can spot it;
- the duty on all staff/employees to report and to whom (this could be tied in with the firm's whistleblowing policy; see **Chapter 9**);
- practical examples of tax evasion in each practice area (e.g. delivering misleading or inaccurate bills which enables a client to evade tax or misstating the value of a property so that less stamp duty land tax (SDLT) is payable or assisting in the creation of corporate or trust structures designed to conceal taxable income; the more practical the examples the better, so staff really understand how it can

happen in their everyday practice and if possible it is a good idea to use examples that have actually occurred in the firm (without naming names of course)).

This policy needs approval from senior management.

6.8.3 Step three – implementation

Now that the risk assessment has been conducted and an appropriate policy written, the policy will need to be communicated to the firm. This could be by email, in a meeting, on the firm's intranet, by internal memo – whatever suits the firm size, is proportionate and appropriate. The firm might want to adopt a different approach for different practice areas. For example, those who work in tax and private client could be called to a meeting as those practice areas may be considered to be higher risk for the purposes of the legislation, and the firm may decide to simply email everyone else. It does not have to be a 'one size fits all' approach, and overall should be proportionate.

Whatever is decided, the firm should document its decision and reasons (remember, if an offence is committed by an associated person, the firm's defence is that it took reasonable steps to prevent the offence occurring – so the firm may need to prove what it has done and why it took the route that it did).

6.8.4 Step four – training

The fourth step is to provide appropriate training. It might be that not everyone in the firm needs to be trained face to face (in person or virtually). Training could be by way of an online module, a meeting/talk, seminar, webinar and so on. Whatever is chosen, it must be proportionate to the risk and the firm size. Again, what is decided should be documented so that the firm can adequately defend itself should a claim that a breach of CFA 2017 has taken place.

6.8.5 Step five – keep reviewing

It is relatively easy to put in place compliance measures at the initial implementation of a new piece of regulation or law – and then not revisit that compliance thereafter. To enable the firm to keep up its ability to defend itself should a claim arise that it had failed to take steps to prevent the facilitation of tax evasion by one of its associated persons, the firm needs to keep its compliance steps up to date.

How often to review compliance is dependent on risk exposure. For example:

- If the firm considers itself low risk, then it could review its compliance going through the steps outlined above every two to three years.
- If the firm considers itself medium risk, then the above steps could be repeated every one to two years, and periodically through file audits/reviews.

CRIMINAL FINANCES AND INVESTIGATIONS

- If the firm considers itself high risk either in all areas of the business or in certain areas, then it may decide to review compliance every year and add an additional question to the file audit/reviews, plus conduct a targeted batch of file audits/reviews every year, six months or quarterly.

What is the right level of continuing review of compliance with CFA 2017 is down to the firm to decide. It is important to write down what the compliance regime will be, but the firm should be realistic about what it can achieve.

6.9 PRACTICAL EXAMPLES OF TAX EVASION

Below are some practical examples of tax evasion that may arise in a law firm. These have been replicated in the template anti-tax evasion policy at **Appendix C2**.

6.9.1 In any practice area

- Delivering a misleading or inaccurate bill which enables a client to evade tax. For example, billing a company for work actually done for its directors or shareholders in order to assist clients to claim a tax deduction to which they are not entitled. This is likely to be VAT fraud.

6.9.2 Property

- Preparing documents which misstate the price of a property to enable a client to evade SDLT or capital gains tax (CGT).
- Assisting in a property being bought using nominees or other structures to enable a client to illegally avoid tax.

6.9.3 Corporate

- Assisting in creating corporate or trust structures designed to conceal a client's taxable income or assets.
- Referring clients to third parties in tax havens to set up accounts or structures which you know are to facilitate tax evasion, rather than tax avoidance.
- Using side letters so that aspects of a transaction with taxable effects are not apparent from reading the main agreement in order to enable a client, or anyone else, to evade tax.

6.9.4 Wills and probate

- Assisting in creating trust or other structures designed to conceal a client's taxable income or assets.
- Giving clients advice on how to make lifetime transfers in ways which HMRC will find difficult to detect.

- Preparing documents which misstate the value of an estate in order to avoid inheritance tax.

6.9.5 Family law

- Helping a client to put forward figures which you know to be false may involve a number of offences, possibly including conspiracy to pervert the course of justice and tax evasion offences.
- Clients who have been ordered to disclose their earnings in connection with family proceedings may tell the solicitor acting that they have committed tax evasion in the past. That information will normally be privileged and is not normally reportable under money laundering regulations. However, in such cases the solicitor should discuss the matter with the money laundering reporting officer (MLRO) or compliance officer for legal practice (COLP) to ensure that their involvement in the case will not create any liabilities or concerns.

6.10 OTHER TAX AVOIDANCE RULES

In addition to, but separate from CFA 2017, there is a body of anti-tax evasion rules that law firms and their solicitors, particularly those who advise on tax planning, should be aware of. These are briefly outlined here. Please remember this is not a book about tax, and so these rules are outlined at a high level.

6.10.1 General anti-abuse rule

The general anti-abuse rule (GAAR) came into effect on 17 July 2013 under Finance Act 2013, Part 5 and was implemented to deter taxpayers from entering into abusive arrangements and to deter would-be promoters of such arrangements (these could be solicitors or accountants). Under the rule, if a taxpayer goes ahead and implements an abusive tax scheme, then the rules allow the tax to be adjusted.

A tax arrangement is deemed to be abusive if one of the main purposes is to obtain a tax advantage. 'Tax advantage' is broadly defined under Finance Act 2013, s.208. Non-abusive tax regimes do not come within the ambit of the rules.

As one would expect, the rule applies to a large range of taxes such as income tax, CGT, inheritance tax, corporation tax, SDLT and so on.

For further reading on the rule, see HMRC, 'General anti-abuse rule (GAAR) guidance' (11 September 2020, **www.gov.uk/government/publications/tax-avoidance-general-anti-abuse-rules**).

CRIMINAL FINANCES AND INVESTIGATIONS

6.10.2 Serial tax avoidance regime

As a consequence of CFA 2017, the serial tax avoidance regime (STAR) came into force on 15 September 2016 and affected those who made use of avoidance schemes from 6 April 2017.

Certain schemes defeated after challenge by HMRC after 5 April 2017 are taken into account when HMRC considers whether a taxpayer is affected by the STAR.

The types of schemes taken into account are those:

- that have been counteracted under GAAR;
- where HMRC has sent a follower notice;
- that fall under the disclosure of tax avoidance schemes (DOTAS) rules;
- that are notified or notifiable under the VAT avoidance disclosure regime (VADR) rules;
- that fall under the disclosure of tax avoidance schemes for VAT and other indirect taxes (DASVOIT) rules.

If a taxpayer has used one of these types of schemes and that was defeated after 5 April 2017 and they have not fully disclosed the scheme, they may receive a warning notice and be requested to send extra information to HMRC.

If the taxpayer has been given a warning notice under the regime, but continues using tax avoidance schemes, they may have sanctions imposed against them, which could include penalties, being publicly named as a serial tax avoider and/or restrictions to direct tax relief.

These rules clearly apply to taxpayers and not solicitors, although if a solicitor is advising a client on such schemes this can of course cause conduct issues as explored below.

6.11 PROFESSIONAL CONDUCT, SRA WARNING NOTICES AND THE SDT

Clearly, assisting clients with avoiding tax by implementing avoidance schemes carries with it significant risk of breaching the SRA Standards and Regulations, and in particular the following SRA principles:

- principle 1 – acting in a way that upholds the constitutional principle of the rule of law, and the proper administration of justice;
- principle 2 – acting in a way that upholds public trust and confidence in the solicitors' profession and in legal services provided by authorised persons;
- principle 3 – acting with independence (perhaps if there is a significant uplift in fee for the use of a scheme designed by a firm);
- principle 4 – acting with honesty;
- principle 5 – acting with integrity;
- principle 7 – acting in the best interests of each client.

To that end, the SRA in 2012 issued a warning notice on the use of SDLT avoidance schemes. This warning notice is no longer available, as the SRA does not make archived notices available (which makes it impossible for firms to assess prior conduct against such warning notices); however, it is summarised below.

The warning notice on SDLT avoidance schemes set out that such schemes were designed to reduce or eliminate the correct level of stamp duty payable on a property. These schemes led to a warning from HMRC which set out: 'Where HMRC find property sale arrangements that have been artificially structured to avoid paying the correct amount of SDLT HMRC will seek to actively challenge those, through the courts where appropriate' ('Guidance: Stamp Duty Land Tax avoidance (Spotlight 10)', 5 August 2010, **www.gov.uk/government/publications/spotlight-10-stamp-duty-land-tax-avoidance-7-june-2010**). The SRA warning notice set out that the *Times* newspaper reported that the loss to HMRC from such schemes was estimated conservatively at £500 million but that it could be as much as £1 billion.

The warning notice set out that the then principles of integrity, independence, acting in the best interests of the client and behaving in a way that maintains the trust the public places in you and the provision of legal services, come into play because buyers will rely on their solicitor to act in line with the principles and promoting/advising a client to adopt such a scheme is counter to those principles.

The warning notice set out that the SRA will scrutinise the implementation of such schemes closely and was taking action in a number of cases (see below for one example).

The warning notice went on to set out some of the factors that may be relevant in determining whether an SDLT scheme was in the best interests of the client. These were:

The SDLT scheme

- SDLT schemes are constantly changing and are usually very complex, bearing in mind what purchasers want to achieve. HMRC publish information on schemes which have been discredited [see HMRC, Spotlight 10 above]
- Be wary of claims by promoters of SDLT schemes that the scheme is backed by a 'robust counsel's opinion'. Based on what we have seen, we warn that you must check that the opinion

  – is genuine,
  – has not been tampered with,
  – is up to date, and
  – specifically covers the scheme which is being promoted.
- Bear in mind that reliance on counsel's opinion is not necessarily a defence to allegations of breaches of the Principles, and such a position is substantially weaker if the opinion has not been obtained by you for the particular client and the transaction in which you are acting;
- Be wary of claims that the SDLT scheme is approved by HMRC. Be aware that disclosure of the scheme to HMRC, and the issue of a scheme reference number by HMRC, is not confirmation the scheme is backed by HMRC;
- Be aware that HMRC can currently challenge SDLT schemes up to four years after the effective date of the transaction and this can be extended if there has been a careless or deliberate error in the submission of the SDLT return;

- Consider carrying out due diligence on the promoter of the SDLT scheme. If the promoter claims they will repay the fee charged for implementing the scheme, robustly check how realistic this is, bearing in mind that HMRC has four years to challenge the scheme. If the promoter is unable to repay the fee, the buyer may look to you to reimburse them;
- If the SDLT scheme is based on a supposed 'no win no fee' basis said to be backed by insurance, robustly check that the policy is suitable and relevant to the purchasers circumstances.

The buyers

- Make sure that you have properly considered all the clients' interests and that no client will be disadvantaged by the scheme;
- Ensure that you account to the buyer for any benefit received by you, and disclose any referral arrangement connected to the scheme.

The lender

- If you act for a lender as well as the buyer, robust consideration needs to be given to whether the scheme could prejudice the interests of the lender. It is our view that it is likely to be very important to ensure that the lender is fully informed that the property is subject to an SDLT scheme with sufficient detail of how the scheme operates. Recent findings by the SDT would support this approach.

Although this warning notice is archived, it is still good guidance.

The SRA's current warning notice on tax is called 'Tax avoidance your duties' (**www.sra.org.uk/solicitors/guidance/tax-avoidance-duties/**). This notice was first published on 21 September 2017 and revised when the new SRA Standards and Regulations were implemented on 25 November 2019.

The notice is aimed at all those the SRA regulates 'involved either directly or indirectly advising clients about tax, handling client matters or transactions involving them in the design, implementation, organisation or management of tax affairs, schemes or arrangements'.

As well as setting out that principles 1, 2, 5 and 7 apply, the warning notice also points out that the following aspects of the SRA Code of Conduct for Solicitors, RELs and RFLs and Code of Conduct for Firms could come into play:

- Paragraphs 1.4 of the codes provide that you must not mislead or attempt to mislead others, either by your own acts or omissions or allowing or being complicit in the acts or omissions of others (including your client).
- Paragraph 3.2 of the code of conduct for solicitors, RELs and RFLs says you must ensure the service you provide to clients is competent and delivered in a timely manner.
- Paragraph 3.4 of the code for conduct of solicitors, RELs and RFLs and 4.2 of the code of conduct for firms says you must consider and take account of your client's attributes, needs and circumstances.
- Paragraph 8.6 of the code for solicitors, RELs and RFLs provides that you must give clients information in a way they can understand and you ensure they are in a position to make informed decisions about the services they need, how their matter will be handled and the options available to them.
- Paragraph 4.3 of the code for firms says you must make sure your managers and employees are competent to carry out their roles, and keep their professional

knowledge and skills, as well as understanding of their legal, ethical and regulatory obligations, up to date. Similarly, paragraph 3.3 of the code for solicitors, RELs and RFLs provides that you must maintain your own competence to carry out your role and keep your professional knowledge and skills up to date.
- Paragraph 1.2 of both codes requires that you do not abuse your position by taking unfair advantage of clients or others.

The notice goes on to state that the SRA is concerned that those it regulates may facilitate tax avoidance schemes, and it references the case of *SRA* v. *Chan, Ali and Abode Solicitors* [2015] EWHC 2659 (Admin) which is outlined below.

The notice sets out that solicitors are in a position of trust and owe duties to their client to act in their best interests whilst ensuring that advice does not go beyond the lawful arrangements of the client's affairs. The SRA expects solicitors to act with integrity and deal with HMRC openly and honestly and to not take advantage of HMRC's lack of knowledge of the client's tax position.

In its notice, the SRA provides the following warning:

> When advising a client on avoidance of tax schemes you should make clear that any avoidance arrangements the client enters into might deliver tax outcomes that were never envisaged or intended by Parliament and may be challenged. You should be clear as to the legal implications, the costs and penalties of non-compliance should the arrangement fail.
> You should also consider your own position in facilitating such an arrangement. Should the arrangement be found to be abusive, your conduct may be called into question. To be involved in such arrangements is likely to reflect badly on you and to damage public confidence in those delivering legal services. You will leave yourself open to the risk of disciplinary proceedings as well as committing a criminal offence. Where you believe, as a consequence of your client's instructions, you are at risk then you should advise your client you cannot comply with their instructions and unless they change instructions you should terminate your retainer.

It should also be said that advising on such schemes and not providing adequate warning to the client that they may be successfully challenged can lead to negligence claims.

The SRA warning notice also sets out that solicitors should be familiar with HMRC's rapidly changing and toughening stance on avoidance schemes as set out in its GAAR (see above).

Finally, the warning notice sets out that the SRA expects solicitors to be familiar with the HMRC-endorsed 'Professional Conduct in Relation to Taxation' (PCRT) (1 March 2019, **www.icaew.com/technical/tax/pcrt**) and adhere to the standards contained therein.

As foreshadowed above, in the case of *SRA* v. *Chan, Ali and Abode Solicitors* the SRA appealed the decision of the SDT to the High Court. This case concerned solicitors Mr Chan, Mr Ali and Abode Solicitors Ltd and their running of schemes designed to avoid or mitigate the impact of SDLT in conveyancing transactions. It was reported that Abode had completed 556 conveyancing transactions involving such schemes between 2009 and 2012, reaping a financial benefit to the firm of approximately £995,000. The SRA's case was that the schemes were aggressive and risky and the solicitors had ignored counsel's advice to inform clients of this fact and that there was no guarantee of success.

In terms of the schemes, there were four separate types, with one scheme facilitated through an offshore company whose directors and shareholders were the very same Mr Chan and Mr Ali.

At first instance the SDT held that the solicitors acted in breach of the Solicitors Code of Conduct 2007 and Solicitors Accounts Rules 2011. It also held that the solicitors were incompetent and did not see their failings. The SDT did not, however, go further to find that the solicitors had acted without integrity or independence or in such a way so as to diminish public trust in the profession. Mr Chan and Mr Ali were fined £15,000 each and the firm had its status as a recognised body to provide legal services revoked.

The SRA appealed the SDT's findings on that basis that in its view the SDT should have gone further and held that the solicitors lacked integrity, acted with a lack of independence, acted in a manner that diminished the public trust in them and in the provision of legal services and that the solicitors had not been connected with a business that was reputable. To that end, the SRA sought the striking off of Mr Chan and Mr Ali.

After chastising the SRA for the unwieldy way that it drafted the allegations which were punctured with many 'and/ors' or 'alternativelys', the High Court held that the SDT was wrong to make the findings that it did on the basis of the facts it established. Further, it held that the solicitors knew what they were doing and put their financial interests before the interests of their clients. The High Court went on to conclude that there had been a lack of integrity, failure to act with independence and that the solicitors had acted in a way that diminishes the trust the public would place in the solicitors and in the provision of legal services. The High Court felt unable to determine whether the solicitors should be struck off, and remitted the case back to the SDT. The SDT subsequently decided to suspend the solicitors for three years and ordered them to pay costs of £5,500.

In another case, law firm Simpson Millar accepted a rebuke and fine of £2,000 from the SRA for its role in promoting SDLT avoidance schemes for which there was an underpayment to HMRC of around £4.5 million. The firm had advised on 234 avoidance schemes and had also advised other law firms in approximately 80 further cases. In total the firm had made nearly £400,000 from the schemes. The SRA reported that the clients were not advised as to the risks arising from the way in which the property would be held as a consequence of the scheme's operation.

The firm admitted that it had acted where there was a conflict of interests or a significant risk of one as it was acting for both borrower and lender and it had not informed the lender of the schemes being adopted. Further, the firm admitted its failure to act in the best interests of the clients. In its defence the firm had taken instructions on these schemes for around 11 months only and had ceased acting on such schemes of its own volition. Further it was said that the monies amounted to less than one per cent of the firm's revenue.

Staggeringly the SRA's investigation took six years, during which time the law firm co-operated fully.

In contrast to the above two cases is the case of Jonathan Peter Mounteney. Mr Mounteney advised corporate clients on the tax element of the SDLT schemes, as opposed to the underlying conveyancing transaction. In each case he had followed the advice of counsel (although in a strange twist, one of those counsel's opinions had in fact been forged by another solicitor, but the SDT held that there was no reason for Mr Mounteney to have known or suspected that to be the case) and two of the schemes actually worked.

The SDT found that Mr Mounteney did not fail in his duties and had in fact ceased his involvement in the schemes when they became too risky. Further, the nature of Mr Mounteney's retainer was that the clients had their own independent conveyancing solicitors and were therefore separately advised. In the light of these facts, the SDT dismissed the case against Mr Mounteney and refused to order costs against him. The SDT did, however, note that the SRA had properly brought the case.

6.12 SRA VISITS

In the SRA's 2020–2021 business plan it announced plans to undertake a thematic review of tax advice given to clients. As the detail provided was vague, it is not clear whether this is to ensure that those who conduct tax advice work are complying with the AML Regulations (Money Laundering, Terrorist Financing and Transfer of Funds (Information on the Payer) Regulations 2017, SI 2017/692) or whether this is to ensure that no avoidance schemes are being implemented by firms – or indeed, both.

CHAPTER 7

Responding to a criminal investigation

7.1 INTRODUCTION

Given the breadth of financial crime legislation and regulation with which law firms need to comply, the fact that law firms are sometimes involved in the commission of financial crime and the fact that they are rich in information pertaining to such crimes, it is possible for law firms to be subject to production orders or disclosure notices.

In this chapter we navigate the substance of these orders and notices and what steps need to be considered when replying to one.

The Law Society's practice note, 'Responding to a financial crime investigation' (22 January 2020, **www.lawsociety.org.uk/en/topics/anti-money-laundering/responding-to-a-financial-crime-investigation**) should be consulted if an order or notice is served on the firm.

7.2 PRODUCTION ORDERS

A production order is granted by a court ordering the recipient to produce specified documents that are not privileged within a certain timeframe. Generally speaking, a production order is applied for by the police and is without notice. However, it is always possible that a police officer will contact the law firm first to ask whether the solicitor will give the information without a production order. Law firms should require an order to be sought and made before providing documentation, as to grant the order a judge needs to assess the merits of such an application and the application for the order may not be successful. Further, a client cannot reasonably be upset if the firm has been ordered to hand information over.

The power to grant a production order is found in Proceeds of Crime Act (POCA) 2002, s.345 which sets out that a judge may make an order if the person specified in the application (that is, the law firm's client) is subject to a confiscation investigation or money laundering investigation, or property specified is subject to a civil recovery investigation. The application must set out that the order is sought for the purposes of the investigation and in relation to the material specified in the application and that the person specified appears to be in possession or control of the material. Finally, s.345 sets out that a production order is an order either requiring the person who appears to be possession or control of the material to produce it to an appropriate officer or requiring that person to give an appropriate officer access to the material.

The normal timeframe for compliance is seven days. However, police officers are often happy to grant more time, depending on urgency.

Failure to comply with such an order could result in proceedings for contempt of court. An order can be challenged if it relates to a criminal investigation, but not if it relates to a civil recovery investigation. Reasons for challenge include inadequate description of the material sought. To prevent challenges to orders, police officers will usually try to gauge from law firms what information they have so that the order is correctly drafted. Law firms need to be careful how much information is given without the protection of an order in the first place, as breach of confidentiality may occur.

Production orders can also be granted under Taxes Management Act 1970, s.20BA and Police and Criminal Evidence Act 1984, Sched.1.

7.3 NOTICE TO DISCLOSE

A notice to disclose is not a court order and is generally made without notice. Notice to disclose can be made under Serious Organised Crime and Police Act (SOCPA) 2005, s.62 and Criminal Justice Act (CJA) 1987, s.2.

Such notices require a person to answer questions, provide information or produce documents to a constable, the National Crime Agency (NCA) or HM Revenue and Customs (HMRC).

The notice will explain what is required and by what date. Failure to comply may mean the investigator will seek to obtain a warrant to enter and seize relevant material or prosecute the non-complying party. Such notices are capable of being challenged by judicial review.

Under SOCPA 2005, s.61 a notice to disclose may be produced where the investigating authority has reasonable grounds to suspect that a relevant offence is being committed, knows that the person to whom the order is being directed has information and has reasonable grounds to suspect that information is likely to be of substantial value to the investigation. The relevant offences are bribery, POCA 2002 lifestyle offences (i.e. leading a criminal lifestyle), terrorism offences, failure to prevent the facilitation of tax evasion and other tax offences.

Such notices can be issued by the Director of Public Prosecutions (DPP), the Lord Advocate or the Director of Public Prosecutions for Northern Ireland or by the authority to which one of those persons delegates the exercise of their powers.

A notice to disclose under CJA 1987, s.2 can be issued if the Serious Fraud Office (SFO) has reasonable grounds for suspecting that an offence involving serious or complex fraud has been committed. The notice itself is issued by the Director of the SFO or any investigator authorised by the Director to exercise such power on their behalf.

CRIMINAL FINANCES AND INVESTIGATIONS

7.4 OTHER ORDERS

There are other orders that can be made as follows.

7.4.1 Notice to produce under Finance Act 2008, Sched.36

This notice will require the recipient to provide information or produce documents in order for HMRC to investigate the tax position of another person. These notices can be issued by inspectors and officers of HMRC and the timeframe for compliance will be set out in the notice. Failure to comply carries a relatively light penalty of £300 plus daily penalties of up to £60 for each day on which the failure continues.

7.4.2 Further information order under POCA 2002, s.336ZH

Here a magistrates' court may make an order requiring a firm to provide information to the NCA following submission of a protected or an authorised disclosure.

The order is applied for by the NCA and the order can be made if the following are satisfied:

- the information required relates to a matter arising from either a protected or an authorised disclosure;
- the person required to provide the information either made the disclosure or is otherwise carrying on business in the regulated sector;
- the information would assist in an investigation into money laundering;
- it's reasonable in all the circumstances for the information to be provided.

This order needs to be made on notice unless a court directs otherwise. The assumption is that an order will be sought when a money laundering reporting officer (MLRO) who has made a suspicious activity report (SAR) refuses to provide further information. The order itself will set out the information ordered to be produced and the timescale.

Failure to comply carries a penalty of up to £5,000 imposed by the magistrates' court. Again, this seems quite lenient in light of the seriousness of the order.

7.5 PRACTICAL CONSIDERATIONS

Below are some practical considerations when in receipt of one of the order types explored above. Again, a visit to the Law Society's practice note, 'Responding to a financial crime investigation' (see **7.1**), would not go amiss.

7.5.1 Check the wording

The firm needs to consider whether the order or notice has been drawn up correctly, citing the correct law, the correct client and correct information. If anything is not correct, then the firm may need to ask for the order or notice to be amended.

7.5.2 Confidentiality and privilege

The SRA Codes of Conduct require solicitors and firms to keep their clients' affairs confidential. For this reason, any enquiries from enforcement agencies about what information the firm may have need to be answered carefully. Once an order has been made or a notice produced, the client's confidential information can be provided.

Generally speaking, it is not a breach of the Data Protection Act 2018 to provide information for the purposes of prevention, detection or investigation of a crime.

Privilege, however, is not eroded by an order or a notice and therefore on production of an order or a notice, careful consideration needs to be given as to whether material needs to be withheld or redacted.

There are two types of privilege that belong to a client: legal advice privilege and litigation privilege. These are briefly outlined below, but also see **3.5.4** for more detailed guidance on privilege.

Legal advice privilege attaches to communications between a client and their lawyer if that communication relates to rights, liabilities, obligations or remedies or is otherwise made in a relevant legal context. When considering legal advice privilege, the test in *Three Rivers District Council and others* v. *Governor and Company of the Bank of England* [2004] UKHL 48 should be considered.

Communications that do not attract legal advice privilege are: notes of open court proceedings; conversations, correspondence or meetings with the opposing side's lawyers; client account ledger, appointments diary and documents that are the lawyer's 'fruits of advice' such as conveyancing documents.

Litigation privilege attaches to communications between a client and their lawyer and other parties if made for the sole or dominant purpose of conducting existing or reasonably contemplated litigation. Again, the *Three Rivers* test should be applied.

The court in *SFO* v. *Eurasian Natural Resources Corporation Ltd* [2018] EWCA Civ 2006 held that the following principles should be applied when considering whether litigation privilege attaches:

1. It is a question of fact as to whether the person asserting privilege was aware of circumstances which rendered litigation a real likelihood rather than a mere possibility.
2. Reasonable contemplation can occur prior to contact from a prosecutor.
3. Uncertainty about the underlying facts by the person asserting privilege does not prevent litigation being in contemplation.

It was further held in that case that heading off litigation or settling contemplated proceedings attracted litigation privilege.

7.5.3 Crime/fraud exception – iniquity exception

Privilege does not arise where a solicitor's assistance has been sought to further a crime or fraud or any other conduct which is a breach of the duty of good faith or contrary to public policy or interests of justice. Knowledge of this fact is not necessary for privilege to not attach.

This exception to privilege does not apply where a client seeks advice on avoiding the commission of a crime.

If in doubt as to whether this exception applies, legal advice should be sought.

7.5.4 Speaking to the client before and after order/notice

It is possible for the client to agree for the release of material and waiver of privilege, saving enforcement agencies time in obtaining an order or producing a notice and solicitor's consideration of confidentiality and privilege.

If an enforcement officer contacts the firm first to ask whether it would need an order or notice to hand over documentation, the answer should invariably be 'yes' until the client consents. Solicitors have a duty under the SRA Codes of Conduct to inform their client of all material information to their matter (see para.6.4 in both the Code of Conduct for Solicitors, RELs and RFLs and the Code of Conduct for Firms). If the solicitor is acting on a live matter in respect of which an order or a notice is contemplated or produced, then the solicitor needs to consider if they have a duty to inform their client of the law enforcement approach or order/notice. When doing so, the solicitor needs to consider whether there is a real risk of tipping off (see **2.4.4** for further guidance on the offence of tipping off).

If the mater to which the contemplated or actual order or notice relates is not an ongoing retainer (perhaps it is a matter which completed years ago and for a client for whom the firm no longer acts), then arguably the solicitor does not have a duty to inform the client of it.

The order or notice itself may confirm whether disclosure to the client/subject is prohibited.

Responding to an order/notice can be time consuming (and depending on the retainer and circumstances, might not be capable of being charged for) and therefore careful thought should be given to how the order/notice can be complied with quickly and efficiently.

7.5.5 Suspicious activity report

Consideration needs to be had as to whether a SAR to the NCA to seek a defence to a possible money laundering offence should be made due to the content and nature of the order/notice. An order/notice may be produced prior to a transaction completing and therefore a defence might need to be sought.

Careful thought needs to be given as to whether the solicitor should cease to act and if to do so might tip off.

For further information about SARs, see **3.5**.

7.5.6 Keeping a copy of the material sent and a comprehensive note

It is important to keep a copy of the material that is sent, and not sent, in response to an order/notice, with a comprehensive file note outlining the rationale. It is possible that the disclosure can be questioned and the firm needs to be in a position to consider the steps it has taken and respond.

7.5.7 Providing a witness statement

Ordinarily the enforcement agent will seek a witness statement from the producing person at the firm simply outlining the materials that have been produced.

If the enforcement agent requests a statement that discusses any retainer, advice given and so on, this should be declined unless the client consents and waives privilege or the crime/fraud exception applies. Thought needs to be given as to whether the solicitor should request to be summoned as a witness before providing any information. Further legal advice should be sought.

PART IV

Sanctions, whistleblowing and reporting concerns

CHAPTER 8
Sanctions

It is vital that all law firms are aware of the sanctions regime and undertake checks on clients for sanctions, on a risk-based approach if not done for all clients regardless of risk.

In this section we will explore the sanctions regime faced by law firms and how to practically implement compliance.

8.1 RELEVANT LEGISLATION

The UK imposes financial sanctions through three key pieces of legislation: the recently enacted Sanctions and Anti-Money Laundering Act (SAMLA) 2018; the Counter-Terrorism Act (CTA) 2008; and the Anti-terrorism, Crime and Security Act (ATCSA) 2001.

SAMLA 2018 was enacted on 31 December 2020 to establish sanctions regimes in the whole of the UK, including in Northern Ireland, post-Brexit. Without the Act in place, the UK would have been at risk of breaching its international obligations following its withdrawal from the EU because as a member of the United Nations (UN) the UK is required to implement sanctions passed by resolution of the UN Security Council. These were previously implemented through EU regulations. Having exited the EU, the UK was therefore left without a mechanism to implement such UN sanctions.

As indicated above, the UN imposes financial sanctions and requires member states to implement them through resolutions passed by the UN Security Council. More information about the UN's work on financial sanctions can be found on its website: **www.un.org/securitycouncil/sanctions/information**.

For guidance on sanctions, readers are advised to consult the Office of Financial Sanctions Implementation (OFSI) report, 'UK financial sanctions: general guidance for financial sanctions under the Sanctions and Anti-Money Laundering Act 2018' (December 2020, **https://assets.publishing.service.gov.uk/government/uploads/system/uploads/attachment_data/file/952150/General_Guidance_-_UK_Financial_Sanctions.pdf**); and the Law Society's practice note, 'UK sanctions regime' (20 January 2020, **www.lawsociety.org.uk/topics/anti-money-laundering/sanctions-guide**). If in doubt, independent legal advice should be sought.

Please note that at the time of writing, sanctions legislation is evolving and readers are urged to check the current legislative framework.

8.2 UK SANCTIONS REGIME KEY PLAYERS

It is important to understand who the key government and department agencies involved in the sanctions regime in the UK are. These are as follows:

- **Foreign, Commonwealth and Development Office (FCDO)** – Responsible for the UK's international sanctions policy, including all international sanctions regimes and designations. It also negotiates all international sanctions.
- **HM Treasury – OFSI** – OFSI is the authority responsible for implementing the UK's financial sanctions on behalf of HM Treasury.
- **Department for International Trade – Export Control Joint Unit (ECJU)** – Implements trade sanctions and embargoes.
- **Department for Transport** – Implements transport sanctions, including controlling movement of ships and aircraft in UK waters and airspace.
- **Home Office** – Implements travel bans.
- **HM Revenue and Customs (HMRC)** – Enforces breaches of trade sanctions.
- **National Crime Agency (NCA)** – Investigates and enforces breaches of financial sanctions.

8.3 WHAT SANCTIONS ARE AND WHY SANCTIONS ARE IMPOSED

In simple terms, sanctions are restrictions put in place to achieve a specific foreign or national security objective.

Financial sanctions put in place by the UK and UN can limit the provision of certain financial services or restrict access to financial markets, funds and economic resources.

The OFSI guidance (at para.1.1) sets out that financial sanctions are generally imposed to:

- **coerce** a regime, or individuals within a regime, into changing their behaviour (or aspects of it) by increasing the cost on them to such an extent that they decide to cease the offending behaviour;
- **constrain** a target by denying them access to key resources needed to continue their offending behaviour, including the financing of terrorism or nuclear proliferation;
- **signal disapproval**, stigmatising and potentially isolating a regime or individual, or as a way of sending broader political messages nationally or internationally; and/or
- **protect the value of assets** that have been misappropriated from a country until these assets can be repatriated.

The main types of sanctions imposed are (para.1.3):

1. **Targeted asset freezes** – These apply to named individuals and entities restricting access to funds and economic resources.
2. **Restrictions on a wide variety of financial markets and services** – These can apply to named individuals, entities, specified groups or sectors. They can take the form of investment bans; restrictions on access to capital markets; directions to cease banking relationships and activities; requirements to notify or seek authorisation prior to certain payments being made or received; and restrictions on the provision of financial, insurance, brokering or advisory services and other financial services. This is not an exhaustive list.
3. **Directions to cease all business** – They will specify the type of business and can apply to a specific person, group, sector or country.

8.4 WHO NEEDS TO COMPLY?

The reporting obligations set out below apply to relevant firms. A relevant firm is defined in the statutory instrument for each sanctions regime. Relevant firms as set out in regulations made under SAMLA 2018 include:

- a person who has permission under Financial Services and Markets Act (FSMA) 2000, Part 4A (permission to carry on regulated activity);
- an undertaking that by way of business operates a currency exchange office, transmits money (or any representations of monetary value) by any means, or cashes cheques which are made payable to customers;
- a firm or sole practitioner that is a statutory auditor or local auditor;
- a firm or sole practitioner that provides by way of business accountancy services, legal or notarial services, advice about tax affairs or certain trust or company services;
- a firm or sole practitioner that carries out, or whose employees carry out, estate agency work;
- the holder of a casino operating licence;
- a person engaged in the business of making, supplying, selling or exchanging articles made from gold, silver, platinum, palladium or precious stones or pearls.

Those who are UK persons or entities but sit outside the UK are still subject to the sanctions legislation.

Law firms are therefore clearly obligated to follow the sanctions regime in place in the UK.

8.5 INTERNATIONAL SANCTIONS – THE REACH OF THE OFFICE OF FOREIGN ASSETS CONTROL

As we have seen so far, UK and UN sanctions apply to those in the UK. Other jurisdictions, however, impose their own sanctions and it is possible therefore for a firm to act (or be asked to act) for an individual or entity that has imposed against them/it a foreign sanction.

One such jurisdiction is the US.

The Office of Foreign Assets Control (OFAC) of the US Department of the Treasury administers and enforces economic and trade sanctions based on US foreign policy and national security. Such sanctions generally attempt to freeze assets anywhere in the world in relation to individuals or entities. To act when a sanction is imposed requires a licence.

US sanctions must be complied with by all persons in the US as well as US citizens and green card holders wherever located. These sanctions also bite on US companies and their foreign branches, unless implementation is blocked by another jurisdiction (such as legislation in the UK which prevents UK entities and individuals from complying with sanctions imposed by the US on companies and individuals associated with Cuba, Iran and Libya – see the Extraterritorial US Legislation (Sanctions against Cuba, Iran and Libya) (Protection of Trading Interests) (Amendment) Order 2018, SI 2018/1357 for more information)).

If a UK company has a person who is a US citizen as part of its board or senior management, this may also mean the US sanction is enforceable against the UK company.

It is possible, therefore, that a UK law firm may be caught by US sanctions; and further, if activity with a US sanctioned person or entity involves an activity that takes place in the US (this is interpreted widely by OFAC), the UK law firm may be opening itself up to being caught by the US sanction.

On the face of it, however, where a UK law firm has no connection to the US and the US sanctioned client is seeking advice that is unconnected with any US assets, the US sanctions regime will not bite.

If, though, the law firm were to be connected with the US, then the US sanctions will need to be checked and considered. Likewise, if a UK law firm is being asked to advise on US assets, a US sanctions check should be considered.

8.6 WHERE TO FIND SANCTIONS LISTS

OFSI maintains two lists for those who are subject to financial sanctions.

The first, 'Financial sanctions targets: list of all asset freeze targets', is the consolidated list which lists all asset freeze targets (**www.gov.uk/government/ publications/financial-sanctions-consolidated-list-of-targets/consolidated- list-of-targets**). Individuals and entities that are included in this list are known as 'designated persons'. When new UN and UK designations are made, the list is usually updated within one working day.

The other list, called 'consolidated list of financial sanction targets in the UK', contains entities subject to restrictions on dealing with transferrable securities or money-market instruments (**https://ofsistorage.blob.core.windows.net/publish live/InvBan.pdf**). These entities are not contained in the consolidated list.

8.7 CHECKING CLIENTS FOR SANCTIONS

8.7.1 When to check

Each firm needs to decide whether it will check all clients for sanctions or whether to check on a risk-based approach. Online platforms are available (at a cost) that enable a user to check sanctions, politically exposed person (PEP) status and adverse media at the same time. If a firm is using one of these platforms, it may decide to check all clients regardless of risk, as to do so will enable checking of PEP status and adverse media at the same time.

On a risk-based approach, firms may decide to only check the consolidated list and only check when the client is from a high-risk jurisdiction or has adverse media surrounding them.

Firms also need to decide whether to check on each new matter and/or periodically. On each new matter would be advisable.

8.7.2 Whom to check

Obviously when acting for an individual client, it is the individual's name that should be checked. Thought should be given to whether maiden names or aliases should also be checked. Likewise, where acting for an entity, it is the entity's name that should be checked.

Where a designated person has ownership or control over an entity, that entity will also be subject to the sanction and its assets can be frozen. It is for this reason that firms need to understand the beneficial ownership and control structure of a client so that those who are the ultimate beneficial owners or controllers can be sanction screened.

For these purposes, an entity is owned or controlled directly or indirectly by an individual in the following ways:

- the person holds (directly or indirectly) more than 50 per cent of the shares or voting rights in an entity;
- the person has the right (directly or indirectly) to appoint or remove a majority of the board of directors of the entity; or
- it is reasonable to expect that the person would be able to ensure the affairs of the entity are conducted in accordance with the person's wishes. This could, for example, include:
    - appointing, solely by exercising one's voting rights, a majority of the

- members of the administrative, management or supervisory bodies of an entity, who have held office during the present and previous financial year;
- controlling alone, pursuant to an agreement with other shareholders in or members of an entity, a majority of shareholders' or members' voting rights in that entity;
- having the right to exercise a dominant influence over an entity, pursuant to an agreement entered into with that entity, or to a provision in its memorandum or articles of association, where the law governing that entity permits its being subject to such agreement or provision;
- having the right to exercise a dominant influence referred to in the point above, without being the holder of that right (including by means of a front company);
- having the ability to direct another entity in accordance with one's wishes. This can be through any means, directly or indirectly. For example, it is possible that a designated person may have control or use of another person's bank accounts or economic resources and may be using them to circumvent financial sanctions.

Where the designated person has a minority interest in an entity, then the entity's assets may not be frozen. However, if the minority owner controls the entity because it conducts its affairs in accordance with the designated person's wishes, the entity may also find itself subject to the sanction.

When acting for an entity, taking the above into account, it is advisable to check the name of the entity, beneficial owners who own or control over 25 per cent of shares or voting rights (whom the firm would be identifying in any event to comply with the AML Regulations (Money Laundering, Terrorist Financing and Transfer of Funds (Information on the Payer) Regulations 2017, SI 2017/692)) and the names of the directors and if possible, board members. Where possible, a risk-based approach should be taken to this task.

8.7.3 Reverse sanction checking

Sanctions lists are updated on a relatively frequent basis. It is possible, therefore, that a client may become sanctioned whilst the firm is acting for it.

For this reason, it is advisable for firms to sign up to alerts for when new lists are released (this can be done at **https://public.govdelivery.com/accounts/UKHMTREAS/subscriber/new**) and then those lists checked against the firm's database of clients. This is what the author calls reverse sanction checking.

Again, firms may wish to take a risk-based approach with this aspect of compliance. If the firm's main client base is UK individuals and companies, the law firm may not wish to conduct these reverse sanctions checks. However, if the client base is more international it is advisable to undertake this task.

There are paid-for platforms that will continually monitor sanctions lists for firms and alert the firm if a client appears on a sanctions list.

8.8 OBLIGATION TO REPORT TO THE OFFICE OF FINANCIAL SANCTIONS IMPLEMENTATION

All firms are required to inform OFSI as soon as reasonably practicable if it is known or reasonably suspected that a person is a designated person or has committed offences under the financial sanctions regulations where the information has been received in the course of carrying on the business. This requirement applies to firms and those that work in firms.

When making a report to OFSI, the firm must set out the information or other matter on which the knowledge or suspicion is based, and any other information the firm holds about the person which identifies them. The firm must also state the nature and amount of funds or economic resources held for the client that the firm suspects or knows is a designated person.

The OFSI financial sanctions guidance sets out the following tables as examples of information to be reported (para.5.2).

Table 8.1 Examples of information to be reported (1)

A designated person or entity	A customer or client of yours is a known or suspected designated person or entity
	As well as providing OFSI with any information you hold about the designated person or entity by which they can be identified, if the designated person is a customer or client you must also inform OFSI of the nature, amount, quantity of any funds or economic resources held on behalf of the customer or client, at the time this knowledge or suspicion arose
Offences	Exact offences will depend on the relevant legislation, but can include: • making funds or economic resources available to a designated person or entity (except where an exception applies or under licence) • dealing with frozen funds or economic resources (except where an exception applies or under licence) • activities that circumvent an asset freeze • breaching licensing conditions

Table 8.2 Examples of information to be reported (2)

A designated person or entity	A customer or client of yours is a known or suspected designated person or entity
	As well as providing OFSI with any information you hold about the designated person or entity by which they can be identified, if the designated person is a customer or client you must also inform OFSI of the nature, amount, quantity of any funds or economic resources held on behalf of the customer or client, at the time this knowledge or suspicion arose
Funds and economic resources	You must include details of the nature, amount or quantity of any funds and economic resources held
	Types of funds or economic resources can include but are not limited to: • cash • cheques • postal orders • crypto assets • bond futures • precious metals or stones • vehicles • antiques
Credits to frozen accounts	A relevant institution must inform OFSI immediately whenever it credits a frozen account: • where it receives funds transferred to it for the purpose of crediting that account

There are also reporting obligations under ATCSA 2001 (see Schedule of Orders under the Act for further detail).

The method by which a report should be made is to OFSI by email (ofsi@hmtreasury.gov.uk), including the detail outlined above and also the designated person's unique ID from the consolidated list.

OFSI has the power to require firms to produce specified documents and provide information for the purpose of establishing the nature and amount of funds or economic resources being owned, held or controlled by or on behalf of the designated person or being made available to the designated person. This is to enable OFSI to understand the nature of any financial transactions being entered into by the designated person. Alternatively, OFSI may seek the information to monitor compliance with sanctions including licensing requirements or obligations to report or to detect or obtain evidence of a crime being committed.

Failure to comply with a request for information from OFSI or within the time given is a criminal offence and could result in prosecution and penalty. Likewise providing false information, destroying documents or being obstructive could result in prosecution, as well as inevitably a referral to the Solicitors Regulation Authority (SRA) and a regulatory investigation.

Note that OFSI can disclose the information provided to it to third parties under the legislation.

8.9 PRIVILEGE

Privilege is a fundamental right and one that can only be overridden by statute. Information obtained may be privileged and therefore incapable of being disclosed without waiver by the holder of the privilege. However, the principle of iniquity needs to be carefully considered. For further guidance on privilege and exceptions, see **3.5.4**.

8.10 EXCEPTIONS AND LICENCES (SPECIFIC AND GENERAL)

If a firm finds itself acting or wanting to act for a designated person, the firm needs to next consider whether the actions it wishes to undertake come under the legislative exceptions or whether a licence is needed from OFSI.

8.10.1 Exception – crediting a frozen account

The legislation permits without a licence the following:

(a) credit to a frozen account with interest or other earnings due on the frozen account, so long as those funds are frozen immediately;
(b) a person to transfer funds to a firm for crediting a frozen account where the transfer is in order to discharge obligations that were concluded or arose before the date the person became sanctioned; and
(c) a firm to credit a frozen account with payments from a third party, provided that the incoming funds are also frozen and that it informs OFSI of the transaction immediately without delay.

8.10.2 Exception – independent person holding legal or equitable interest in frozen funds or economic resources

Independent persons who wish to transfer their legal or equitable interests in frozen funds or economic resources to other persons are able to do so as long as the conditions below are met:

(a) the independent person is not a designated person;
(b) the independent person holds the interest in the funds or economic resources;
(c) the independent person doesn't hold the interest jointly with a designated person; and
(d) the independent person isn't owned or controlled, directly or indirectly by a designated person.

8.10.3 Exception – ring-fencing

Although this applies to the actions of banks, it is useful for law firms to understand.

Large banks are required to separate out their core retail banking from the rest of their business as per the Financial Services (Banking Reform) Act 2013. This is known as ring-fencing.

These banks are permitted under the UK sanctions legislation to transfer funds from an account that is not ring-fenced to a ring-fenced account where both accounts are held or controlled directly or indirectly by a designated person.

8.10.4 Licensing

OFSI is able to grant a licence for acts that fall within the licensing grounds set out in the legislation.

General licences issued by OFSI allow multiple parties to undertake specific acts without the need for specific licences. However, OFSI will not accept applications for a general licence, but rather such licences are issued when deemed appropriate by HM Treasury.

The OFSI guidance sets out an example (at para.6.8):

> For example, a general licence could be used to respond to a situation where it may be necessary for persons to undertake otherwise prohibited financial activity because the Government has introduced an unrelated financial services policy that would otherwise be hindered by sanctions law, provided that it does not contradict the policy intent of the sanctions regime. A general licence is not limited to the derogations (licencing grounds) set out in the relevant legislation (except for UN sanctions regimes, in relation to which a general licence would be limited to the derogations set out in the relevant UN resolution). A general licence can be issued under the counter-terrorism regimes.

Applications for licences need to be specific and a relevant ground for the licence must be established. Common grounds for licences are set out in the OFSI guidance as follows (para.6.5).

Table 8.3 OFSI's approach to licensing grounds

Licensing ground	OFSI's approach

Basic needs	• The legislation confirms that the ground is present to enable the basic needs of a designated person, or (in the case of an individual) any financially dependent family member of such a person to be met.
	• Expenditure to meet basic needs of an individual should be expenses which are necessary to ensure that designated persons or financially dependent family members are not imperilled.
	• In respect of a person other than an individual e.g. **an entity**, the legislation confirms that basic needs *includes*:
	  – payment of insurance premiums
	  – payment of reasonable fees for the provision of property management services
	  – payment of remuneration, allowances or pensions of employees
	  – payment of tax
	  – rent or mortgage payments
	  – utility charges
	• The list of basic needs detailed above is not exhaustive but is indicative of the type of basic needs intended to be caught. Therefore, expenditure to meet the basic needs of an entity should be expenses strictly necessary to ensure the continued existence of the designated entity.
	• Basic needs licences do not necessarily enable a designated person to continue the lifestyle or business activities they had before they were designated.

Fees for the provision of legal services	• Both legal fees and disbursements must be reasonable. It is for the applicant to demonstrate to OFSI that the legal fees and disbursements are reasonable.
	• In most cases, you can provide legal advice to or act for a designated person without an OFSI licence, however, you cannot receive any payment for that advice without first obtaining an OFSI licence.
	• OFSI can only authorise payment of reasonable legal fees and disbursements in relation to legal services provided to a designated person. You are strongly encouraged to apply for a licence in advance of providing substantive legal services in order for you to have certainty as to the fees that will be recoverable whilst the designated person remains listed.
	• In support of your application, you should:
	  – provide an estimate of the anticipated fees and/or fees that have already been incurred;
	  – provide a breakdown of how the fees will be charged and/or have been charged; and
	  – identify any disbursements, such as payments for counsel and/or expert witnesses.

SANCTIONS, WHISTLEBLOWING AND REPORTING CONCERNS

Licensing ground	OFSI's approach
	• OFSI considers that the Supreme Court Cost Guides or the sums that could be expected to be recouped if costs were awarded, provide a useful starting point for assessing the reasonableness of legal fees and disbursements. • If you are seeking fees of a level in excess of those, you need to demonstrate why those increased fees are reasonable in the given case. • Fees and disbursements must relate specifically to the provision of legal advice, involvement in litigation or in dispute resolution.
Routine maintenance of frozen funds and economic resources	• The fees or service charges must be reasonable and result in the routine holding or maintenance of frozen funds or economic resources. • The re-design, refurbishment or redevelopment in order to improve the value of a frozen economic resource is generally not covered, although each application will be considered on a case by case basis.
Extraordinary expenses	• This must be extraordinary in nature (unexpected, unavoidable and not recurring). • It cannot be used where other licensing grounds are more suitable or as a way of avoiding the clear limitations of those other grounds.
Pre-existing judicial decisions etc.	• This enables the use of frozen funds or economic resources that are the subject of a judicial decision or lien which was established before the date of designation and enforceable in the UK. The use of the funds or economic resources must be to implement or satisfy in whole or in part the pre-existing judicial decision or lien and cannot be for the direct or indirect benefit of a designated person.
Humanitarian assistance activity etc.	• This enables payments to facilitate: – any humanitarian activity; or – where applicable, any activity where its purposes are consistent with the objectives of UN Security Council Resolutions (which will be set out in the applicable Sanctions Act regulations). • Humanitarian assistance includes the work of international and non-governmental organisations carrying out relief activities for the benefit of the applicable civilian population, which may include the delivery of humanitarian aid or peace-building programmes. • A licence may still be required even if this activity is using government funds.
Diplomatic missions	• This enables anything to be done in order that the proper functions of a diplomatic mission or consular post or an international organisation enjoying immunities in accordance with international law, may be carried out.

Licensing ground	OFSI's approach
Extraordinary situations	• This must be extraordinary in nature (unexpected, unavoidable and not recurring). • This applies to non-UN designated persons and enables anything to be done to deal with an extraordinary situation. This will enable a situation which is extraordinary in nature but does not necessarily involve an expense. • This may, for example, allow for funds to be released to support disaster relief or provide aid in extraordinary situations. It cannot be used where other grounds are more suitable or as a way of avoiding the clear limitations of other grounds.
Prior obligations	• The obligation must have arisen prior to the date of designation and cannot relate to trade provisions (specified in the regulations). In addition, it cannot result in funds or economic resources being made available (directly or indirectly) to the designated person.

It follows that whilst law firms are not prevented from providing legal advice to a designated person, to have legal fees paid does require a licence. If a sanction prohibits specific action, e.g. asset movement, then the law firm/individual advising needs to consider whether they are facilitating a breach of the sanction imposed.

Payments into court for security for costs need to be licensed specifically. Court fees may be paid without a licence, but only if not 'significant', which is to be determined on the facts. A scenario could arise where a client has a cause of action in respect of which limitation is about to expire and the law firm wishes to issue a claim to preserve it. In that scenario it might not be possible to obtain a licence in time and it is likely the payment of the court fee will not require a licence. If in doubt, legal advice should be sought.

The OFSI guidance sets out that ATCSA 2001 and CTA 2008 do not have specific licensing grounds contained within them but do contain a general power to issue licences (para.6.7).

8.10.5 Applying for a specific licence

To apply for a licence, firms need to fill in a licence application form – found at: **www.gov.uk/guidance/licences-that-allow-activity-prohibited-by-financial-sanctions** – and email it to OFSI (ofsi@hmtreasury.gov.uk).

The application requires the following information to be provided:

(a) the licensing ground(s) being relied upon in the application including supporting arguments;
(b) full information on the parties involved in the proposed transaction, e.g.:

    – the designated person(s);

SANCTIONS, WHISTLEBLOWING AND REPORTING CONCERNS

- any financial institution(s) involved (e.g. remitter, correspondent, beneficiary);
- the ultimate beneficiary of the transaction.

(c) the complete payment route, including account details;
(d) the amount (or estimated amount) of the proposed transaction.

Licences cannot be given retrospectively and so should a firm consider that it acted without a licence, legal advice should be taken straight away.

The OFSI guidance sets out that if a firm is seeking a licence under (a) the ISIL (Da'esh) and Al-Qaida (United Nations Sanctions) (EU Exit) regime; (b) the Counter-Terrorism (International Sanctions) (EU Exit) regime; or (c) the Counter-Terrorism (Sanctions) (EU Exit) regime, the firm should email OFSI (at the email address above) setting out the full details of the proposed transaction (para.6.9.3).

OFSI further sets out in its guidance that specificity is best when applying for a licence. Note that licences only apply to activity subject to the UK jurisdiction, and if the prohibited activity engages another jurisdiction the licence applicant needs to consider whether additional licences need to be sought from those jurisdictions.

8.10.6 Timeframe for a licence to be granted

The OFSI guidance sets out that OFSI aims to 'engage with applicants' on their application within four weeks of it being submitted, though this does not mean a licence will be granted by then (para.6.10). Should the application not be deemed to have all the information needed for OFSI to consider a licence, it will be sent back to the applicant. Though it is not clear when that might happen, presumably it could happen four weeks after submission. Urgent and humanitarian cases are prioritised.

One reason for the length of time it may take for OFSI to provide a licence is its need to seek approval from the relevant United Nations Sanctions Committee and OFSI guidance sets out that in fact such approval-seeking can prevent a licence from being issued.

8.10.7 Amending a licence

If amendment of a licence is needed, a request needs to be sent to OFSI by email as soon as possible. Again, OFSI aims to engage with the request within four weeks but this does not mean it will be granted within that timeframe.

8.10.8 Refusal of a licence

If a licence is refused, then the specific act for which a licence was requested may not be lawful. Although OFSI will provide written reasons for refusing the request, firms should take legal advice if the refusal places them in a difficult professional position.

Firms that have had their request for a licence refused can ask OFSI to review the decision; apply for a new licence with new information; apply for a different licence; or seek to challenge the decision in court.

8.11 COMPLIANCE AND BREACHING THE TERMS OF A LICENCE

Licences should be shared with relevant persons but not published.

All actions undertaken need to come within the terms of the licence. If this is unclear, then OFSI can be asked for clarification and will aim to respond to such queries within two weeks. The OFSI guidance warns that firms should not assume that OFSI agrees with the firm's interpretation.

Breaching a licence is of course very serious and carries heavy penalties of custodial sentences of up to seven years on indictment or 12 months on a summary conviction in England and Wales and Scotland (six months for Northern Ireland).

Firms can also be fined up to 50 per cent of the total breach value up to £1 million.

Deferred prosecution agreements can be entered into; see **6.4** for more information about those agreements.

Further, a serious crime prevention order can be imposed to prevent further action being taken by a firm. Such an order may be obtained from court on the civil standard of proof.

8.12 OTHER REPORTING OBLIGATIONS – SUSPICIOUS ACTIVITY REPORTS

Whilst a firm is considering whether it needs a licence for actions it wishes to undertake, thought needs to be given as to whether there is an obligation to make a suspicious activity report (SAR) to the NCA and seek a defence. The Proceeds of Crime Act (POCA) 2002 may be triggered due to the underlying reason for the sanction (UK or otherwise) imposition. See **3.5** for more information about the SARs regime.

CHAPTER 9

Whistleblowing and reporting concerns

9.1 INTRODUCTION

All law firms need to have a good understanding of whistleblowing, an adequate policy and a good culture to ensure that internal reports are made in good time and dealt with swiftly. Further, the Solicitors Regulation Authority (SRA) Codes of Conduct set out reporting obligations alongside whistleblowing type protection.

In this chapter we will explore what whistleblowing is under the UK and global whistleblowing legislation; reporting obligations and protections under the SRA Codes of Conduct; and how law firms can create a good whistleblowing and reporting culture.

9.2 WHISTLEBLOWING LEGISLATION

9.2.1 What is whistleblowing?

First of all, it is important to understand what whistleblowing is and is not.

Whistleblowing is the act of reporting wrongdoing of an organisation, normally the person's place of work (often it is an employee who is the first to find out or suspect that something is going wrong). This wrongdoing could be something criminal, illegal, immoral or unethical.

Although a whistleblower may not ultimately feel that they have a choice about it, they are able to bring the information to light internally at the organisation they work for, bring it to the public's attention or not say anything at all. In many different types of organisations whistleblowers can suffer great personal detriment by blowing the whistle with little or no personal gain and so decisions to blow the whistle are not taken lightly.

Whistleblowing is not the act of raising a grievance in the workplace, though some employees may try to use whistleblowing policies in this way. An organisation's grievance procedure should respond to those scenarios and they should not be conflated with whistleblowing. It is therefore important that firms make this distinction clear.

9.2.2 Why is whistleblowing important?

Whistleblowing is vital as a way of revealing criminal, illegal, immoral or unethical activity and potentially preventing events that could lead to catastrophes. Whistleblowing is a way of creating an environment of self-checking. This would not be possible, however, without the appropriate legislative protections and organisational culture.

Wrongdoing can have disastrous consequences on organisations, reputationally and financially (perhaps think of Mossack Fonseca & Co, which assisted many people with hiding their assets to evade tax, which ultimately led to the closure of the firm). Whistleblowing can provide protection against catastrophic results so long as the organisation has processes in place and acts quickly.

Further, having appropriate and accessible processes means that organisations are more likely to keep the information that is being disclosed internal and investigate it rather than providing the whistleblower with little or no choice, in their mind, but to make it public. Internal-only disclosures must be a far better choice than facing an external disclosure and the reputational damage that could bring.

9.2.3 Whistleblowing legislation in the UK

The UK has specified legislation for whistleblowing protection in the workplace by virtue of the Employment Rights Act 1996 which incorporates the Public Interest Disclosure Act 1998. These pieces of legislation provide protection for employees against dismissal if the reason or principal reason for the dismissal is that the employee made a 'protected disclosure'. Such dismissals are deemed to be automatically unfair, leaving the employer open to an employment tribunal claim. The UK legislation also provides protection against retaliation or detriment due to the protected disclosure.

A protected disclosure under UK legislation is a disclosure that in the reasonable belief of the worker is made in the public interest and tends to show that:

- a criminal offence has been committed, is being committed or is likely to be committed;
- a person is failing to comply with a legal obligation;
- a miscarriage of justice has occurred or is likely to occur;
- the health and safety of someone has been or is likely to be put into danger;
- the environment has been or is likely to be damaged; or
- any of these activities mentioned is being or is likely to be concealed.

Further, for the disclosure to be protected it needs to be made to a person specified by the legislation, that being:

- the worker's employer;
- the person responsible for the relevant failure;
- legal advisers;

- government ministers; or
- other persons, providing certain conditions are met.

Since 2013 there has been no requirement for the disclosure to have been made in good faith. Presumably then, it can be made in bad faith.

Employers can be held vicariously liable for the retaliation on the whistleblower by other co-workers unless the employer took all reasonable steps to prevent that from happening.

It worth noting that the Public Interest Disclosure Act 1998 does not override the legal privilege belonging to another party, and such information cannot therefore form part of a protected disclosure.

The Law Society has published a useful practice note, 'Raising concerns and whistleblowing – guidance for staff' (22 November 2019, **www.lawsociety.org.uk/topics/hr-and-people-management/raising-concerns-and-whistleblowing-guidance-for-staff**). For an outline of whistleblowing provisions in the SRA Codes of Conduct, please see **9.3**.

9.2.4 Whistleblowing legislation across the globe

Dozens of countries have now adopted some form of legislative whistleblower protection. That protection, however, varies from country to country. Below is a summary of some of the protections offered by countries in Europe, South Africa, Asia and the US.

9.2.4.1 European Union

Note there is a new EU directive on whistleblowing (**https://eur-lex.europa.eu/legal-content/EN/TXT/PDF/?uri=CELEX:32019L1937**) which was published late 2019. Member states have until December 2021 to transpose the directive into national law.

The EU directive requires the creation of safe channels for reporting of whistleblowing within organisations both private and public where there are more than 50 employees. The directive also requires a high level of protection for whistleblowers against retaliation and will cover whistleblowing in areas such as public procurement, financial services, prevention of money laundering and public health.

GERMANY

It is surprising that Germany, as a European powerhouse, does not have specific legislation protecting whistleblowers. However, whistleblowers do have protection under Germany's general employment laws and in particular the Dismissal Protection Act. This Act provides that employees can only be dismissed 'for reasons'. These reasons can be related to conduct or serious breaches of contract.

Making an external disclosure without trying to do so internally first may, in Germany, be valid reason for dismissal.

The Act protects all employees after six months' service so long as the employer employs more than 10 people.

There are no specific provisions governing the nature of protected disclosures, and vicarious liability will only arise if the employee has acted as an agent for the employer and acted tortiously. Those who cause deliberate harm (injury, or interfere with a property or other right of the person) by retaliating against a whistleblower may be personally liable for their actions.

FRANCE

The Labour Code in France provides some whistleblowing protection but it is not extensive. Under this legislation an individual cannot be denied access to recruitment or training, be dismissed or subjected to discrimination for having disclosed when exercising their functions to their employer, or to the judicial or administrative authorities, their concerns as to corruption.

Whistleblowing in France is further regulated by the Data Protection Act and the French Data Protection Authority which has produced guidelines and requires that whistleblowing procedures in businesses in France must be declared to the French Data Protection Authority prior to being implemented so that the scope and operation can be considered.

The guidelines provide that a whistleblower must not be subjected to sanctions if the whistle is blown in good faith using an authorised procedure even if it turns out later that the allegation was not borne out.

Protected disclosures are those relating to activity in accounting; banking; financial audit; anti-corruption; anti-competitive behaviour; harassment and discrimination, health and safety; and environmental concerns.

In terms of vicarious liability for the acts of other employees against the whistleblower, if the employee is seen to be harassing or placing any pressure on the whistleblower then the employer must take disciplinary action which could ultimately lead to the dismissal of the harasser. The employee harassing may also face criminal prosecution, a fine and imprisonment.

9.2.4.2 South Africa

South Africa has an advanced whistleblowing protection regime by way of statutory framework and a body of case law. The statutory framework comes in the form of the Protected Disclosures Act 2000, the Labor Relations Act and the Companies Act 2008. Employees who disclose information in the manner prescribed relating to criminal, unlawful or irregular conduct are protected from any form of detriment such as retaliation under the Protected Disclosures Act 2000. This protection is limited to paid employees and excludes contractors and volunteers. However, the Companies Act 2008 does offer some whistleblowing protection to suppliers of goods or services which may therefore protect those that are unprotected by the Protected Disclosures Act 2000.

For a disclosure to be protected, it needs to relate to certain categories of information as set out in the legislative framework.

A disclosure is defined by the Protected Disclosures Act 2000 as any disclosure of information regarding any conduct of an employer or employee of the employer made by an employee who has reason to believe that the information concerned shows or tends to show that wrongdoing has occurred, is occurring, or is likely to occur. That wrongdoing must relate to a criminal offence, failure to comply with any legal obligation, a miscarriage of justice, danger to the health and safety of any individual, damage to the environment, unfair discrimination and the deliberate concealing of information about any of these categories.

Disclosures under the Protected Disclosures Act 2000 are protected if they are made to a legal adviser in the course of obtaining legal advice, an employer substantially in accordance with any prescribed procedure, a member of cabinet or of the executive council of a province about an individual, body or organ of state appointed by or falling in the area of responsibility of that member or the public protector, the auditor-general or a person or body prescribed by regulation.

The above is very similar to the UK provisions; however, there is a requirement in South Africa for protection only to be afforded if the disclosure is made in good faith, founded on information that the whistleblower believes to be true, the whistleblowing is not made for financial gain and the employee has reason to believe that they would be subjected to an occupational detriment and evidence would be concealed or destroyed if disclosure was made to the employer. The requirements are therefore quite far-reaching and hurdles have to be jumped.

Vicarious liability for the acts of other employees against the whistleblower exists if the employer fails to protect the whistleblower from detriment.

9.2.4.3 United States

The US legislation protecting whistleblowers is spread across multiple statutes reflecting the type of worker to be protected.

By way of example, the Corporate and Criminal Fraud Accountability Act 2002 (known as Sarbanes-Oxley) protects employees as well as their contractors, sub-contractors and agents of certain publicly traded companies and companies with certain reporting requirements with the Securities and Exchange Commission (SEC) from whistleblowing retaliation. Whistleblowing has a statutory footing in other areas including the Affordable Care Act which protects whistleblowers on issues related to healthcare reform; and the Occupational Safety and Health Act 1970 which protects whistleblowers who have reported workplace safety and health issues.

What disclosure is protected will depend on the legislation being used for protection. Complaints about retaliation or discrimination based on a whistle-blowing event need to be addressed to the Department of Labor or the Occupational

Safety and Health Authority, depending on the statute being utilised. These institutions are responsible for enforcing the relevant legislation. If certain criteria are met, then the complainant can file a complaint in the federal court.

As in other countries, in the US an employer has vicarious liability for retaliation by an employee against the whistleblower. Further, an individual employee may be personally liable under Sarbanes-Oxley if they are both materially involved with the retaliation effort plus in a position to modify the terms of the whistleblower's employment. Being found guilty of the latter action can result in a fine or up to 10 years in prison if the whistleblowing related to a report to a law enforcement agency about the commission of any federal offence. Such hefty consequences send a clear message that the US wants to encourage whistleblowing and heavily restrict retaliation against it.

9.2.4.4 Asia

PEOPLE'S REPUBLIC OF CHINA

China has specific legislation for the protection of whistleblowers contained within the Regulation on Labor Security Supervision and Criminal Procedure Law of the PRC. Detailed rules are contained within the Rules of the People's Procuratorate on Whistleblowing Work, which aim to encourage the reporting of illegal activities.

Chinese regulation sets out that any person who wishes to whistleblow about any breach of the law or regulations can do so to a labour bureau. Interestingly, and not seen in many jurisdictions the whistleblower may also be rewarded if the information provided is genuine. However, equally the whistleblower is also informed about the potential liability which exists where a false accusation is made which in turn would potentially discourage disclosure.

If the whistleblower is seen to be retaliated against due to their whistleblowing, then the employer can be compelled to take rectification action but there is no penalty for not doing so.

Interestingly, the Basic Standard of Enterprise Internal Control which applies to listed companies also sets out that those companies must set up whistleblowing procedures to include a hotline.

Under Chinese law, the protected disclosures relate to disclosure of an employer's violation of labour security related laws, regulations and rules and disclosure of crimes or suspects to the public security authority, people's procuratorate or people's court.

Retaliation by co-workers can leave the co-worker personally liable, but there does not seem to be a doctrine of vicarious liability in China.

HONG KONG

Hong Kong is quite a contrast to China, with no statutory protection for whistleblowers. Employees are, however, protected to some extent under the Employment

Ordinance if they give over information relating to an inquiry about the enforcement of legislation relating to industrial accidents or breach of health and safety laws. Further protection may be given if disclosure is made under certain statutory footings such as the Organised and Serious Crimes Ordinance or the United Nations (Anti-Terrorism) Ordinance. Also, if the disclosure is made in the public interest, common law may assist.

Interestingly, under certain legislation when an employee knows or has reasonable grounds to know of a criminal activity then they have an obligation to report (not too dissimilar to the UK's anti-money laundering regime with submitting suspicious activity reports (SARs) to the National Crime Agency (NCA)).

Hong Kong provides no specific legislative framework for retaliation against whistleblowers which makes employers vicariously liable. Co-workers can be liable to whistleblowers under other aspects of law, such as tort or criminal laws.

9.2.5 Why are there differences between countries?

It is clear that many developed countries offer some form of whistleblowing protection. There are, however, differences between countries. Some countries offer full protection set out in dedicated legislative frameworks, and others do not. Some countries make disclosure a legal requirement (the US by virtue of Sarbanes-Oxley, for example), and others do not.

Some countries offer reward, whilst many countries do not. Some countries create vicarious liability for a co-worker retaliating against the whistleblower, whilst in some countries this does not exist – though in most countries there is personal liability, but this will not encourage employer protection of an employee.

One possible reason why whistleblowing protection has developed at a more comprehensive rate in the US is because there is a lack of employment rights there and thus whistleblower protection is more needed. In Europe, employees have extensive rights and as such the whistleblowing legislation may not have had to grow at such a fast pace.

9.3 REPORTING CONCERNS UNDER THE SRA CODES OF CONDUCT

9.3.1 The rules old and new

On 25 November 2019, the SRA Standards and Regulations came into force, producing two new Codes of Conduct: the Code of Conduct for Firms and the Code of Conduct for Solicitors, RELs and RFLs (we shall call these the Code for Firms and the Code for Solicitors, respectively) (**www.sra.org.uk/solicitors/standards-regulations/**).

These new Codes brought in newly worded provisions dealing with the obligations of law firms and solicitors to report certain conduct.

Under the prior SRA Code of Conduct 2011, Outcome 10.3 dealt with the obligation to report material changes as follows:

> you notify the SRA promptly of any material changes to relevant information about you including serious financial difficulty, action taken against you by another regulator and serious failure to comply with or achieve the Principles, rules, outcomes and other requirements of the Handbook;

Further, Outcome 10.4 set out the obligation for firms and solicitors to report conduct as follows:

> you report to the SRA promptly serious misconduct by any person or firm authorised by the SRA, or any employee, manager or owner of any such firm (taking into account, where necessary, your duty of confidentiality to your client);

The SRA consulted on its proposed changes to these Outcomes in August 2018 (**https://www.sra.org.uk/sra/consultations/consultation-listing/reporting-concerns/?s=c**).

In its post-consultation document, 'Reporting concerns: our post-consultations position' (January 2019, **www.sra.org.uk/globalassets/documents/sra/consultations/reporting-concerns-post-consultation-position.pdf?version=4a1abb**) the SRA set out that firms' and individuals' understanding of when the duty to report was triggered differed, and in particular the SRA identified that some considered they did not need to report concerns until an internal investigation had occurred and a determination as to whether serious misconduct had taken place was reached. This is at odds with how the SRA viewed when reporting should occur. The consultation documentation is useful (in the absence of further guidance from the SRA) as an insight into what the SRA expects from those it regulates.

Having felt there was confusion across the profession about what to report and when, in its consultation the SRA posed a number of questions to firms, including the following:

- Do you agree that a person should report facts and matters that are capable of resulting in a finding by the SRA, rather than decide whether a breach has occurred?
- Where do you think the evidential threshold for reporting should lie?
- Do you think that an objective element – such as 'reasonable belief' or 'reasonable grounds' would assist decision makers, or unnecessarily hamper their discretion?
- Do you have a preferred drafting option [from among the SRA's suggestions]?
- What else can the SRA do to help those we regulate report matters in a way that allows us to act appropriately in the public interest …?

The SRA proposed a number of different possible drafts of the reporting concerns requirement based on different threshold tests, such as reasonable grounds and belief. After 29 responses had been received (far too few for something so important), the new rule was drafted and is now enshrined in the new Codes.

The relevant reporting concerns obligations under the 2019 Code for Firms can be found at paragraphs 3.9–3.12 as follows:

SANCTIONS, WHISTLEBLOWING AND REPORTING CONCERNS

3.9 You report promptly to the SRA, or another approved regulator, as appropriate, any facts or matters that you reasonably believe are capable of amounting to a serious breach of their regulatory arrangements by any person regulated by them (including you) of which you are aware. If requested to do so by the SRA, you investigate whether there have been any serious breaches that should be reported to the SRA.

3.10 Notwithstanding paragraph 3.9, you inform the SRA promptly of any facts or matters that you reasonably believe should be brought to its attention in order that it may investigate whether a serious breach of its regulatory arrangements has occurred or otherwise exercise its regulatory powers.

3.11 You do not attempt to prevent anyone from providing information to the SRA or any other body exercising regulatory, supervisory, investigatory or prosecutory functions in the public interest.

3.12 You do not subject any person to detrimental treatment for making or proposing to make a report or providing, or proposing to provide, information based on a reasonably held belief under paragraph 3.9 or 3.10 above or 9.1(d) or (e) or 9.2(b) or (c) below, or under paragraph 7.7 or 7.8 of the SRA Code of Conduct for Solicitors, RELs and RFLs, irrespective of whether the SRA or another approved regulator subsequently investigates or takes any action in relation to the facts or matters in question.

The relevant reporting obligations under the 2019 Code for Solicitors can be found at paragraphs 7.7–7.9 as follows:

7.7 You report promptly to the SRA or another approved regulator, as appropriate, any facts or matters that you reasonably believe are capable of amounting to a serious breach of their regulatory arrangements by any person regulated by them (including you).

7.8 Notwithstanding paragraph 7.7, you inform the SRA promptly of any facts or matters that you reasonably believe should be brought to its attention in order that it may investigate whether a serious breach of its regulatory arrangements has occurred or otherwise exercise its regulatory powers.

7.9 You do not subject any person to detrimental treatment for making or proposing to make a report or providing or proposing to provide information based on a reasonably held belief under paragraph 7.7 or 7.8 above, or paragraph 3.9, 3.10, 9.1(d) or (e) or 9.2(b) or (c) of the SRA Code of Conduct for Firms, irrespective of whether the SRA or another approved regulator subsequently investigates or takes any action in relation to the facts or matters in question.

It is not entirely clear where business services/support services personnel (such as human resources (HR), finance, IT and so on) come into the Codes and it is assumed they must therefore need to abide by the requirements as set out in the Code for Firms.

There are some key differences between the old and the new regimes. Whereas under the old Outcome 10.4 the firm or solicitor was obliged to report 'serious misconduct', the new requirement is for the firm or solicitor to report 'any facts or matters that you reasonably believe are capable of amounting to a serious breach'. The emphasis has changed and is arguably wider in application.

In its consultation documentation, the SRA says this change is to reflect that as a regulator it expects to receive information at an early stage where it may result in it taking regulatory action. The SRA sets out that it does not want to receive reports or

WHISTLEBLOWING AND REPORTING CONCERNS

allegations that are unmeritorious or frivolous but it does want to know whether it is possible that a serious breach of its standards or regulations has occurred.

Further, the SRA says in the consultation that it agrees with one respondent's comment that 'It is not the role of a Compliance Officer to make a final determination as to whether or not an act or omission amounts to a breach of the Code of Conduct' (para.26). The SRA wants to conduct its own investigation and wants the legal profession to make reports. This doesn't mean, however, that the compliance officer for legal practice (COLP) cannot or should not investigate, but the decision about what is serious misconduct is for the SRA and not compliance officers, or anyone in the firm for that matter.

Interestingly the Code for Solicitors sets out at paragraph 7.12 that a solicitor's obligations to make reports to the SRA are satisfied if the report/information was made to the firm's COLP or compliance officer for finance and administration (COFA) on the 'understanding that they will do so', i.e. that the COLP or COFA will then make a report. This may cause tension between a solicitor who considers that a report should be made and a COLP/COFA who does not. If that were to happen, then it is advised that the parties take independent legal advice about whether a duty to report has arisen.

The 'notwithstanding' provision found at paragraph 3.10 in the Code for Firms and paragraph 7.8 in the Code for Solicitors seeks to be a 'catch all' requirement in that notwithstanding the assessment made as to whether there are indeed facts or matters which the firm or solicitor believes is capable of amounting to a serious breach of regulatory arrangements, if the facts or matters are something that is considered would interest the SRA enough for it to want to investigate or exercise its regulatory powers, a report should be made.

9.3.2 What to report?

The SRA wants reports to be made where facts or matters point to a potential serious breach. There are situations that are clear-cut, such as theft of money or other forms of dishonesty, fraud and the like. However, sometimes allegations that are just that – allegations. It may not be known until an investigation has taken place whether the allegations are meritorious. Reporting is serious and should not be taken lightly.

The SRA does not define within the Codes what is meant by 'serious breach'; however it does set out its approach to enforcement in its 'SRA enforcement strategy' (updated 25 November 2019, **www.sra.org.uk/sra/corporate-strategy/sra-enforcement-strategy/**), which lists what factors it takes into account when deciding whether something is serious. These factors include:

(a) **Nature of the allegation** – Some types are inherently more serious than others, for example dishonesty, taking unfair advantage of clients, sexual misconduct.
(b) **Intent and motivation** – Conduct may be more serious because of the intent behind it.

- (c) **Harm and impact** – Has there been significant impact on the victim or little/no impact at all?
- (d) **Vulnerability** – Was the victim vulnerable and did the solicitor take advantage of that?
- (e) **Role, experience and seniority** – Is the individual junior or well seasoned?
- (f) **Regulatory history and pattern of behaviour** – Has this happened before?
- (g) **Remediation** – Is there a risk of future harm or has any risk been mitigated?

9.3.3 When to report?

The new Codes do not provide clarity on *when* the reporting should happen. However, the consultation provides big clues as to what the SRA expects. It says ('Reporting concerns: our post-consultation position', paras.25–29):

> … it is important for us, as the regulator, to receive information at an early stage where this may result in us taking regulatory action.
>
> … we require reporting of facts or matters which could comprise a serious breach, rather than allegations identifying specific and conclusively determined breaches.
>
> … it is our job to investigate those concerns that are capable, if proven, of amounting to a serious breach of our requirements. Early reporting is important because it allows us to do so; and although a firm itself, having identified a breach may be best placed to gather evidence, this will not always be the case – for example where this sits in another firm or with a client.
>
> …
>
> Early engagement with the SRA also allows us to make sure that we can understand any patterns or trends using information we already hold. Sometimes we will want to gather information regarding particular types of risk to consumers, to understand patterns and trends (eg cybercrime), even where this may raise no concerns about the conduct or behaviour of regulated individuals or firms.

So, should you investigate first before you report? The SRA says (para.30):

> This is not to suggest that firms shouldn't investigate matters nor that compliance officers shouldn't exercise their judgment in deciding whether a potential breach has occurred – indeed we want to encourage firms to resolve and remedy issues locally where they can. However, we are keen for firms to engage with us at an early stage in their internal investigative process and to keep us updated on progress and outcomes. In these circumstances, we are likely to be happy for the firm to conclude their investigation and to provide us with a copy of their report and findings. However, we may, on occasion wish to investigate a matter (or an aspect of a matter) ourselves – for example because our focus is different, or because we need to gather evidence from elsewhere.

9.3.4 Why reporting obligations matter to fighting financial crime

Failure to adhere to regulatory and legislative obligations that are enacted to tackle financial crime may amount to a serious breach of regulatory arrangements. For example, failure to report a suspicion of money laundering to the firm's money laundering reporting officer (MLRO) or for the MLRO to have failed to report a suspicion to the NCA would be deemed serious enough to warrant a report to the SRA. However, failing to conduct a client and matter risk assessment on a new client and matter, where this is a one-off omission, would not be deemed serious enough to warrant a report, and internal remedying measures such as messaging and training are enough.

What is important is that the thought process behind whether a report should or should not be made is documented for future reference. The documenter should also reference guidance that was reviewed at the time and consider saving that guidance electronically, as the SRA does not keep available old guidance that it has amended, and today's guidance can be quite different from the guidance considered at the time of deciding whether a report should be made or not.

9.4 HOW TO IMPLEMENT COMPLIANCE IN YOUR FIRM

The most vital aspect to whistleblowing and the SRA reporting obligations is having the right culture in the firm, where people feel they can report, be heard and not be persecuted for reporting.

Policies, procedures and messaging will help with this, but ultimately actions speak louder than words and so when a report is made it should be handled correctly.

To assist in creating the right culture, below are some steps firms may wish to take.

9.4.1 Policy and guidance

First of all, firms should write and implement an easy to understand and accessible whistleblowing policy (see **Appendix D1** for a template policy). This policy should set out what whistleblowing is and is not; the firm's approach to whistleblowing (that it takes whistleblowing seriously); the legislative framework (though this is not strictly necessary); examples of whistleblowing; and whom to report whistleblowing to.

The whistleblowing policy should be supported at board level and say so in the policy. Further, the board needs to appreciate that whistleblowing policies do not create a culture of over-reporting, which is often the fear, but instead could prevent a catastrophic event from occurring.

Firms should consider producing guidance on the reporting obligations found in the SRA Codes. See **Appendix D2** for template guidance.

SANCTIONS, WHISTLEBLOWING AND REPORTING CONCERNS

9.4.2 Appoint a whistleblowing officer and make sure everyone knows who the COLP is

It is a good idea (if not mandated by a firm's country's legislation) to appoint a whistleblowing officer to whom reports can be made. Also consider separating whistleblowing from the firm's HR function so that employees see the distinction between the firm's whistleblowing and grievance procedures.

Firms should ensure that everyone in the firm understands who the COLP is; and if that COLP is supported by a risk team, whether to report concerns to the COLP or the risk team in the first instance.

9.4.3 Whistleblowing hotline

Depending on the size of firm, consider making available a whistleblowing hotline. There are companies who are able to supply this service. Think carefully about confidentiality regarding information about the business.

9.4.4 Communicate about whistleblowing and reporting obligations – and not just once

Communicate policy and guidance to the firm. Further, firms should discuss it in team meetings and training, and put it in newsletters and the like.

Firms should diarise to mention whistleblowing/reporting obligations and the fact that the firm has a policy and guidance – say, twice a year, or more frequently if considered necessary. The firm should try and keep the content fresh by using a recent news story about whistleblowing or reporting concerns and then link back to the firm's policy and guidance to remind everyone it exists.

9.4.5 Training

Everyone in the firm should receive some form of training. Training does not need to be via just one method and can be in person, virtual/video, online, through guidance notes, attendance at team meetings and so on.

Firms should consider training for those to whom a person may blow the whistle or report concerns. Those individuals need to understand when a concern is being raised such that it needs to be looked at properly.

Firms should also consider arranging for an external person to come and speak to people in the firm. There are charitable organisations such as Protect, who offer free, confidential whistleblowing advice (**https://protect-advice.org.uk/**), who may be able to assist, or recommend others who can. Obtaining external speakers can sometimes drive home messages better.

9.4.6 Act quickly

Firms should have a documented procedure in place to act on a whistleblowing report or where a report is being made as per the SRA Codes of Conduct.

When a whistleblowing situation arises, firms need to act quickly and professionally and should not dismiss the concerns being raised without documented consideration and, where appropriate, should investigate what is being reported.

If an employee, who reports something which they consider serious, feels they are not taken seriously, the firm risks that feeling spreading across the firm and the firm could gain an internal (or external) reputation for not listening. This then discourages further whistleblowing or reporting of concerns.

9.4.7 To that end – practise

If at all possible, firms should consider practising on paper whistleblowing or reporting concerns scenarios (just like a firm might practise a business continuity situation).

Firms should think about what kind of whistleblowing claim or reporting concern could be made, such as an illegal activity (money laundering for example) or the breaching of the non-banking rule (SRA Accounts Rules, rule 3.3) and plan on paper how the firm would proceed to investigate that report. Firms would do well to also consider in advance who they would involve in such an investigation, and what filing system they would use to store what is bound to be highly confidential information.

9.5 WHAT IF YOU HAVE OFFICES IN DIFFERENT COUNTRIES?

Firms with offices in different countries may decide to implement a policy in each office that follows the legal requirements in each location. This might be quite tricky to implement and supervise.

Firms may decide to implement a policy which is the same across all offices. If a firm does this, it will need to adopt the highest standard required, dependent on the location of the offices but ensuring it does not cut across some legislation requirements in certain countries.

However, on the other hand, firms may not want to hold themselves to a policy that goes way beyond local legal requirements.

Whatever a firm decides to do, what is ultimately important is that the firm has some form of whistleblowing policy and process in place, and that this is communicated, if the firm wants to have any chance of preventing a catastrophic event and/or information going public before being discussed internally.

APPENDIX A

Anti-bribery and corruption

APPENDIX A1

Template anti-bribery and corruption risk assessment

This assessment should be adapted to suit the firm's business.

This risk assessment was completed on [*insert date*] and last reviewed on [*insert date*] by [*insert name*].

Area of risk	Assessment of risk (what is the firm's work type – how likely is bribery to happen in firm)	Mitigation steps in place (policies and procedures)	Likelihood of bribery (low, medium or high)	Mitigation steps to take	Completion of steps and date
Country risk Does the firm work in or with high-risk jurisdictions? Does the firm have sufficient oversight of staff working in these countries or with high-risk clients?					

APPENDIX A1

Area of risk	Assessment of risk (what is the firm's work type – how likely is bribery to happen in firm)	Mitigation steps in place (policies and procedures)	Likelihood of bribery (low, medium or high)	Mitigation steps to take	Completion of steps and date
Sector risk Is the firm working with clients in high bribery risk sectors? Does the firm work in sectors that have a higher risk of bribery?					

TEMPLATE ANTI-BRIBERY AND CORRUPTION RISK ASSESSMENT

Area of risk	Assessment of risk (what is the firm's work type – how likely is bribery to happen in firm)	Mitigation steps in place (policies and procedures)	Likelihood of bribery (low, medium or high)	Mitigation steps to take	Completion of steps and date
Supplier risk Does the firm ensure that contracts make it clear that offering or accepting bribes could lead to termination of the contract? Are there clear payment terms within the contract that are appropriate for the services provided? Does the firm have a robust procurement process to assess whether suppliers are compliant?					

APPENDIX A2

Template anti-bribery and corruption policy

INTRODUCTION

We value our reputation and are committed to maintaining the highest ethical standards in the conduct of our business.

This policy applies to all employees, partners, agents, consultants, contractors and to any other people or bodies associated with the practice.

THE LEGISLATION

The Bribery Act 2010 came into force on 1 July 2011. It creates three main offences: bribing a person to induce or reward them to perform a relevant function; improperly requesting, accepting or receiving a bribe as a reward for performing a relevant function; and improperly using a bribe to influence a foreign official to gain a business advantage.

Bribery is not always a matter of handing over cash. Gifts, hospitality and entertainment can be bribes if they are intended to influence a decision.

Under the Act, bribery by individuals is punishable by up to 10 years' imprisonment and/or an unlimited fine. If the firm is found to have taken part in bribery or to lack adequate procedures to prevent bribery, it too could face an unlimited fine.

A conviction for a bribery or corruption related offence would have severe reputational and financial consequences for us.

MANAGERIAL RESPONSIBILITIES

The Anti-Bribery Officer (ABO) is [*insert name and consider whether you would like to name a deputy*]. The ABO is responsible for overseeing our policy on anti-bribery and corruption and ensuring it is upheld in both word and spirit.

This responsibility includes:

- an annual review of the policy;
- an annual risk assessment of issues relating to the policy;
- overseeing training and communications relating to the topic.

The ABO has authority to make amendments to this policy but ultimately all partners of the practice remain accountable for its implementation.

THIRD PARTY DUE DILIGENCE

The scope of the Bribery Act 2010 requires us to identify third party business relationships which may give opportunity for that third party to use bribery while acting on our behalf. Appropriate due diligence should be undertaken before a third party is engaged. Third parties should only be engaged where there is a clear business rationale for doing so, with an appropriate contract. Any payments to third parties should be properly authorised and recorded. [*Note – you may wish to cross-refer to your procurement process.*]

GIFTS AND HOSPITALITY

Gifts and hospitality are commonly used in business circles to build relationships and market services or products. Hospitality often takes the form of entertainment, meals or tickets to events. If the provider of the hospitality does not attend, then it should be regarded as a gift. Businesses often pay expenses for a potential client to attend business-related conferences or events.

While this is all normal practice, it is recognised that gifts and hospitality can be used to influence and corrupt third parties, and on occasion to manoeuvre employees into a position of obligation. When considering whether to accept a gift, what matters is the intention behind it. If it is offered as a bribe, it should be refused; but if it is offered as a genuine gift, it may be accepted provided that all aspects of this policy are complied with.

We want to prevent the giving or receiving of gifts, hospitality or paying of expenses if it might influence or be perceived to influence a business decision. Accordingly, gifts, entertainment and hospitality over the value of £[*insert value which fits your firm – this might be say £100 or may be £500*] either given or received must be reported to the ABO and logged in the Gift Register by either the ABO or the business development team as appropriate [*adapt as appropriate*]. This allows us to monitor both the level and the number of instances to assess whether the nature of the relationship is appropriate.

RISK ASSESSMENT

We will conduct a risk assessment to assess the extent and nature of the risk of bribery or corruption to which we might be liable in our activities. This assessment will record the type of risk and the means by which we can prevent or mitigate our exposure to such risk. [*Note – you may wish to create a document setting out your risk assessment or combine it with your firm-wide anti-money laundering (AML) risk assessment.*]

COMMUNICATION AND TRAINING

It is important that we are all aware of this policy, and for this reason we will ensure that:

- it is available via our intranet;
- you are notified of any amendments via email and the intranet;
- new staff are made aware of the policy as part of their induction;
- training will be provided, as necessary.

PERSONAL RESPONSIBILITIES

We must all take personal responsibility for upholding the principles of this policy. Aside from the risk of criminal liability, you should be aware that any breach of procedure in relation to its letter or spirit may be interpreted as a matter of misconduct and could result in disciplinary proceedings.

You should not hesitate to contact the ABO if you have any questions about the Anti-Bribery and Corruption Policy, its implementation or implications.

You are all actively encouraged to contact the ABO if you have any suspicions about another member of staff or any third party in relation to bribery and corruption. Such reports will be dealt with on a strictly confidential basis.

APPENDIX B

Anti-money laundering

APPENDIX B1

Template firm-wide anti-money laundering risk assessment

[Note to user – remember that this risk assessment must be tailored to suit your firm.]

Review notes by money laundering reporting officer (MLRO) – enter these on this row or in a different document								
Area of risk	**Type of risk**	**Explanation of risk and likelihood of it occurring**	**Policies**	**Procedures**	**Controls**	**Next steps**	**Completion notes**	**Completion date**
Clients	High turnover of clients v. stable client base							
	Politically exposed persons (PEPs)							
	Sanctioned individuals							

219

APPENDIX B1

	Adverse media	Large cash operators	Offshore companies	Complex corporate structures	Reside or operate in a high-risk jurisdiction	Operate in a high-risk sector	Require work done urgently unnecessarily – behavioural warning signs	Evasive when providing client due diligence (CDD)	Size and value of transaction

TEMPLATE FIRM-WIDE AML RISK ASSESSMENT

Area of practice/ type of transaction	Transactions that don't fit with the firm's or client's normal transaction type	Transactions or products that facilitate anonymity	New products, delivery mechanisms or technology	Complex transactions	Combining services
[Insert here your practice areas and types of transactions, along with associated risks]					

APPENDIX B1

Geographical areas in which we operate	[Insert here the geographical areas you operate in and assess the risk of each]						
Delivery channels	[Suggestions below]						
	Non face-to-face						
	Face-to-face						
	Through intermediary						
Other aspects considered	[Insert here other risks you considered. Below are some suggestions]						
	Suspicious activity reports (SARs)						
	High-risk register						

TEMPLATE FIRM-WIDE AML RISK ASSESSMENT

Monies being received before full CDD being completed	Misuse of client account

APPENDIX B2

Template suspicious activity report

We, [*name of law firm*], are a law firm located in [*insert location*] and we provide a wide range of legal services for our clients [*amend as necessary*]. We make this disclosure under section 330 of the Proceeds of Crime Act (POCA) 2002.

The proposed activity to which we seek a defence is [*set out the actual act you are seeking a defence for as succinctly as possible*].

We suspect these monies may be proceeds of crime for the reasons outlined below and that offences under sections [*insert specific sections that apply – s.327 and/or s.328 and/or s.329*] of POCA 2002 may be committed.

In this matter [*outline the matter including, who the firm acts for, details of the retainer, monies in, monies out, proposed activity and when it will be taking place*].

For the avoidance of doubt, this suspicious activity report (SAR) is being filed in discharge of our obligation to make disclosure of suspected money laundering pursuant to section 330 of POCA 2002.

APPENDIX B3

Privilege decision template from Legal Sector Affinity Group anti-money laundering guidance

[*See Legal Sector Affinity Group, 'Anti-money laundering guidance for the legal sector 2021', January 2021, para.13.8.1.*]

Question	Answer	Evidence
What are the specific terms of your retainer/ terms of engagement with the client? What have you been asked to do for your client?		
Has the retainer been varied at any stage? Was the variation express or implied?		
How has the retainer developed? What is the nature of the **'relevant legal context'** and the **'continuum of communication'** in relation to the document or conversation?		
What are the specific requirements set out in your **Rules of Professional Conduct** relating to your **professional obligations** relating to **confidential information** and **LPP [legal professional privilege]**? Is the right of the client to LPP based on the common law or statute?		

APPENDIX B3

Question	Answer	Evidence
Is the exchange or the material **confidential**? If so, why?		
On your analysis, does a **particular type of LPP (legal advice or litigation) apply?** If so, why?		
Why do you believe that a **disclosure obligation** may have arisen under the AML [anti-money laundering] legislation?		
Do you have knowledge of/formed a suspicion relating to money laundering? What is the precise nature of the suspicion? Is there a reasonable basis for the suspicion? Review the relevant test, such as *R* v. *Da Silva* [2006] and *R* v. *Anwoir* [2008].		
Has your client **agreed to waive LPP** in this exchange or document to make a joint disclosure?		
If your client has not agreed to waive privilege, **which exemption applies to displace** the primary duty to uphold **client confidentiality and LPP (statutory abrogation or the crime/fraud exception)**?		
Is this a case in which the **'privileged circumstance' exception** applies under s.330(6) POCA? Does common law LPP also apply?		
Based on the answers to the questions set out above, is this a **'marginal case'** or is the position unclear for any other reason?		

PRIVILEGE DECISION TEMPLATE FROM LSAG AML GUIDANCE

Question	Answer	Evidence
DECISION 1 **COMMUNICATION IS COVERED BY LPP**	Crime/fraud exception does not apply/no statutory abrogation and cannot make a disclosure without a breach of (i) retainer and (ii) Code of Conduct . . .	Note of retainer and Code.
DECISION 2 **COMMUNICATION RECEIVED IN 'PRIVILEGED CIRCUMSTANCES' within POCA**	Crime/fraud exception does not apply/no statutory abrogation and cannot make a disclosure without a breach of (i) retainer and (ii) Code of Conduct . . . You are exempt from making a disclosure to the NCA [National Crime Agency].	Note of retainer and Code.
DECISION 3 **COMMUNICATION NOT PRIVILEGED BUT CONFIDENTIAL**	If disclosable under POCA and not covered by LPP, disclosure can be made to avoid a breach of s.330.	
DECISION 4 **MARGINAL CASE**	A marginal case could turn in a definitional issue regarding the nature of the document or other communication. Review with MLRO [money laundering reporting officer] and/or external counsel.	

APPENDIX B4

Flowchart from Legal Sector Affinity Group anti-money laundering guidance

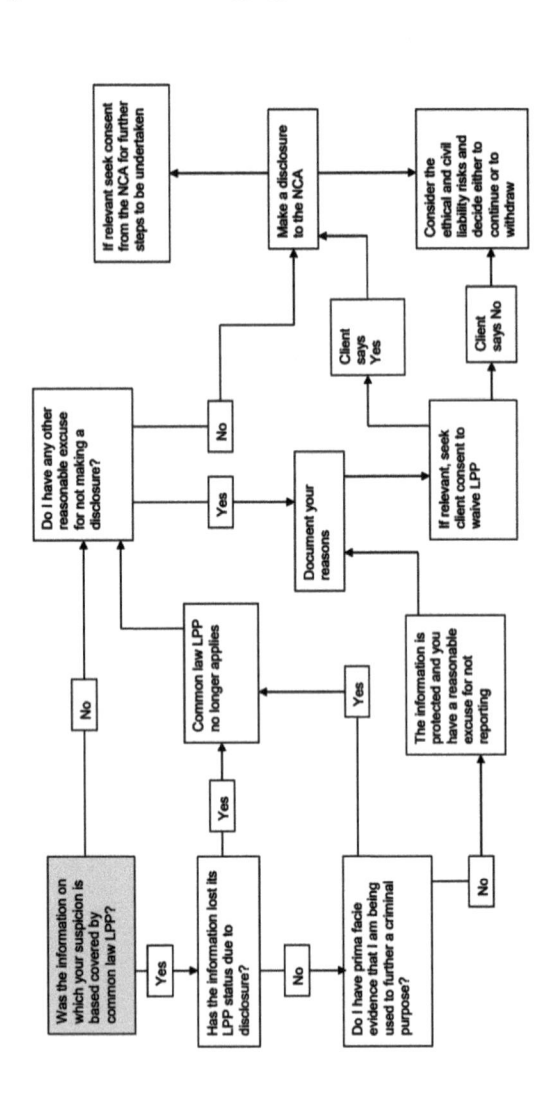

Legal Sector Affinity Group, 'Anti-money laundering guidance for the legal sector 2021', January 2021, Annex II Flowchart B, p.210

APPENDIX B5

Template anti-money laundering policy

[*Note – This template anti-money laundering (AML) policy is one way of writing a policy and must be adapted by firms if used. It is written on the basis of certain assumptions and these will need to be amended as appropriate. Firms must amend their AML policy to sit in line with their firm-wide risk assessment, and also the Legal Sector Affinity Group (LSAG) AML guidance (LSAG, 'Anti-money laundering guidance for the legal sector 2021', January 2021).*]

INTRODUCTION

Law firms are key players in the financial and business world, facilitating vital transactions that underpin the UK economy. As such, we have an important role to play in ensuring that our services are not used to further a criminal purpose. The objective of this policy is to help us all comply with our obligations under the UK anti-money laundering and counter-terrorist financing regime. All those who have any questions regarding this policy should speak to the money laundering reporting officer (MLRO) and where appropriate are encouraged to read the Legal Sector Affinity Group (LSAG) guidance found on the Law Society's website. This policy has been approved by the firm's MLRO and money laundering compliance officer (MLCO) and was last reviewed [*insert date*].

WHAT IS MONEY LAUNDERING?

Money laundering is generally defined as the process by which the proceeds of crime, and the true ownership of those proceeds, are changed so that they appear to come from a legitimate source. It is designed to disguise the true origin of criminal proceeds to give them legitimacy to enable their subsequent use.

HOW ARE LAWYERS AND LAW FIRMS AT RISK?

Law firms are at risk of being used by criminals to launder the proceeds of crime by channelling money through client accounts to make it look as if it came from a legitimate source. Proceeds of crime is widely defined and as well as covering things such as the illicit sale of drugs, it can include small profits and savings from relatively minor crimes, such as regulatory breaches, tax evasion and benefit fraud.

It is vital to note that whilst all European Union (EU) countries were required to introduce legislation to cover all serious crime, the UK went further and included all 'proceeds of crime' in its legislation. This means that UK legislation applies to all 'proceeds of crime', however minor and regardless of when the crime was committed. It may also apply if the criminal activity concerned took place abroad.

Our policy is that we will take no avoidable risks and will co-operate fully with the authorities where necessary. No matter how much we want to help our clients, we must not be a party to any form of dishonesty. We must be alert to the possibility that transactions might involve money laundering and follow our policy to reduce the risk. Any failure to do so could

APPENDIX B5

result in disciplinary action and put you at personal risk of prosecution under the Proceeds of Crime Act (POCA) 2002.

APPOINTMENT OF MONEY LAUNDERING REPORTING OFFICER AND OFFICER RESPONSIBLE FOR COMPLIANCE WITH THE REGULATIONS

Under the regulations, we are required to appoint a money laundering reporting officer (MLRO) to deal with the reporting/disclosure requirements and an Officer to be responsible for compliance with the regulations. We are also required to establish and maintain risk-sensitive policies and procedures in order to prevent activities related to money laundering and terrorist financing. [*Insert name*] is our MLRO, and [*insert name*] is our Deputy MLRO. [*Insert name*] is the officer with overall responsibility for compliance with the money laundering regulations. Any questions about these guidelines or money laundering issues generally (including any queries from law enforcement agencies) should be addressed to [*insert name*] or in their absence [*insert name*].

THE MONEY LAUNDERING, TERRORIST FINANCING AND TRANSFER OF FUNDS (INFORMATION ON THE PAYER) REGULATIONS 2017

In accordance with the requirements of the 2017 Regulations, we will carry out the following steps (this is not an exhaustive list):

- conduct an annual risk assessment which will assess the risk level particular to our firm and ensure that we implement reasonable and considered controls to minimise those risks;
- review our policies, procedures and controls annually to ensure that we fulfil our regulatory obligations. A review may also be carried out if a change in legislation occurs that requires a change to our approach;
- when a new client is on-boarded, all due diligence carried out on a client is checked and any concerns or issues reported to the MLRO;
- conduct risk assessments on our clients and their matters at the outset of the matter or as soon as practicable and where necessary conduct ongoing monitoring;
- screen all new relevant members of staff prior to them joining the firm;
- undertake appropriate screening on existing staff who are involved in the detection, identification, prevention or mitigation of money laundering risk to include annual checks using [*insert tool*] or an equivalent supplier and the Solicitors Regulation Authority (SRA) register;
- regularly train staff about the law and our procedures regarding money laundering taking into account changes in legislation or practice. Anti-money laundering (AML) training is included as part of staff induction and must be completed within three months of starting. Refresher training will take place every two years and where necessary (i.e. for high-risk practice areas) more frequently. Records of staff training are kept to ensure that no one is overlooked; and
- maintain records of evidence of identity for at least five years from the end of the client relationship.

BEWARE OF POTENTIAL RISKS

The money laundering process has traditionally been described as being divided into three stages:

1. **Placement** – Cash generated from crime is placed into the financial system.
2. **Layering** – Once the proceeds of crime are in the financial system, layering obscures

their origins by passing the money through complex transactions. These often involve different entities such as companies and trusts, and can take place in multiple jurisdictions.
3. **Integration** – Involves the translation of the laundered funds into a legitimate asset, such as the purchase of property through a conveyancing solicitor.

We can be targeted by criminals at any of these stages. We must therefore be vigilant to minimise the risks of:

- exposure to potential civil or criminal liability because of fraud, money laundering or the financing of terrorism, even where that exposure is as a result of innocent involvement in fraudulent transactions;
- reputational damage;
- claims from the true owner of property that we may have been involved in unlawful dealings;
- claims from the UK or other authorities; and
- disciplinary action from our professional regulator, the SRA.

YOUR ROLE

To protect yourself and us from potential prosecution for being involved in money laundering, you should act as follows:

- During the course of any transaction you should be alert to the possibility of money laundering activity and satisfy yourself that the transaction in question is legitimate and does not involve criminal property.
- If, during the course of any transaction, you become aware or suspect that criminal property is involved you should immediately discuss the circumstances with the MLRO. They will then advise you on the next steps after considering the circumstances. In particular, they will advise whether it is necessary to submit a formal disclosure.
- Once you have referred your knowledge or suspicion to the MLRO, you must not take any further steps in the transaction unless authorised in writing by the MLRO.
- Having reported the circumstances, unless authorised by the MLRO, you must not discuss your concerns with the client or anyone else.

CONFIDENTIALITY AND PRIVILEGE

Clients who instruct us are entitled to expect that their affairs are kept confidential. Everyone in the firm has a duty, under the SRA Codes of Conduct, to keep clients' affairs confidential. However, this duty can be overridden in very limited circumstances and these include situations where we have a statutory obligation to report known or suspected money laundering activity.

If anyone acquires knowledge or becomes suspicious about any form of activity which involves criminal property, they will have a statutory duty to report the circumstances to the MLRO. However, in certain circumstances, where the knowledge or suspicion is acquired in privileged circumstances, there will be no requirement to report.

The law relating to legal privilege is very complicated. You will not be breaching any privilege by discussing the circumstances of a case with the MLRO with a view to seeking their advice as to your disclosure obligations under POCA 2002. The MLRO will be solely responsible for determining issues relating to privilege and external reporting obligations to the National Crime Agency (NCA).

APPENDIX B5

PRIVILEGE AND LITIGATION WORK

In 2005 the Court of Appeal in the case of *Bowman* v. *Fels* [2005] EWCA Civ 226 effectively ruled that in general the money laundering offences do not apply to most forms of litigation including family work and mediation. Whilst therefore (in litigation work) there will be no requirement to formally report knowledge or suspicions of activity involving criminal property, it will still be necessary to provide the MLRO with all the relevant details so that the information can be recorded against the particular client or the property in question. This will enable us to 'flag up' the relevant client and property in the event that we are ever instructed in the future outside the litigation context in relation to the property in question.

DETECTING MONEY LAUNDERING – GENERAL GROUNDS FOR SUSPICION OF MONEY LAUNDERING

It is not possible to provide an exhaustive list of circumstances or situations that might give rise to a suspicion. However, please consider the following (this is not an exhaustive list and please also see the firm's client and matter risk assessment which sets out the risk factors you need to consider).

- Be vigilant at all times and be alert to the possibility of money laundering by clients or third parties. In most situations it should be obvious that the transaction in question is perfectly legitimate.
- Where a third party (such as the other person in a transaction) or a client we have not yet fully on-boarded sends us monies, **NEVER** send those monies back or use those monies for the transaction until we are satisfied as to the sender's identity, and where appropriate, source of funds and wealth. Sending the monies back can in effect clean them, and you should be suspicious of any third party sending monies to us uninvited.
- Always take care when dealing with a client who has no obvious reasons for using our services – e.g. clients with distant addresses who could find the same service nearer to home; or clients whose requirements do not fit into the normal pattern of our business and could be more easily serviced elsewhere.
- If you are in any way suspicious about the circumstances of a particular transaction, discuss it with the MLRO before getting involved.
- Be aware of higher risk factors – e.g. handling high value items such as art for which ownership is not clear; or dealing with a transaction that is creating or facilitating anonymity of ownership or a transaction which is unnecessarily complex, unusually large or has an unusual pattern of transactions within it. What is considered to be complex or unusually large should be judged in relation to the normal activities of the firm and client.
- The view of the SRA is that we should also be aware of clients who combine services. These can be services that may not be inherently risky but when combined with other services may become so. For example, setting up a company to purchase a property and disguise beneficial ownership. Combining services may also be where the client is using our firm for one aspect of a transaction and another firm for a different aspect of the transaction. This may obscure what would otherwise cause suspicion.
- The SRA also sets out that we should be cautious of transactions or products that facilitate anonymity or that do not fit in with our profile as a firm or the client's normal type of transaction.
- There may be good reasons why a client wishes to pay money to us in cash. However, it should be a warning signal to you if this happens. You must satisfy yourself that there is a good and legitimate reason for this method of payment. Do not be afraid of asking the client for a full explanation. Always make a note on the file of the explanation and if in any doubt seek guidance from the MLRO.
- Cash payments from clients will only be accepted for sums up to £500, but even then

TEMPLATE ANTI-MONEY LAUNDERING POLICY

enquiries will be made as to why the payment has to be made in cash. Where any larger cash payments are offered, the matter will be referred to the MLRO and only accepted with their authorisation.
- Under no circumstances must our client account be used except in cases where there is a genuine underlying legal transaction or some other valid reason for clients' money to be held. This is a fundamental requirement and must be observed at all times.
- Where possible, meet new clients in person. Be very cautious about third parties introducing clients whom you do not meet.
- If anything about the circumstances of a transaction gives cause for concern, then ask more questions. The answers may deal with your initial cause for concern. If they do not, then the answers may give foundation to a suspicion and you may have to consider whether or not the circumstances need to be reported.
- Sometimes it is the details of 'the deal' itself that just do not make sense. Try to get full details of the transaction, its structure and its funding source before you become involved. If your instructions change dramatically or they change at the last minute be very wary. Watch out if it appears on the face of it that the client is overpaying for something, or selling something at a significant loss.
- Another area which should raise warning signals is where the transaction involves the client insisting on paying monies direct to the other party, as opposed to through solicitors.
- People may wish to avoid paying tax. Sometimes they attempt to achieve this by laundering money through a solicitors' firm. You must be careful not to become unwittingly involved in such activity.
- A client who refuses to co-operate with you about identification and other 'client due diligence' procedures should not remain a client.
- A client who gives confusing and/or misleading identification and other required information about the source and flow of funds should be questioned.
- Be extremely vigilant if a client wishes to use offshore funds for a particular transaction. There may be a very good and legitimate reason why offshore funds are being used. If in doubt, please refer to the MLRO.
- Be wary if the client tells you that they have just 'won the lottery' or have inherited a large sum of money. It may be true, but you should seek information to satisfy yourself that it is.
- A flow of funds through our client account that is out of character with your actual knowledge of the financial standing of the client or with the circumstances of the transaction may give rise to suspicion.
- There may be cases where the client provides instructions and transfers funds to us and suddenly, for no obvious reason, the matter becomes abortive and the funds are returned to the client. We are not suggesting that all abortive work should be regarded as suspicious, we are simply saying that you should be careful. It is well known that money launderers often use solicitors in this way.
- Be on your guard if a client asks you to simply prepare paperwork to reflect the transfer of an asset in circumstances where they have already paid the full consideration to the other party.
- If you know that your client is bankrupt or you have suspicions about their financial position, be wary if the client wishes to deal in cash.
- Believe it or not, money launderers do go to the extremes of inventing legal disputes. This type of money laundering is often difficult to detect, but if a case suddenly takes an unexpected turn and settles quickly without any apparent reason, your suspicions may be raised.

APPENDIX B5

The identity information that you have obtained should ensure that you know enough about your client and your client's normal expected activities to recognise unusual or suspicious instructions or matters. A suspicious instruction or matter should give rise to further enquiry.

REPORTING A SUSPICIOUS ACTIVITY

If you do have any concerns of whatever nature, that either your client or any third party is engaged in money laundering, then you should immediately discuss the matter with the MLRO. Under no circumstances should you discuss your suspicion with your client or any third party or generally in the office. To do so could amount to the criminal offence of 'tipping off.'

If you have concerns about the client, any other party to the transaction or any aspect of any matter, you **MUST**:

- review and immediately follow our procedures which requires you to discuss the matter with the MLRO. Your suspicion or concern can relate to a major or minor crime and it matters not where or when it was committed, so long as it would have been a criminal offence if it had happened in the UK;
- not fail to report your suspicion or concern because you believe the matter may be privileged. This is a matter for the MLRO to determine;
- if you continue to have concerns report your concerns to the MLRO as a suspicion following our firm's procedures. If you have reported to the MLRO and they consider the report to be justified, they will report to the NCA and if appropriate, obtain their express or deemed permission to continue to act. In the meantime, you should take no steps to progress the transaction without the MLRO's consent;
- refer any enquiries from the SRA, NCA or the police to the MLRO immediately to allow them to deal with the enquiries with urgency, if required;
- keep the fact that a report has been made confidential, even within the office;
- take care as to what is recorded on the client file;
- strictly and fully observe our firm's reporting procedures in order to gain the protection afforded to you personally by the legislation.

You **MUST NOT**:

- do anything to indicate to the client, or anyone else, that a report has been made to the MLRO or to NCA; and in particular, you **MUST NOT** report directly to NCA.

CLIENT DUE DILIGENCE

The money laundering regulations require us to carry out 'client due diligence' ('CDD') and 'ongoing monitoring' on clients who retain our services. Clients we can identify are less likely to be conducting money laundering.

The importance of thorough CDD

Our reputation is our greatest asset. Thorough CDD will not only ensure compliance with the law, but will tend to deter undesirable clients from instructing us.

When taking instructions from new clients, you must explain your obligation to carry out due diligence and the reason why this must be done. Where appropriate, ask questions about the source of the client's wealth and how any transaction is to be financed. Few honest clients will resent such questions. Our client care letter explains our CDD obligations, and you may wish to draw that explanation to your clients' attention when you speak or meet with them.

We also have available information sheets which can be accessed on the Risk & Compliance page of the intranet which outline the identification documents that we would like to see

TEMPLATE ANTI-MONEY LAUNDERING POLICY

from clients according to their type. You should send this to your clients, as appropriate, when carrying out client due diligence.

CDD involves a number of elements:

These are:

1. identifying the client and verifying their identity on the basis of documents, data or information obtained from a reliable and independent source (this can be on a simplified, standard or enhanced due diligence basis);
2. identifying where there is a beneficial owner who is not the client and taking adequate measures, on a risk sensitive basis, to verify their identity so that you are satisfied that you know who the beneficial owner is. This includes understanding the ownership and control of a legal person, trust or similar arrangement;
3. identifying where clients operate in a high-risk jurisdiction and taking appropriate ongoing monitoring measures;
4. verifying the identity of those who purport to act on behalf of the client ;
5. undertaking sanctions, politically exposed persons (PEPs) and adverse media checks;
6. understanding the source of funds and wealth (for example, when dealing with the purchase of assets and also handling assets which were made/created/bought in a high-risk jurisdiction); and
7. obtaining information on the purpose and intended nature of the business relationship.

In relation to point 4, the legal requirement is in line with other law firms in that this requirement is seeking to capture situations such as family members giving instructions on behalf of the client. It is not intended to capture, for example, a bank employee who clearly has the correct job role to provide us instructions on behalf of the bank.

Our procedure

It is our policy to verify the identity of all new clients and all existing clients that we have not acted for within the last [X] years at the start of a new matter [*amend as appropriate to suit the firm*].

For all matters, the client's full name, address and telephone number should be obtained and recorded correctly on our database. For companies, we also require the full names of those who sit on the Board, the senior people responsible for the operations of the body and the usual entity information such as registered address, company number and the laws to which it is subject.

Particular care must be taken when acting on the instructions of someone on behalf of the true client or where our client is clearly an agent for a third party. In those circumstances, you must ensure that steps are taken to establish and verify the identity of both parties.

A client's identity must be verified within five working days of a file opening (when work begins) or files will be locked with no ability to time record or bill [*amend as appropriate*].

No client money should be accepted from the client for payment into client account until the verification process has been satisfactorily completed.

You should be satisfied that any documents offered to verify identity are originals so as to guard against forgery. Ensure that any photographs provide an actual likeness of the client. Take copies of the relevant evidence and sign and date the copies to certify that they have been compared with the originals. If you do not see the originals, you can accept copies provided they have been certified by a regulated professional.

We categorise our clients into three risk levels: low; medium; high. Low-risk clients might include financial institutions, listed companies and public authorities where the work that is being conducted can also be considered to be low risk and the client operates in a low-risk

APPENDIX B5

jurisdiction. High-risk clients can include those where there is no face-to-face meeting or where the client is a PEP.

If a client is a PEP, then their details must be passed to the Risk & Compliance team so that the MLRO can approve the firm acting for the PEP and so that the PEP may be added to our high-risk register. At the outset of a matter, the Risk & Compliance team will conduct a PEP check using an online database. However, if you are aware early on in your interaction with a potential client that they are or may be a PEP, you must contact the Risk & Compliance team as soon as possible so that they may conduct checks at an early stage. This will help prevent any delays in on-boarding a client later on.

When acting for a PEP, you must also consider whether it is appropriate to:

- seek further verification of the client's or beneficial owner's identity;
- obtain more detail on the ownership and control of the client;
- request further information on the purposes of the retainer or the source of the funds; and
- conduct enhanced ongoing monitoring.

Please note you can only act for a PEP with the approval of the MLRO as required by the Regulations.

Our CDD checks include identifying whether clients are subject to sanctions. The Risk & Compliance team do this by way of [*insert tool*] check on matter inception.

Financial sanctions aim to safeguard international security and prevent terrorism. **It can be an offence to do business with someone who is subject to sanctions.** We conduct a sanctions check on all clients at matter inception and any adverse results are reported back to the fee earner with conduct of the case. Identifying whether a client is subject to counter-measures by the Financial Action Task Force or the UK Treasury, where the Treasury has imposed financial restrictions, can be checked by accessing the restrictions list at **www.gov.uk/government/publications/financial-sanctions-consolidated-list-of-targets/ consolidated-list-of-targets**. Identifying whether clients are subject to financial sanctions following designation by the United Nations or the European Commission can be checked by accessing the full list at **www.gov.uk/government/publications/financial-sanctions-consolidated-list-of-targets**. If you have any concerns relating to sanctions, you should speak to a member of the Risk & Compliance team.

Enhanced due diligence (EDD)

EDD is required to be undertaken under the following non-exhaustive circumstances:

- the client is a PEP and we are undertaking a transaction for them;
- where the transaction is complex;
- where the transaction is unusually large;
- where the client is established in a high-risk jurisdiction;
- where there is an unusual pattern of transactions, or the transaction or transactions have no apparent economic or legal purpose;
- there are unfavourable answers to the client and matter risk assessment meaning the client and matter are not deemed low or medium risk.

Whether a transaction is 'complex' or 'unusually large' should be judged in relation to the normal activity of the firm and the normal activity of the client.

The Fifth EU Directive on Money Laundering sets out additional factors to take account of in deciding whether EDD should be applied:

- whether the person is a beneficiary of a life insurance policy (whether the person is a beneficiary of a life insurance policy is only likely to be indicative of higher AML risk where the retainer bears direct relevance to the policy);

- whether the person is seeking residence/citizen rights in exchange for investments in that EEA state;
- whether you act without face-to-face meeting and without electronic identity systems to mitigate this;
- whether the person is involved in the trade of oil; arms; precious metals; tobacco products; cultural artefacts; ivory and other items related to protected species; and other items of archaeological, historical, cultural and religious significance, or of rare scientific value.

Client has changed

Where the client has changed (for example, the underlying client has altered which purchase vehicle will be used or formed a new purchase vehicle), the CDD process must be repeated for that new client and the new client set up in the appropriate way.

Beneficiaries of trusts

There are additional requirements in relation to the identification of beneficiaries. Before we are able to make any distribution or the beneficiary is able to exercise their rights in the trust, we must ensure that we have established and verified the identity of that beneficiary.

There are also additional obligations for reporting the details of trusts and beneficial owners to HM Revenue and Customs (HMRC) as set out in the regulations and our Private Client team are aware of these obligations.

Third party reliance

As a firm, our starting point is that we do not rely on a third party's analysis of a client's due diligence documentation. The reason for this is that we will be liable for any failure by the third party to carry out the identity checks properly. If a third party such as another solicitor, financial institution or accountant has obtained CDD, you may ask that the CDD is sent to you for you to analyse to see whether it is satisfactory according to the firm's standards.

A third party may request to rely on the firm's due diligence documents for the purpose of satisfying their money laundering requirements. These third parties can be other solicitors or estate agents for example.

While we consider that we satisfy our due diligence requirements accurately, there is always the chance that we could get it wrong. By allowing a third party to place reliance on our due diligence, we may become liable to them if the documents we hold are not accurate. **We do not therefore allow others to rely on our assessment of the client's CDD.**

Subject to the client's consent, we would be willing to provide the third party with the CDD documents. However, it is for the third party to decide whether or not to rely on the documents for satisfying their money laundering requirements.

If you receive such a request, you are asked to adopt the following wording in your response:

> Subject to obtaining our client's consent, we will provide you with a copy of the due diligence we hold on our file to assist your due diligence requirements under the money laundering regulations. However, it is for you to form your own opinion of these documents.
>
> For the avoidance of doubt, [*insert firm name*] does not consent to the application of Regulation 39 of the Money Laundering, Terrorist Financing and Transfer of Funds (Information on the Payer) Regulations 2017 and you cannot place reliance on this firm's assessment.

If you have any queries, please contact the Risk & Compliance team.

APPENDIX B5

Identification requirements

For details on what documents are required to identify our clients, please see the information sheets found on the intranet.

Please note that the money laundering regulations do not allow the firm to automatically apply simplified due diligence where a client is regulated or listed (i.e. use their regulated or listed status as evidence of identity) without first assessing the risk (by analysing the type of operation the client undertakes and jurisdiction of the client and its operations). The firm's client and matter risk assessment therefore covers this requirement when completed.

We recognise that more and more clients do not have physical/original proof of address because it is held electronically only. We will accept an electronic proof of address, but only where the client is unable to provide physical/original proof of address.

The importance of obtaining documentary evidence

Evidence of identity must be kept with the individual client file and uploaded into [*insert*]. This ensures that any other fee earner wanting to check the identity documents for a client will know where those documents are located.

It needs to be borne in mind at all times that the dual objectives of seeking CDD are to meet statutory requirements as well as to 'know your client' and understand its business.

A common sense approach should be adopted. For example, you should check the client's correspondence address against the verification evidence and any discrepancy must be satisfactorily explained. It may not be possible to obtain all of the documents specified and there will be some circumstances in which judgment needs to be exercised. If you are in any doubt, the Risk & Compliance team is on hand to help you make the correct judgment call.

Where you inspect an original document, a copy should be taken and the copy should be marked 'original seen' and signed by the relevant fee earner or the fee earner should apply the usual certification.

Documentary evidence from prospective and actual clients and information from other sources obtained when undertaking client due diligence form an essential record of the steps we have taken as a firm to comply with our money laundering obligations. Such records may be subject to inspection by the regulatory authorities.

Failure to comply with these regulatory requirements can amount to an offence, irrespective of whether any money laundering has taken place.

The requirements should be applied to all new clients but we are also under an obligation to monitor client relationships.

We are required to retain documentary evidence of ID for a minimum period of five years after the end of the client relationship.

Renewing ID evidence

Once we have evidence of identification on file for a particular client there will be no need to obtain similar evidence if we are instructed by that client on a new matter unless we have not acted for them in the last [X] years in which case fresh identification evidence should be obtained. If we become aware during a matter or at the beginning of a new matter that the structure or details of the client has or have changed, then we must refresh our CDD regardless of the [X] year rule.

If you are in any doubt about what evidence to obtain or whether the evidence that you have is adequate, you should consult the Risk & Compliance team.

Where joint instructions are received, identification procedures should be applied to each client. If joint clients have the same name and address (e.g. spouses) the verification of the address for one client only is sufficient.

RISK ASSESSMENTS

As part of our assessment of the client and the matter at hand, we conduct a risk assessment at the outset of a matter and where necessary select the client for ongoing monitoring.

The risk assessment is split into two parts – client and matter. The first part of the client risk assessment is conducted by the Risk & Compliance team as soon as possible after client opening and includes the PEP, sanctions, and adverse media checks and a thorough review of the client identification documents. The conducting fee earner is tasked with completing the second part of the client assessment and matter risk assessment as soon as possible and within five working days of the client opening or work beginning, whichever is the earliest.

Depending on the client and/or matter assessment, the client may be selected for ongoing monitoring by the Risk & Compliance team or the conducting fee earner. If this is the case, that decision will be recorded and the method of ongoing monitoring selected and carried out. Please see the firm-wide client and matter risk assessment and guidance for more information.

MORTGAGE FRAUD

This AML policy and procedure should be read in conjunction with the policy relating to mortgage fraud.

APPENDIX B6

Template client and matter risk assessment

[*Note: There are many ways in which to conduct a client and matter risk assessment and this is just one way. The questions below have been designed based on the anti-money laundering (AML) regulations and Solicitors Regulation Authority (SRA) guidance. This assessment template is based on a firm having a centralised on-boarding process by a Risk & Compliance team. If this is not the case, the firm will need to amend the client assessment parts 1 and 2 to make it clear that the fee earner completes all client risk assessment questions.*]

Client and matter number: ....

Client name and matter description: ....

Solicitors are required to identify and assess risk on each and every client and matter as soon as possible and on an ongoing basis. This is not only to ensure compliance with the money laundering legislation but also as part of firm-wide good practice. The risk assessment is split into two parts – client and matter.

The Risk & Compliance team will complete the first client assessment section of this form as soon as possible after a new client is opened. Fee earners should complete their sections as soon as possible and keep it under review and amend as necessary as the matter progresses.

The Risk & Compliance team will place this risk assessment in [*insert location*]

CLIENT ASSESSMENT FOR NEW CLIENTS OR CLIENTS WE HAVE NOT ACTED FOR IN PAST 3 YEARS [AMEND TO SUIT YOUR FIRM POLICY]

Part 1 – initial assessment by Risk & Compliance

When answering Yes to any question, enhanced due diligence should be considered. When answering Yes to a question denoted with a * enhanced due diligence must be applied.

		Y/N/NA
1.	Is the client a regulated person or entity, or is the client listed on a regulated market?	
2.	Is the client resident in, operating from or controlled from a high-risk jurisdiction set out in Schedule 2 below?*	

TEMPLATE CLIENT AND MATTER RISK ASSESSMENT

3.	Does the client operate in any of the following sectors which are regarded as potentially high risk?: (a) High end art/goods (b) Cultural artefacts (c) Public works contracts and construction (d) Real estate and property development (e) Oil and gas (f) Nuclear industry (g) Mining (of any sort) (h) Tobacco products (i) Arms manufacturing/supply and the defence industry	
4.	Is simplified due diligence satisfactory for this client?	
5.	Is the client, director or beneficial owner a politically exposed person (PEP)?* This includes UK and foreign PEPs, their family members and known close associates.	
6.	Is the client, director or beneficial owner sanctioned?*	
7.	Is the client, director or beneficial owner resident in or a national of a country which is the subject of UK financial sanctions (refer to Schedule 1 below)?*	
8.	Are we aware of any adverse media about the client, a director or beneficial owner?	
9.	Have any of the client's shares been issued in the form of bearer shares (corporates only)?	
10.	Has the client been evasive or obstructive in relation to our anti-money laundering (AML) checks (especially regarding beneficial ownership or source of funds or wealth)?	
11.	Has the firm previously had to file a suspicious activity report (SAR) about this client?	
12.	If the client is unregulated does the client's ownership structure seem unusual or unnecessarily complex/opaque?*	
13.	Do we have satisfactory due diligence documentation?	
14.	Does the information provided by the client match the people with significant control (PSC) register? If not consider obligation to report.	

RISK RATING given by Risk & Compliance

If any of the factors for questions 1–13 apply, the client may be assessed as being high risk.

Client risk rating by Risk & Compliance (High/Medium/Low – if all answers are of a favourable nature then the risk is likely to be low depending on work type. However, answers of an unfavourable nature may indicate a medium- or high-risk rating): [*insert rating*] ....

Reasons if necessary: [*insert reasons*] ....

Has this client been selected for ongoing monitoring: Y/N

APPENDIX B6

Part 2 – to be completed by the conducting fee earner

When answering Yes to any question, enhanced due diligence should be considered. When answering Yes to a question denoted with a * enhanced due diligence must be applied.

		Y/N/NA
1.	Have we met the client (for companies this could be a director, beneficial owner or person with authority such as a general counsel)?	
2.	Does the client's business involve dealing with large amounts of cash?	
3.	As far as you are aware, has another law firm refused to accept the client or terminated their retainer?	
4.	If the client is unregulated, does the client's ownership structure seem unusual or unnecessarily complex/opaque?*	

MATTER ASSESSMENT FOR ALL MATTERS – TO BE COMPLETED BY THE CONDUCTING FEE EARNER

When answering Yes to any question, enhanced due diligence should be considered. When answering Yes to a question denoted with a * enhanced due diligence must be applied as the regulations require this. Please see separate guidance.

		Y/N/NA
1.	Are instructions for this matter being given by a third party? If so, ensure you have identified and verified that third party as appropriate.	
2.	Is there an underlying legal transaction?*	
3.	Is the client asking us to create a corporate structure or trust structure that is unnecessarily complex and/or could lead to tax evasion?*	
4.	Is the transaction unusually large or is there an unusual pattern of transactions?*	
5.	Does the transaction carry with it additional risk, e.g. it is handling high-value items such as art for which ownership is not clear; or does it create or facilitate anonymity of ownership; or is the transaction unnecessarily complex?	
6.	Does the value of the transaction exceed our professional indemnity cover of £[*insert*]? Please ensure that liability is capped.	
7.	Is the transaction consistent with what you know about the client's business or level of wealth generally?	
8.	Do you understand the source of funds for this transaction? Do you understand the client's source of wealth? Does the information you are being given tally with what you know? Please document below. **Please insert detail here.**	

TEMPLATE CLIENT AND MATTER RISK ASSESSMENT

9.	Will funds for the transaction be sent from a sanctioned jurisdiction OR high-risk country listed in Schedules 1 and 2 below?* If yes, please inform [*insert role or name*]	
10.	If funds are coming from a third party, are you satisfied that you know who the third party is and why they are funding? Consider whether you need to undertake CDD.	
11.	Is the client insisting that you proceed on an urgent basis without a reasonable explanation, and this is unusual for this client?	
12.	Is there anything else of concern to you? (Remember, if you suspect money laundering, please speak to the money laundering reporting officer (MLRO) straight away.)	

RISK RATING given by conducting fee earner

Client and Matter risk rating (High/Medium/Low – if all answers are of a favourable nature then the risk is likely to be low depending on the work type. However answers of an unfavourable nature may indicate a medium- or high-risk rating. If the latter please inform [*insert role or name*]. Please see accompanying guidance to assist your rating): [*insert rating*] ....

Reasons if necessary: [*insert reason*] ....

Remember you must tell [*insert role or name*] if your client changes address, ownership, directorship or corporate structure so that we can consider refreshing the CDD that the firm holds.

SCHEDULE 1

UK AND UN FINANCIAL SANCTIONS REGIMES

[*Note – firms need to check this list is accurate at the time of using this template by checking the Office of Financial Sanctions Implementation HM Treasury website (**www.gov.uk/ government/organisations/office-of-financial-sanctions-implementation**).*]

Afghanistan (UK)	Mali (UN)	South Sudan (UK & UN)
Belarus (UK)	Republic of Guinea (UK)	Sudan (UK & UN)
Burundi (UK)	Republic of Guinea-Bissau (UK & UN)	Syria (UK)
Burma (UK)	Iran	Tunisia (UK)
Central African Republic (UK & UN)	Iraq (UK & UN)	Ukraine
Democratic Republic of the Congo (UK & UN)	Lebanon and Syria (UK)	Venezuela (UK)
Egypt (UK)	Libya (UK & UN)	Yemen (UK & UN)

APPENDIX B6

Eritrea (UK & UN)	North Korea (Democratic People's Republic of Korea DPRK) (UK & UN)	Zimbabwe (UK)
ISIL (Da'esh) and Al-Qaida organisations (UK & UN)	Somalia (UK & UN)	

SCHEDULE 2

OTHER HIGH-RISK JURISDICTIONS

[*Note – firms need to check this list is accurate at the time of using this template and may wish to place below high-risk countries that the firm is more likely to encounter in its business.*]

Clients based in high-risk jurisdictions (individuals and corporates)

Transparency International publishes a list every year which ranks countries in order of their perceived levels of corruption (the Corruption Perceptions Index). The list of countries in the table below takes this into account together with the guidance on high-risk and non-co-operative jurisdictions published by the Financial Action Task Force (FATF).

The following list includes countries you are most likely to encounter. It is not intended to be exhaustive. To view the list visit **www.transparency.org/en/cpi/2020/index/nzl**

Afghanistan	Kenya	Russia
Bahrain	Kuwait	Saudi Arabia
Bosnia and Herzegovina	Lao PDR	South Africa
Brazil	Lebanon	South Sudan
China	Liberia	Sri Lanka
Cyprus	Libya	Sudan
Democratic People's Republic of Korea	Kazakhstan	Syria
Egypt	Malaysia	Thailand
Ethiopia	Malta	Trinidad and Tobago
Ghana	Mauritius	Tunisia
Greece	Mexico	Turkey
Grenada	Morocco	Uganda
India	Nigeria	Ukraine
Iran	North Korea (DPRK)	Vanuatu
Iraq	Oman	Venezuela
Italy	Pakistan	Yemen
Jamaica	Panama	Zimbabwe

APPENDIX B7

Template high-risk register

Active clients						
Client name	Client number	Fee earner	Reason for entry (politically exposed person (PEP), sanction or adverse media)	Date added	Frequency of check	Ongoing monitoring notes including who has conducted monitoring

Inactive clients								
Place here clients that have moved from active monitoring to inactive								
Client name	Client number	Fee earner	Reason for entry (PEP, sanction or adverse media)	Date added	Frequency of check	Ongoing monitoring notes, including who has conducted monitoring	Date of removal from active High-Risk Register	Reason for removal

Suspicious activity reports (SARs) register						

APPENDIX B7

Record here all SARs made internally or externally						
Name of client	Client number	Fee earner	Date SAR made	Content of SAR	Was SAR made to National Crime Agency (NCA)?	Outcome of NCA SAR
						[*Suggest here – defence given, no defence given, no reply, info only SAR*]

APPENDIX B8

Template ongoing anti-money laundering risk monitoring form

Name or reviewer:	
Fee earner:	
Date:	
Client name:	
Client number:	

[*Insert name*] has carried out the following:

- Politically exposed person (PEP), sanction, adverse media check [*comment – via a third party provider if this is possible*] – results are: [*insert results*]
  ....
- Google search – results are: [*insert results*]
  ....

[*Option 1:*] [*insert name if not the fee earner completing this form*] has spoken to [*name of fee earner*] and asked the following questions, responses underneath each point:

[*Option 2:*] I am the fee earner on this matter and I have considered the questions below and set out my answers:

- Is the transaction consistent with knowledge of client/business and risk profile?
- Has the structure of company changed? If so, obtain evidence.
- Has nature of the work changed?
- Source of funds, if appropriate?
- Do you have any concerns?

Please save this form [*insert place*].

APPENDIX B9

Template anti-money laundering audit table

[*Note: This is a basic anti-money laundering (AML) audit table – this audit table goes through the key regulations found under the Money Laundering, Terrorist Financing and Transfer of Funds (Information on the Payer) Regulations 2017, SI 2017/692 as amended, that need to be complied with, but firms are able to add more or audit less. This audit table will need reviewing by firms should the regulations change.*]

Area	Regulation	Requirement	Finding	Action
Firm-based risk assessment	Regulation 18(1)	The firm must take appropriate steps to identify and assess the risks of money laundering.		
	Regulation 18(2)(a)	In carrying out the risk assessment, the firm must take into account information made available to it by its supervisor (in the case of law firms, the Solicitors Regulation Authority (SRA)).		
	Regulation 18(2)(b)	In carrying out the risk assessment, the firm must take into account risk factors including factors relating to: (a) its customers; (b) the countries or geographic areas in which it operates; (c) its services; (d) its transactions; (e) its delivery channels.		
	Regulation 18(3)	In carrying out the risk assessment, the firm must take into account the size and nature of the firm.		
	Regulation 18(4)	The firm must keep an up-to-date record of all the steps taken to carry out the risk assessment.		

TEMPLATE AML AUDIT TABLE

Area	Regulation	Requirement	Finding	Action
Policies, controls and procedures (PCPs)	Regulation 19(1)(a) Regulation 19(3)	The firm must establish and maintain policies, controls and procedures to mitigate and manage effectively the risk of money laundering and terrorist financing. The policies controls and procedures must include: • risk management practices; • internal controls; • customer due diligence (CDD); • reliance and record-keeping; • monitoring and management of compliance with and the internal communication of such policies controls and procedures.		
	Regulation 19(1)(b)	The firm must regularly review and update the policies, controls and procedures.		
	Regulation 19(2)(a)	The policies, controls and procedures must be proportionate with regard to the size and nature of the firm.		
	Regulation 19(2)(b)	The policies, controls and procedures must be approved by its senior management.		

APPENDIX B9

Area	Regulation	Requirement	Finding	Action
	Regulation 19(4)	The policies, controls and procedures must: • provide for the identification and scrutiny of any case which is complex or unusually large or where there is an unusual pattern of transactions and there is no apparent legal or economic purpose; • specify the taking of additional measures where appropriate to prevent money laundering and transactions which might favour anonymity; • require a person who suspects money laundering or terrorist financing to comply with the relevant legislation.		
	Regulation 19(6)	The firm must communicate the policies, controls and procedures to its branches that are outside the UK.		
Internal controls	Regulation 21(1)(a)	With regard to the size and nature of its business, the firm must appoint one individual who is a member of the board, or senior management as the officer responsible for the firm's compliance with these regulations. This is the money laundering compliance officer (MLCO).		

TEMPLATE AML AUDIT TABLE

Area	Regulation	Requirement	Finding	Action
	Regulation 21(1)(b) and (2)	With regard to the size and nature of its business the firm must carry out screening of relevant employees, both before appointment is made and during the course of the appointment. 'Screening' means an assessment of the skills, knowledge and expertise of the individual and an assessment of their conduct and integrity. 'Relevant employee' means an employee whose work is relevant to compliance with these regulations or is otherwise capable of contributing to the identification or mitigation of the risk of money laundering and terrorist financing or the prevention or detection of money laundering or terrorist financing.		
	Regulation 21(1)(c)	The firm must establish an independent audit function.		
Training	Regulation 24(1)(a)	The firm must take appropriate measures to ensure that its relevant employees and any agents it uses for the purposes of the work under reg.24(2) are made aware of the law relating to money laundering and terrorist financing and the data protection requirements in the regulations and regularly given training to recognise transactions which may be related to money laundering or terrorist financing.		
Customer due diligence	Regulation 27(1)	The firm must apply customer due diligence measures if the person establishes a business relationship.		

APPENDIX B9

Area	Regulation	Requirement	Finding	Action
	Regulation 27(9)	When determining when it is appropriate to take customer due diligence measures in relation to existing customers, the firm must take into account: (a) any indication that the identity of the customer or of the customer's beneficial owner has changed; (b) any transactions which are not reasonably consistent with the relevant person's knowledge of the customer; (c) any change in the purpose or intended nature of the firm's relationship with the customer; (d) any other matter which might affect the firm's assessment of risk.		
Client identification and verification	Regulation 28	The firm must identify and verify its customer when undertaking regulated activity. The firm must understand what this means for each type of customer.		
Enhanced due diligence (EDD)	Regulation 33	The firm must apply EDD measures in any case which is identified as high risk, is with a person in a high-risk third country, where the customer is a politically exposed person (PEP) or where the transaction is unusually large, complex or unusual, or has no economic or legal purpose. If customer is established in a high-risk third country, then specific EDD measures need to be undertaken as set out in regulation 33(3A).		

TEMPLATE AML AUDIT TABLE

Area	Regulation	Requirement	Finding	Action
Ongoing monitoring	Regulation 28(11)	The firm must conduct ongoing monitoring, including scrutiny of transactions undertaken during the business relationship and undertaking review of existing records and keeping the due diligence up to date.		
Matter-based risk assessment	Regulation 28(12)(a)(ii)	The way in which the firm complies with the requirement to take customer due diligence measures must reflect the firm's risk assessment and the firm's assessment of the level of risk arising from any particular case.		
Purpose and nature of the transaction	Regulation 28(13)	In assessing the level of risk in a particular case, the firm must take account of the purpose of the transaction or business relationship, the level of assets to be deposited or size of transaction and regularity and duration of business relationship.		
Timing of verification	Regulation 30	The firm must comply with the requirement to verify the identity of the customer before the establishment of a business relationship, unless it would interrupt the normal conduct of business and there is little risk of money laundering, provided that verification is completed as soon as practicable.		
Politically exposed persons (PEPs)	Regulation 35(1)	The firm must have in place appropriate procedures to determine whether a customer or beneficial owner is a PEP or a family member or a known close associate of a PEP.		
	Regulation 35(5)	Where the firm intends to act for a PEP, there must be senior management approval; adequate measures taken to establish source of funds and wealth; and EDD conducted.		

APPENDIX B9

Area	Regulation	Requirement	Finding	Action
Simplified due diligence	Regulation 37	The firm may apply simplified due diligence measures where it determines the risk of money laundering or terrorist financing is low. The firm should have a procedure to determine whether simplified due diligence is appropriate.		
Reliance	Regulation 39	The firm may rely on a third party to apply due diligence provided that it immediately obtains from the third party all the information needed for due diligence and that it enters into arrangements with the third party to enable the firm to obtain copies of CDD information, and that the third party will retain the information. If the firm does not do this, is this documented in a policy.		
Record-keeping	Regulation 40(1), (2), (3)	The firm must keep copies of customer due diligence information and supporting documentation in relation to a transaction for five years after the end of the business relationship.		
	Regulation 40(5)	Once the period of retention has expired, the firm must delete any personal data obtained for these purposes unless the firm is required to retain the data by law, for court proceedings or the data subject has given consent for the retention.		

APPENDIX C

Criminal finances and investigations

APPENDIX C1

Template Criminal Finances Act 2017 risk assessment

The risk assessment below has been carried out by [*insert name*] and forms the firm's risk assessment further to the implementation of the Criminal Finances Act 2017. This risk assessment will be revisited and expanded upon, if appropriate, each year on the anniversary of the legislation coming into force or during the year if necessary. The last review of this risk assessment was [*insert date*]. [*Note – the frequency of review is a matter entirely for the firm to decide and this is just a suggestion.*]

[*Steps for use – Complete the assessment below by ticking or marking with a cross where appropriate. Then decide whether the firm has a low, medium or high risk of being involved with tax evasion and write down the steps the firm will take to mitigate these risks. There are some suggested steps below.*]

OUR CLIENTS	Never	Rarely	Sometimes	Often
Do we act for clients whom we have reason to suspect of past or present involvement in tax evasion?				
Do we otherwise act for clients who may pose particular tax evasion risks? For example: • cash-based businesses or their owners; • clients with assets in high-risk jurisdictions; • clients who hold assets through complex or obscure ownership structures.				
Do we have clients who for some other reason present a substantial tax evasion risk?				
OUR SERVICES	**Never**	**Rarely**	**Sometimes**	**Often**
Do we set up arrangements which have as a major objective the minimisation of tax?				
Do we assist in creating corporate or trust structures which may be sought by clients in order to facilitate tax evasion?				
Do we act in matters with connections to tax havens, or other jurisdictions which may provide facilities for tax evasion?				

APPENDIX C1

	Never	Rarely	Sometimes	Often
Do we otherwise act in matters which may involve substantial tax liabilities? For example: • purchases of property subject to stamp duty land tax (SDLT); • sales of businesses or property subject to capital gains tax (CGT); • inheritance and estate matters involving inheritance tax (IHT) issues.				
OUR PEOPLE	**Never**	**Rarely**	**Sometimes**	**Often**
Does any member of staff or partner display ignorance of or indifference to their ethical and legal obligations?				
Do we lack appropriate oversight of anyone in the firm?				
Do we recruit people without suitable references or other checks upon their ethical record?				
Does our bonus and remuneration system encourage a win-at-all-costs approach to doing business?				
Do we use third parties to carry out work on our behalf, where that third party may be involved in facilitating tax evasion?				

OVERALL ASSESSMENT

Overall, we regard the firm as being [*insert risk rating*].

RISK AREAS

The following types of client are considered to be higher risk:

[*Note – these are examples, but the firm may be exposed to different risks.*]

Private clients who engage us to advise on mitigating their tax position.
Corporate clients who engage us to advise on mitigating their tax position.
Family clients who do not wish to disclose certain assets or income in order to avoid tax.

The following practice areas are considered to be higher risk:

[*Note – these are examples, but the firm may be exposed to different risks.*]

Private client and tax team – tax mitigation planning.
Corporate – corporate structuring so as to mitigate tax liability.
Family – clients who do not wish to disclose assets or income to their spouse so as to avoid tax.

TEMPLATE CRIMINAL FINANCES ACT 2017 RISK ASSESSMENT

We have the following other significant risks:

[Note – this is an example, but the firm may be exposed to different risks.]

In respect of billing, when clients ask us to change the name of the client/entity to be billed.

MITIGATION

[Set out here mitigation steps for the risks identified. Below are some suggestions.]

- Billing guide will be written and circulated by *[insert date]*. This provides guidance relating to billing third parties.
- Anti-tax evasion policy will be published to all staff by *[insert date]*.
- A reminder to all staff as to that policy will be sent on *[insert date]*.
- Training will be mandatory for all relevant personnel *[Note – consider here who should receive the training as it may not be necessary to train all]* and will take place by *[insert date]*.
- The file review process will have a question added as to whether there are any tax evasion concerns on the file.
- A procedure will be put in place requiring third parties who provide services to high-risk clients through the firm to demonstrate their anti-tax evasion credentials and where necessary commit to improving them. *[Note – this is a suggestion, and the firm will need to consider how practically to implement this. Firms may decide where that third party is itself regulated that the risk is mitigated and no further steps are needed. However, if the third party is unregulated the firm needs to consider what steps should be taken.]*

APPENDIX C2

Template anti-tax evasion policy

This is the firm's Anti-Tax Evasion Policy and applies to all staff in the firm.

This document has been approved by the firm's money laundering reporting officer (MLRO) and compliance officer for legal practice (COLP). They are collectively responsible for this policy. [*Note – it is up to you who approves the policy, but it needs to be someone in senior management in the firm.*]

If you have any concerns about this policy or are aware of any tax evasion, please contact either of these people or your supervisor (if appropriate) in the first instance.

Failure to adhere to this policy may be treated by the firm as gross misconduct and could result in formal disciplinary action, in addition to any other professional or criminal sanctions which may apply.

1. CRIMINAL FINANCES ACT 2017

The Criminal Finances Act 2017 came into force on 30 September 2017 and creates a criminal offence for any entity that fails to prevent the criminal facilitation of tax evasion by associated persons. The offence is not so much about tax law, but about behaviours and indicators which are dishonest.

The offence of tax evasion will be committed where an associated person:

(a) is knowingly concerned in, or takes steps with a view to, the fraudulent evasion of tax by another person; or
(b) aids, abets, counsels or procures the commission of a UK tax evasion offence by another person; or
(c) is involved in the commission of an offence consisting of being knowingly concerned in, or taking steps with a view to, the fraudulent evasion of tax.

There are three stages to the offence:

1. the criminal evasion of UK tax, i.e. the underlying tax evasion offence;
2. the criminal facilitation of this offence by a person associated with the firm;
3. the firm failing to prevent the associated person from committing that facilitation.

An 'associated person' is defined as a person who is an employee of the firm who is acting in the capacity of an employee (this includes partners and consultants); an agent of the firm who is acting in their capacity as an agent; or any other person who performs services for and on behalf of the firm who is acting in the capacity of a person performing such services.

Those who act as agents may be experts that we instruct including counsel. These parties may therefore be construed as being associated persons. Most if not all such persons themselves will be regulated persons, and so will be subject to their own regulators' requirements and the Criminal Finances Act 2017 and therefore we consider these associated persons as being low risk. [*Note – you need to make this assessment for your firm but this is my suggested stance.*]

However, if you are instructing a non-regulated person to provide a service which may cause them to be seen as an associated person and they are providing advice which may include tax advice, you need to consider whether we should ask questions concerning their own anti-tax evasion policy.

For further guidance, please consult the Law Society 'Criminal Finances Act 2017' Practice Note.

If in doubt, please speak to [*insert name*] in the first instance.

2. OUR COMMITMENT

Our firm is committed to doing business ethically and in accordance with our professional and legal obligations.

Our commitment to avoiding facilitating tax evasion is one aspect of that.

Moreover, under Part 3 of the Criminal Finances Act 2017, the firm is expected to have reasonable procedures to prevent the criminal facilitation of tax evasion by staff or other associated persons. Without such procedures, the firm may be exposed to criminal sanctions.

This document explains those procedures.

3. WHAT WE EXPECT OF YOU, AND WHY

Your work for the firm may present you with opportunities to facilitate tax evasion by clients or others.

We expect you to resist any temptation to engage in such behaviour and to immediately report any improper behaviour by others.

If you were to facilitate tax evasion you would commit a serious criminal offence.

You would also leave yourself open to professional sanctions and internal disciplinary action and you could expose the firm to liability.

4. WHAT IS 'FACILITATION OF TAX EVASION'?

Tax evasion is fraudulent activity.

Tax evasion is quite different from tax avoidance or tax mitigation (the lawful minimisation of tax liability). It is also different from honest errors in tax affairs, even where such errors amount to an offence.

To be more specific, fraudulent activity intended to divert funds from the public revenue constitutes the common law offence of cheating the public revenue.

There are also statutory offences of 'fraudulently evading' various taxes.

It is not necessary that any tax actually be successfully evaded.

Facilitating tax evasion is a crime, if done deliberately and dishonestly.

That can apply even if you are outside the UK at the time. Facilitating the evasion of foreign tax may likewise be a crime. It is not necessary for your client to be convicted for you to face conviction.

5. YOUR DUTY TO REPORT

It is not enough merely to avoid personally facilitating tax evasion. As with all aspects of your professional work, you should be open, report any concerns about questionable behaviour, past or present and, if in doubt, seek guidance.

If someone within or outside the firm suggests anything which might be regarded as tax evasion, you must report it.

APPENDIX C2

6. WHISTLEBLOWER PROTECTION – OUR PROMISE TO YOU

As per our Whistleblowing Policy, you will not be subject to any retaliation or retribution for reporting your concerns about a suspected breach of this policy.

Anyone who retaliates against someone who has made such a report will be subject to disciplinary action.

Whilst we would prefer you to report any concerns openly, you may do so anonymously.

Whistleblower protection applies even if your concerns turn out to be unjustified, so long as you made the report in good faith. It may not apply in other circumstances, for example if someone maliciously makes allegations which they know to be false.

If you do have such concerns, please report them to the firm's whistleblowing officer, [*insert name*].

7. EXAMPLES

The following are non-exhaustive examples where opportunities to facilitate tax evasion might arise within our practice areas and to which you should be alert.

If you are in any doubt, please contact [*insert name*] for guidance.

In any practice area:

- Delivering a misleading or inaccurate bill which enables a client to evade tax. For example, billing a company for work actually done for its directors or shareholders in order to assist clients to claim a tax deduction to which they are not entitled. This is likely to be VAT fraud.

Property:

- Preparing documents which misstate the price of a property to enable a client to evade stamp duty land tax or capital gains tax.
- Assisting in a property being bought using nominees or other structures to enable a client to illegally avoid tax.

Corporate:

- Assisting in creating corporate or trust structures designed to conceal a client's taxable income or assets.
- Referring clients to third parties in tax havens to set up accounts or structures which you know are to facilitate tax evasion, rather than tax avoidance.
- Using side letters so that aspects of a transaction with taxable effects are not apparent from reading the main agreement in order to enable a client, or anyone else, to evade tax.

Wills and probate:

- Assisting in creating trust or other structures designed to conceal a client's taxable income or assets.
- Giving clients advice on how to make lifetime transfers in ways which HM Revenue and Customs (HMRC) will find difficult to detect.
- Preparing documents which misstate the value of an estate in order to avoid inheritance tax.

Family law:

- Helping a client to put forward figures which you know to be false may involve a number of offences, possibly including conspiracy to pervert the course of justice and tax evasion offences.
- Clients who have been ordered to disclose their earnings in connection with

family proceedings may tell the solicitor acting that they have committed tax evasion in the past. That information will normally be privileged and is not normally reportable under money laundering regulations. However, in such cases the solicitor should discuss the matter with the MLRO or COLP to ensure that their involvement in the case will not create any liabilities or concerns.

APPENDIX D

Sanctions, whistleblowing and reporting concerns

APPENDIX D1

Template whistleblowing policy

This policy does not form part of any contract of employment and it may be amended at any time.

1. PURPOSE AND SCOPE

1.1 All organisations face the risk of things going wrong or of unknowingly harbouring malpractice.
1.2 [*Insert name of firm*] takes malpractice very seriously. The partners are committed to conducting their business with honesty and integrity and expect all of our people to maintain high standards too. They encourage open communication from all those who work for them and want everyone to feel secure about raising genuine concerns.
1.3 All employees have protection under whistleblowing laws if they raise concerns in the correct way. This policy is designed to give our employees that opportunity and protection.
1.4 It does not matter if an individual who raises a concern is mistaken about it – our people do not have to prove anything about the allegation they are making, but they must reasonably believe that the disclosure is made in the public interest and that the information they have tends to show some malpractice.
1.5 This policy applies to all employees, officers, consultants, contractors, partners, interns, casual workers and agency workers.

2. WHAT IS WHISTLEBLOWING?

2.1 Whistleblowing is the reporting of suspected malpractice, wrongdoing or dangers in relation to the firm's activities. This includes: bribery; fraud or other criminal activity; miscarriages of justice; health and safety risks; damage to the environment; any breach of legal, professional or regulatory obligations; or the deliberate concealment of any of the above matters.
2.2 There is a difference between whistleblowing and raising a grievance:
  2.2.1 whistleblowing is where an individual has a concern about a danger or illegality that has a public interest aspect to it, for example because it threatens clients, third parties or the public generally; but
  2.2.2 a grievance is a complaint that generally relates to an individual's own employment position or personal circumstances at work.
2.3 This policy should not be used for raising a grievance. In those cases, employees should use the firm's Grievance Procedure.

APPENDIX D1

3. HOW TO RAISE A CONCERN

3.1 If an individual is concerned about any form of malpractice covered by this policy, the individual should normally raise the issue with their immediate superior.

3.2 If an individual feels they cannot tell their immediate superior, for whatever reason, they should raise the issue with their head of department [*amend as necessary*].

3.3 If an individual has raised concerns and is still concerned, or the matter is so serious that they feel they cannot discuss it with either of the two persons named above, they should raise the matter with the whistleblowing officer – [*insert name*].

3.4 A concern can be raised by telephone, in person or in writing. It is preferable if it is made in writing. Although the individual is not expected to prove the truth of their concern beyond doubt or provide evidence, the individual will generally need to provide the following information as a minimum:

3.4.1 the nature of the concern and why the individual believes it to be true; and
3.4.2 the background and history of the concern (giving relevant dates where possible).

4. RESPONDING TO A CONCERN RAISED

4.1 The firm is committed to ensuring that all disclosures raised will be dealt with appropriately, consistently, fairly and professionally.

4.2 We will arrange a meeting as soon possible to discuss the concern raised. The individual may bring a colleague or trade union representative to any meeting that takes place. The companion must respect the confidentiality of the disclosure and any subsequent investigation. We may ask the individual for further information about the concern raised, either at this meeting or at a later stage.

4.3 After the meeting, we will decide how to respond. Usually this will involve making internal enquiries first, but it may be necessary to carry out an investigation at a later stage which may be formal or informal depending on the nature of the concern raised. We will endeavour to complete investigations within a reasonable time.

4.4 We will keep the individual who raised the concern informed of the progress of the investigation carried out and when it is completed, and give an indication of timings for any actions or next steps that we will take, but we will not be able to inform the individual of any matters which would infringe any duty of confidentiality owed to others.

5. CONFIDENTIALITY

5.1 All concerns raised will be treated in confidence and every effort will be made not to reveal the identity of an individual who raises a concern if that is their wish. If disciplinary or other proceedings follow the investigation, it may not be possible to take action as a result of a disclosure without the help of the individual who raised the concern, so the individual may be asked to come forward as a witness. If they agree to this, they will be offered advice and support.

5.2 We hope that our people will feel able to voice their concerns openly under this policy. Although a concern may be made anonymously, we encourage individuals to put their name to their allegation whenever possible. If this is not done, it will be much more difficult for us to protect the individual's position or to give feedback on the outcome of investigations.

5.3 Concerns that are expressed completely anonymously are much less powerful and are difficult to investigate. We will consider them at our discretion, taking into account factors such as the seriousness of the issue raised, the credibility of the concern and the likelihood of confirming the allegation from other sources.

6. EXTERNAL DISCLOSURES (EXCEPTIONAL CASES)

6.1 The aim of this policy is to provide an internal mechanism for reporting, investigating and remedying any wrongdoing in the workplace. We would expect in almost all cases raising concerns internally would be the most appropriate course of action and that you should not find it necessary to alert anyone externally.

6.2 However, if for whatever reason, an individual feels they cannot raise their concerns internally and they reasonably believe the information and any allegations are substantially true, the law recognises that it may be appropriate for them to raise the matter with another prescribed person, such as a regulator or professional body or an MP. A list of the relevant prescribed people and bodies for this purpose and the areas for which they are responsible is available from Protect (see paragraph 8 – Further information and contacts, below) and on the GOV.UK website at **www.gov.uk/government/publications/blowing-the-whistle-list-of-prescribed-people-and-bodies–2**.

6.3 We strongly encourage you to seek advice before reporting a concern to anyone external.

7. PROTECTION AND SUPPORT FOR THOSE RAISING CONCERNS

7.1 We are committed to good practice and high standards and to being supportive to anyone who raises genuine concerns under this policy, even if they turn out to be mistaken.

7.2 Any individual raising a genuine concern must not suffer any detriment as a result of doing so. If an individual believes that they have suffered such treatment, they should inform the firm's whistleblowing officer [*insert name*] immediately. If the matter is not dealt with to the individual's satisfaction, the individual should raise it formally using the Grievance Procedure.

7.3 Nobody must threaten or retaliate against an individual who has raised a concern and the firm will not tolerate any such harassment or victimisation. Any person involved in such conduct may be subject to disciplinary action.

7.4 However, to ensure the protection of our people, those who raise a concern frivolously, maliciously and/or for personal gain and/or make an allegation they do not reasonably believe to be true and/or made in the public interest will also be liable to disciplinary action.

8. FURTHER INFORMATION AND CONTACTS

8.1 If you have any queries about the application of this policy, please contact the firm's whistleblowing officer [*insert name and contact details*].

8.2 Protect is a source of further information and advice at **protect-advice.org.uk/**. It also provides a free helpline offering confidential advice on 020 3117 2520.

APPENDIX D2

Guidance note: Solicitors Regulation Authority reporting obligations – what are they and when do they kick in?

On 25 November 2019 the new Solicitors Regulation Authority (SRA) Codes of Conduct came into force. This brought with it a change in the reporting obligations for both the firm and solicitors. You will find the new Codes on the SRA website and you are encouraged to visit them (**www.sra.org.uk/solicitors/standards-regulations/**).

The reporting obligations are as follows:

- You report promptly to the SRA, or another approved regulator, as appropriate, **any facts or matters that you reasonably believe are capable of amounting to a serious breach** of its regulatory arrangements by any person regulated by it (including you).
- Notwithstanding the paragraph above **you inform the SRA promptly of any facts or matters that you reasonably believe should be brought to its attention** in order that it may investigate whether a serious breach of its regulatory arrangements has occurred or otherwise exercise its regulatory powers.
- **You do not subject any person to detrimental treatment** for making or proposing to make a report or providing or proposing to provide information based on a reasonably held belief under the first paragraph above irrespective of whether the SRA or another approved regulator subsequently investigates or takes an action in relation to the facts or matters in question.

The Code for Solicitors, RELs and RFLs further sets out that a solicitor's obligation to report will be fulfilled if they have informed the compliance officer for legal practice (COLP) or compliance officer for finance and administration (COFA) of the matter on the understanding that they will make a report.

When considering whether an obligation to report has occurred you need to consider whether the facts or matters before you could amount to a **serious breach**. What therefore needs to occur is an assessment of what is serious.

The SRA does not define what serious means, but it does inform us via its Enforcement Strategy what factors it takes into account when it decides whether something is serious. These factors include but are not limited to:

1. **Nature of the allegation** – Some types are inherently more serious than others, for example dishonesty, taking unfair advantage of clients, sexual misconduct.
2. **Intent and motivation** – Conduct may be more serious because of the intent behind it.
3. **Harm and impact** – Has there been significant impact on the victim or little/no impact at all?
4. **Vulnerability** – Was the victim vulnerable and did the solicitor take advantage of that?
5. **Role, experience and seniority** – Is the individual junior or well seasoned?
6. **Regulatory history and pattern of behaviour** – Has this happened before?
7. **Remediation** – Is there a risk of future harm or has any risk been mitigated?

WHAT SHOULD YOU DO IF YOU ARE CONCERNED YOU HAVE A REPORTING OBLIGATION?

To begin with, consider whether you have facts or matters before you that could amount to a serious breach taking into account the above factors. If you are unsure or believe that you do have such facts or matters before you, please speak to [*insert name ad role, such as Risk & Compliance Manager or COLP*].

Please do not make any reports to the SRA about any other person inside or outside the firm without speaking to [*insert name and role*] first.

Index

Account freezing orders 6.7
Adequate consideration defence 2.4.2.3
Adverse media check 4.2.3
Alexander Dobrovinsky and Partners LLP 5.9.4
AML compliance
    AML governance 5.10.1
    AML policies, controls and procedures 3.6, 5.10.4
    client due diligence 5.10.5
    client/matter level risk assessment 5.10.3
    generally 5.10
    high-level compliance actions 5.10.11
    internal controls 5.10.9
    practice-wide risk assessment 5.10.2
    record-keeping 5.10.10
    suspicious activity reporting 5.10.6
    technology 5.10.7
    training 5.10.8
AML legislation
    EU directives 2.3.1, 5.8
    offences *see* Money laundering offences
    prior AML legislation 2.3.1
    summary 2.3.2
AML Regulations
    generally 2.1, 2.3.2
    internal controls *see* Internal controls
    policies, controls and procedures 3.6, 5.10.4, App.B5
Audits
    audit table template App.B9
    independent audit 3.7.1
    SRA thematic review 5.5.3.1

Brexit regulations 5.8
Bribery and corruption
    anti-bribery officer 1.3.3
    Bribery Act 2010 1.1
    COLPs 1.4
    corporate offence 1.1.2
    countries with high levels of
        instructing firms based in 1.2.3
        setting up operations in 1.2.2
    donations to charities 1.3.6
    examples 1.2
    foreign public officials 1.1.1.3
    gifts 1.2.1, 1.3.4
    grease payments 1.2.4, 1.3.5
    hospitality 1.3.4
    implementing compliance 1.3
    individual offences 1.1.1
    inducement/reward to perform relevant function 1.1.1.1
    internal report 1.4
    MLROs 1.4.2
    penalties 1.1.3
    policy 1.3.2, 1.3.7, App.A2
    practical examples 1.2
    privileged disclosures 1.4.1
    public international organisations 1.1.1.3
    reputation 1.4.4
    requesting etc. reward for performing relevant function 1.1.1.2
    risk assessment 1.3.1, App.A1
    SARs 1.4.2
    SRA Principles and Codes 1.4.3
    suspicions 1.4
    third-party due diligence 1.3.8

Charities
    donations to 1.3.6
    identity of client 4.1.1.8
Child & Child 5.9.3
Christmas gifts *see* Gifts
Churches
    identity of client 4.1.1.10

INDEX

Client account
    use as banking facility 5.3.3
Client due diligence
    adverse media check 4.2.3
    centralisation 4.7.1
    client and matter risk assessment
        4.1.2, 5.5.3.4, 5.10.3, App.B6
    compliance 5.10.5
    enhanced due diligence 4.1.4.1, 4.1.7
    generally 4.1
    high-risk registers 4.1.5, App.B7
    identification *see* Identity of client
    non-regulated work 4.7.2
    ongoing monitoring 4.1.5, App.B8
    politically exposed persons (PEPs)
        4.2, 4.2.1
    pooled client accounts 4.5
    purpose and nature of work 4.1.3
    record-keeping 4.3.2
    regulated work 4.7.2
    reliance 4.3.1
    sanctions check 4.2.2, 5.5.3.6, 8.7
    simplified due diligence 4.1.6
    source of funds and wealth *see*
        Source of funds and wealth
    SRA 2019/20 thematic review 5.5.3
    SRA approval
        application procedure 4.6.4
        beneficial owner 4.6.1
        manager 4.6.3
        officers 4.6.2
    trustee obligations 4.4
Client and matter risk assessment
    4.1.2, 5.5.3.4, 5.10.3, App.B6
Clubs and associations
    identity of client 4.1.1.9
Clyde & Co and partners 5.9.5
Colleges
    identity of client 4.1.1.10
Compliance officer for finance and administration (COFA)
    overlap with other officers' roles 3.4.2
    role of 3.4.1
Compliance officer for legal practice (COLP)
    overlap with other officers' roles 3.4.2
    role of 3.4.1
    suspected bribery 1.4
    whistleblowing 9.4.2
Corruption *see* Bribery and corruption

Councils
    identity of client 4.1.1.10
Criminal Finances Act 2017
    account freezing orders 6.7
    background to Act 6.1
    compliance 6.8
        implementation 6.8.3
        policy implementation 6.8.2
        reviewing 6.8.5
        risk assessment 6.8.1, App.C1
        training 6.8.4
    HMRC research 6.5
    outline 6.2
    prosecutions to date 6.5
    serial tax avoidance regime (STAR) 6.10.2
    tax evasion *see* Tax evasion
    unexplained wealth orders 6.6.1, 6.6.2.1, 6.6.2.2, 6.6.2.3
Criminal investigations
    check wording of order/notice 7.5.1
    comprehensive file note 7.5.6
    copying material sent 7.5.6
    further information order 7.4.2
    generally 7.1
    notice to disclose 7.3
    notice to produce 7.4.1
    practical considerations 7.5
    privilege 7.5.2, 7.5.3, 7.5.4
    production orders 7.2
    suspicious activity report 7.5.5
    witness statement 7.5.7
Criminal record checks 3.7.1

Disciplinary action
    Alexander Dobrovinsky and Partners LLP partner 5.9.4
    Child & Child partner 5.9.3
    Clyde & Co and partners 5.9.5
    generally 5.9
    Seatons Law Limited 5.9.2
    solicitor described as 'puppet' 5.9.6
    Taylor Vinters LLP 5.9.1
Due diligence *see* Client due diligence

Electronic verification 4.1.1.12, 5.5.3.3, 5.10.7
Employee screening 3.7.1, 5.5.3.8
EU money laundering directives 2.3.1, 3.1, 5.5.3
    Sixth (6AMLD) 5.8

INDEX

Financial Action Task Force (FATF)
    assessing compliance 2.2
    blacklist 2.2
    generally 2.2, 3.2.1
    grey list 2.2
    High-Risk Jurisdictions subject to a Call for Action 2.2
    Jurisdictions Under Increased Monitoring 2.2
    methodology 2.2
    objectives 2.2
    recommendations 2.2
    role of 2.2
Foreign public official
    bribing 1.1.1.3
Further information order 7.4.2

General anti-abuse rule (GAAR) 6.10.1
Gifts
    Christmas gifts 1.2.1
    intention behind 1.2.1, 1.3.4
    policy on 1.3.4
    reporting and recording 1.3.4
Government agencies
    identity of client 4.1.1.10
Grease payments 1.2.4, 1.3.5

High-risk registers 4.1.5, App.B7
Hospitality
    policy on 1.3.4
    see also Gifts

Identity of client
    certification 4.1.1.11
    charities 4.1.1.8
    churches 4.1.1.10
    clubs and associations 4.1.1.9
    colleges 4.1.1.10
    company identification 4.1.1.3
    councils 4.1.1.10
    electronic verification 4.1.1.12, 5.5.3.3, 5.10.7
    examples of ID documentation 4.1.1.15
    generally 4.1.1.1
    government agencies 4.1.1.10
    identifying third parties on behalf of client 4.1.1.13
    inability to identify beneficial owner of body corporate 4.1.1.4
    individual person identification 4.1.1.2
    partnerships 4.1.1.6

    pension funds 4.1.1.10
    places of worship 4.1.1.10
    PSC register discrepancy reporting 4.1.1.5
    schools 4.1.1.10
    SRA thematic review 5.5.3.3
    timing of verification of ID 4.1.1.14
    trusts and estate administration 4.1.1.7
    universities 4.1.1.10
    see also Client due diligence
Internal controls
    criminal record checks 3.7.1
    generally 3.6, 3.7, 5.10.9
    independent audit 3.7.1
    LSAG guidance 3.7.4
    MLCO appointment 3.7.1
    MLRO appointment and role 3.7.2
    requests for information 3.7.3
    SRA risk assessment 3.7.4
    staff screening 3.7.1, 5.5.3.8
    training 3.7.5
    see also Policies, controls and procedures

Joint Money Laundering Steering Group (JMLSG) 3.2.7

Law Society of England and Wales guidance 3.2.5, 5.2
Legal advice privilege *see* Privilege
Legal Sector Affinity Group (LSAG) AML guidance 2.4, 3.2.6, 3.6, 3.7.4, 5.1
    flowchart App.B4
    privilege decision template App.B3

Money laundering compliance officer (MLCO)
    appointment 3.7.1
    overlap with other officers' roles 3.4.2
    role of 3.4.1, 3.7.1
    SRA thematic review 5.5.3.5
    SRA visit 5.7.2
Money laundering offences
    criminal property
        acquisition, use or possession 2.4.1.5
        arrangements 2.4.1.4
        concealing 2.4.1.3
        definition 2.4.1.2
    defences 2.4, 2.4.2, 2.4.3
        adequate consideration 2.4.2.3

INDEX

Money laundering offences – *continued*
   defences – *continued*
      authorised disclosure 2.4.2.1
      lack of training 2.4.3.3
      privileged circumstances 2.4.3.2
      reasonable excuse 2.4.2.2, 2.4.3.1
      tipping off offences 2.4.4.2
   failure to disclose 2.4.1.6
   generally 2.4, 2.4.1
   legal advice 2.4.1.1
   nature of 2.3.2
   SRA warning notice 5.3.1
   stages of 2.3.2
   suspicion 2.4
   terrorist financing 2.5.1.4
   tipping off *see* Tipping off offences
   UK National risk assessment 3.1.1
Money laundering reporting officer (MLRO)
   appointment 3.7.2
   overlap with other officers' roles 3.4.2
   reporting suspicions to 1.4, 1.4.2, 2.4
   role of 3.4.1, 3.7.2
   SRA visit 5.7.2

National Crime Agency (NCA) 3.2.4
   National strategic assessment of serious and organised crime 2020 3.1.3
Notice to disclose 7.3
Notice to produce 7.4.1

Office of Financial Sanctions Implementation (OFSI) *see* Sanctions
Office for Professional Body Anti-Money Laundering Supervision (OPBAS) 3.2.2, 5.4
   review of SRA 5.4
Overseas operations 1.2.2

Partnerships
   disciplinary action 5.9
   identifying partners 4.1.1.6
Pension funds
   identity of client 4.1.1.10
Places of worship
   identity of client 4.1.1.10
POCA 2002 offences *see* Money laundering offences; Terrorist financing; Tipping off offences
Policies, controls and procedures
   generally 3.6, 5.10.4

   template policy App.B5
   see also Internal controls
Politically exposed persons (PEPs) 4.2.1
Pooled client accounts
   client due diligence 4.5
Pre-employment checks 3.7.1, 5.5.3.8
Privilege
   crime/fraud or iniquity exception 3.5.4.4, 7.5.3
   criminal investigations 7.5.2, 7.5.3, 7.5.4
   generally 1.4.1, 3.5.4
   legal advice privilege 3.5.4.1, 7.5.2
   litigation privilege 3.5.4.2
   LSAG privilege decision template App.B3
   privileged circumstances 3.5.4.3
   reporting suspicions 1.4.1
   sanctions checking 8.9
   speaking to client before/after order/notice 7.5.4
Production orders 7.2
Public international organisations 1.1.1.3

Record-keeping
   client due diligence 4.3.2
   compliance 5.10.10
Reporting obligations *see* SRA reporting obligations
Reputation 1.4.4
Risk assessment
   bribery and corruption 1.3.1, App.A1
   client and matter risk assessment 4.1.2, 5.5.3.4, 5.10.3, App.B6
   compliance with CFA 2017 6.8.1, App.C1
   firm-wide risk assessment 3.3, 5.10.2
      checklist 3.3
      compliance 5.10.2
      guidance 3.3
      review 3.3
      SRA thematic review 5.5.2
      template App.B1
   internal controls and 3.7.4
   NCA National strategic assessment 3.1.3
   SRA AML risk assessment 3.1, 3.1.2, 3.7.4
   SRA warning notice 5.3.2
   tax evasion 6.8.1, App.C1
   UK national risk assessment 3.1, 3.1.1

INDEX

Sanctions
    checking clients for 4.2.2, 5.5.3.6, 8.7
    definition 8.3
    exceptions
      crediting frozen accounts 8.10.1
      independent persons holding
        interests 8.10.2
      ring-fencing 8.10.3
    international sanctions 8.5
    licences
      amending 8.10.7
      breach of terms 8.11
      compliance 8.11
      general licence 8.10.4
      grounds for 8.10.4
      refusal of 8.10.8
      specific licence 8.10.5
      suspicious activity reports and 8.12
      timeframe for grant 8.10.6
    lists 8.6
    main types 8.3
    name checks 8.7.2
    nature of 8.3
    Office of Financial Sanctions
      Implementation (OFSI)
      guidance 8.3
      licensing 8.10.4
      lists of targets 8.6
      reporting obligations 8.8
    privilege 8.9
    purpose of 8.3
    relevant legislation 8.1
    reporting obligations 8.4
    reverse sanction checking 8.7.3
    risk-based approach 8.7.1
    SRA thematic review 5.5.3.6
    UK sanctions key players 8.2

Schools
    identity of client 4.1.1.10

Screening of employees 3.7.1, 5.5.3.8

SDLT avoidance schemes 6.11

Seatons Law Limited 5.9.2

Serial tax avoidance regime (STAR) 6.10.2

Solicitors Disciplinary Tribunal 3.2.3
    tax evasion 6.11

Solicitors Regulation Authority (SRA)
    agenda for 2021 and beyond 5.6.3
    approval of beneficial owners,
      officers and managers 4.6
    business plan 2020/21 5.6.1
    disciplinary action *see* Disciplinary
      action

    guidance 5.1
    OPBAS review 5.4
    Principles and Codes 1.4.3
    reporting obligations *see* SRA
      reporting obligations
    risk assessments 3.1, 3.1.2, 3.7.4, 5.5.2
    Risk Outlook 2020/21 5.6.2
    role of 3.2.3
    thematic reviews
      2019/20 *see* SRA 2019/20 AML
        thematic review
      firm-wide risk assessments 5.5.2
      trust and company providers 5.5.1
    visits *see* SRA visits
    warning notices *see* SRA warning
      notices

Source of funds and wealth
    categories 4.1.4.1
    documentation 4.1.4.2
    generally 4.1.4.1
    policy on 4.1.4.3
    practical examples 4.1.4.4
    SRA thematic review 5.5.3.7
    see also Client due diligence

SRA 2019/20 AML thematic review
    audits 5.5.3.1
    due diligence 5.5.3.2
    electronic verification 5.5.3.3
    generally 5.5.3
    matter risk assessments 5.5.3.4
    MLCOs and their roles 5.5.3.5
    next steps/actions with firms 5.5.4
    sanctions 5.5.3.6
    SARs 5.5.3.9
    source of funds 5.5.3.7
    staff screening 5.5.3.8
    training 5.5.3.10

SRA reporting obligations
    codes of conduct 9.3.1
    communicating to firm 9.4.4
    guidance 9.4.1, App.D2
    importance of 9.3.4
    matters to report 9.3.2
    offices in different countries 9.5
    practising 9.4.7
    prompt action 9.4.6
    serious breach 9.3.2
    timing of report 9.3.3
    training 9.4.5
    see also Whistleblowing

SRA visits
    debrief 5.7.3
    during the visit 5.7.2

INDEX

SRA visits – *continued*
    generally 5.7
    interviews with MLRO/MLCO and fee earners 5.7.3
    letter after visit 5.7.4
    letter prior to visit 5.7.1
    preparation for 5.7.5
    selection for 5.7.1
    tax advice review 6.12
SRA warning notices
    client account used as banking facility 5.3.3
    firm risk assessment 5.3.2
    generally 5.3
    money laundering 5.3.1
    SDLT avoidance schemes 6.11
    suspicious activity reports 5.3.4
    tax evasion 6.11
    terrorist financing 5.3.1
Staff screening 3.7.1, 5.5.3.8
Suspicious activity report (SAR)
    after submission 3.5.3.5
    bribery 1.4, 1.4.2
    compliance 5.10.6
    content of 3.5.3.4
    criminal investigations 7.5.5
    disclosing 2.4.4.1, 2.5.5.1
    information to client 3.5.3.6
    licence applications 8.12
    making 3.5.3.2
    privilege *see* Privilege
    purpose of 3.5.3.3
    SRA thematic review 5.5.3.9
    SRA warning notice 5.3.4
    suspicion 3.5.1
    template App.B2
    terrorist financing 2.5.5.1
    tipping off offences 2.4.4.1, 2.5.5.1
    unexpected proceeds of crime 3.5.2

Tax evasion
    associated persons 6.3
    bills/billing 6.9.1
    corporate/trust 6.9.3
    definition of offence 6.2
    family law 6.9.5
    general anti-abuse rule (GAAR) 6.10.1
    HMRC research 6.5
    investigations 6.4
    penalties 6.4
    policy 6.8.2, App.C2
    practical examples 6.9

    probate 6.9.4
    professional conduct 6.11
    property transactions 6.9.2
    prosecutions 6.5
    risk assessment 6.8.1, App.C1
    SDLT avoidance schemes 6.11
    serial tax avoidance regime (STAR) 6.10.2
    Solicitors Disciplinary Tribunal 6.11
    SRA visits 6.12
    SRA warning notices 6.11
    stages of offence 6.2
    training 6.8.4
    wills 6.9.4
    see also Criminal Finances Act 2017
Taylor Vinters LLP 5.9.1
Technology 5.10.7
Terrorist financing
    defences 2.5.2
    consent 2.5.2
    failure to disclose offences 2.5.4
    permitted disclosures 2.5.5.2
    police co-operation 2.5.2
    prior consent 2.5.2
    reasonable excuse 2.5.2
    tipping off offences 2.5.5.2
    definition of 'terrorist property' 2.5
    failure to disclose offences 2.5.3
    defences 2.5.4
    FATF and 2.2
    funding arrangements 2.5.1.3
    fundraising 2.5.1.1
    generally 2.5
    money laundering 2.5.1.4
    principal offences 2.5.1
    SRA warning notice 5.3.1
    tipping off offences
        defences 2.5.5.2
        disclosing an investigation 2.5.5.1
        disclosing a SAR 2.5.5.1
    UK National risk assessment 3.1.1
    use and possession offence 2.5.1.2
Tipping off offences
    defences 2.4.4.2, 2.5.5.2
    disclosing an investigation 2.4.4.1, 2.5.5.1
    disclosing a SAR 2.4.4.1, 2.5.5.1
    generally 2.4
    penalties 2.4.4.1
    prejudicing an investigation 2.4.4.1
    terrorist financing 2.5.5.1, 2.5.5.2
Training
    bribery policy 1.3.7

compliance 3.7.5, 5.10.8
lack of training as defence 2.4.3.3
reporting obligations 9.4.5
SRA thematic review 5.5.3.10
tax evasion 6.8.4
whistleblowing 9.4.5
Trustees
client due diligence 4.4
Trusts and estate administration
identity of client 4.1.1.7

Unexpected proceeds of crime 3.5.2
Unexplained wealth orders (UWOs) 6.6.1
examples 6.6.2
first use 6.6.2.1
implemented to its end 6.6.2.2
unsuccessful cases 6.6.2.3
Universities
identity of client 4.1.1.10

Whistleblowing
COLP and 9.4.2
communicating policy to firm 9.4.4
definition 9.2.1
generally 1.4, 9.1
grievances distinguished 9.2.2
hotline 9.4.3
implementing compliance 9.4
importance of 9.2.2
legislation
China 9.2.4.4
differences between countries 9.2.5
Europe 9.2.4.1
France 9.2.4.1
Germany 9.2.4.1
Hong Kong 9.2.4.4
South Africa 9.2.4.2
UK 9.2.3
US 9.2.4.3
offices in different countries 9.5
policy 9.4.1, 9.4.4, 9.5, App.D1
practising 9.4.7
prompt action 9.4.6
training 9.4.5
whistleblowing officer 9.4.2
see also SRA reporting obligations
Witness statements 7.5.7